Hew Ainslie, Thomas Carstairs Latto

A Pilgrimage to the Land of Burns

And Poems

Hew Ainslie, Thomas Carstairs Latto

A Pilgrimage to the Land of Burns
And Poems

ISBN/EAN: 9783744712835

Printed in Europe, USA, Canada, Australia, Japan

Cover: Foto ©Thomas Meinert / pixelio.de

More available books at **www.hansebooks.com**

A Pilgrimage to the Land of Burns

And Po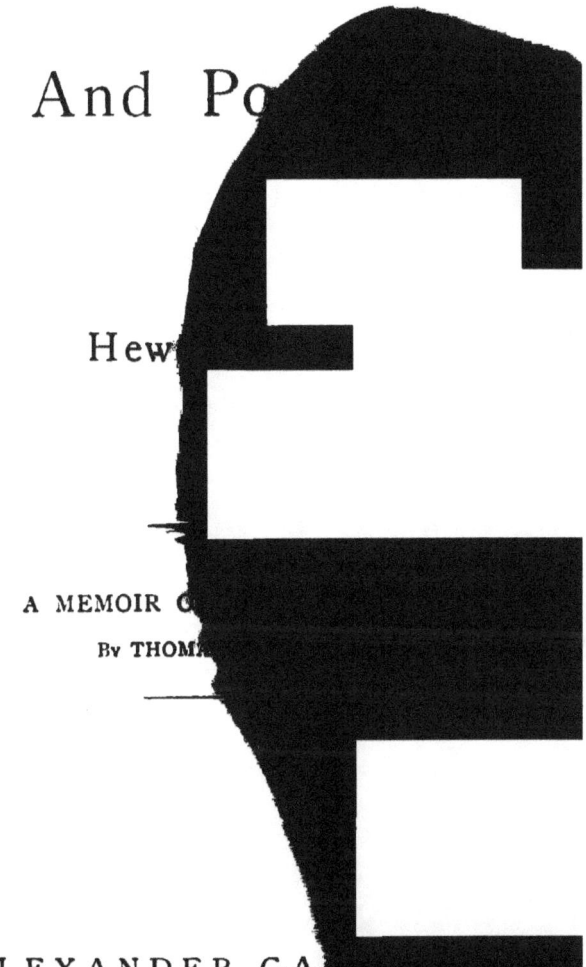

Hew

A MEMOIR O

By THOM

ALEXANDER GA

Publisher to Her Majesty th

PAISLEY; AND 26 PATERNOSTER SQU

1892

PUBLISHER'S PREFACE.

THE Publisher has pleasure in submitting the first complete collection of the writings of HEW AINSLIE that has been printed since his PILGRIMAGE TO THE LAND OF BURNS was given to the world from an obscure press in Deptford in 1822. That work, which includes some of the Poet's finest lyrics, has long been so scarce as to be almost unattainable, and the present reissue will no doubt be warmly welcomed by a large circle of his admirers. The New York collection of the Poems, published in 1855, is also here reproduced, with the addition of a large number of pieces which have not hitherto been published, or which have only appeared in a fugitive form. For copies of these, and for other assistance rendered in the preparation of this work, the Publisher's thanks are due to Mr. Thomas C. Latto, New York, whose fresh and highly interesting Memoir of AINSLIE is prefixed to the Poet's writings; Mr. James Wellstood Ainslie, of Louisville, Kentucky, and Mrs. Campbell, the only two surviving children of the Poet; Miss Annie Ainslie, his grand-daughter; Mr. John G. Wellstood, of Greenwich, Conn., and Mr. William Wellstood, of New York, the eminent engravers; Mrs. Margaret M. Wellstood Spence, 135th Street, New York; Mrs Annie Wellstood Johns, the poetess, Frogmore, Westzaan, Holland; Mr. George Taylor, London, whose contributions were very numerous; Miss Katie H. Crist, Montgomery, New York; Mr. James B. Smith, of Clifford

Park, Stirling ; and Mr. George Dunlop of the *Kilmarnock Standard*, who has given valuable help in the way of editing and supervision of the press.

The portrait which faces the title page is from a photograph taken while Ainslie was staying with the late Mr. Stephen Wellstood at Bonnybridge, some thirty years ago. The other portrait, which appears in the body of the volume, formed the frontispiece of the New York edition of the Poems ; and the profiles of the three "pilgrims" are engraved from a photo-copy of a miniature, received from Mrs. Johns. To these illustrations have been added reproductions of the three engravings which appeared in the original edition of the " PILGRIMAGE," from drawings made by Ainslie and his companion, Mr. James Wellstood, in the course of their memorable tour. One of these is particularly interesting, as showing Mauchline Old Kirk of the time of Burns, with Gavin Hamilton's house and Mauchline Castle.

CONTENTS.

Park, Stirling ; and Mr. George Dunlop of the *Kilmar-nock Standard*, who has given valuable help in the way of editing and supervision of the press.

The portrait which faces the title page is from a photograph taken while Ainslie was staying with the late Mr. Stephen Wellstood at Bonnybridge, some thirty years ago. The other portrait, which appears in the body of the volume, formed the frontispiece of the New York edition of the Poems ; and the profiles of the three "pilgrims" are engraved from a photo-copy of a miniature, received from Mrs. Johns. To these illustrations have been added reproductions of the three engravings which appeared in the original edition of the "PILGRIM-AGE," from drawings made by Ainslie and his companion, Mr. James Wellstood, in the course of their memorable tour. One of these is particularly interesting, as showing Mauchline Old Kirk of the time of Burns, with Gavin Hamilton's house and Mauchline Castle.

CONTENTS.

ILLUSTRATIONS.

MEMOIR OF HEW AINSLIE.

By THOMAS C. LATTO.

———◇◆◇———

ON the 5th day of April, 1792, just four years before the death of Robert Burns, and while the dark clouds in which his brief but brilliant career was to close were already impending, there was born in a wild and secluded district of Ayrshire, on the estate of an ancient and distinguished family, situated in the parish of Dailly, on the banks of "Girvan's fairy haunted stream," a chubby, cheerful, and remarkably lively infant, to the joy of a fond mother and an equally proud father.

On the 25th of July, 1796, while the "awkward squad" fired a straggling volley in Gray Friars' kirkyard, Dumfries, over the remains of "Scotland's darling son," that infant, now a "royt" urchin of four, with yellow curling hair and rosy lips, was scampering about the lanes in the "Bourocks o' Bargeny," afterwards to be immortalized in one of the sweetest and completest songs in the whole compass of Scottish lyrical poetry. It was those rosy lips that were to sing it. That lively infant—that "royt" urchin—was—let us pronounce his name with admiring affection—

HEW AINSLIE.

It is interesting to note that in the same cottage (of which no trace now remains) there had been born, nineteen years previously, the Rev. Hamilton Paul, also a poet of undoubted genius, and one of the early bio

a

graphers of Burns.   The subject of this memoir was
the only son of George Ainslie, who held pretty much
the same position under Sir Hew Dalrymple Hamilton
that Willie Laidlaw, author of "Lucy's Flittin'," did
under Sir Walter Scott.   The Dalrymples were direct
descendants of the "Stair" dynasty, notable for the
production of at least two remarkable characters,—the
statesman celebrated in legendary lore as "Sir William
Ashton," the usurping proprietor of Ravenswood, at
whose instigation it is believed William of Orange was
hounded on to consent to the Massacre of Glencoe—
and Lucy Ashton, known to her family as the "Bride of
Baldoon," and to the wide world as the "Bride of
Lammermoor."

George Ainslie was the father of three children,
Eleanora, Hew and Jean.   He was a counterpart of
Burns' father, without his austerity, and even *minus* the
failings which are sometimes said to lean to Virtue's side.
He was respected by high and low, well meriting the
brief but glowing tribute afterwards conferred upon him
by changeless filial affection :

> " Father ! if thou hast not the rest
> Eternal heaven hath named the best,
> There's not a living man on earth,
> Who knew thy virtues and thy worth,
> But what would say with all his heart :
> Ainslie ! thou hast not thy desert."

Young Hew throve fairly well, though his constitu-
tion was somewhat delicate, giving small promise
of the strength and agility he displayed in manhood.
A Dominie Sampson sort of body was engaged to initiate
him into the mysteries of the three R's in his father's
house, whence he was promoted to the benches of the
parish school at Ballantrae, and then entered a pupil at

Ayr Academy.   At fourteen he shot up almost suddenly into a tall raw-boned lad, the cuffs of his jacket getting ridiculously near the elbow, while the corduroys crept half way to his knee.   He was Hood's "rising son" in *propria persona*.   This rapid growth diminished his vital forces, and as it was feared he was going into a decline, the youthful giant was summoned home.   Here, under his mother's careful nursing, he soon began to pick up, and in a few months was as hearty as ever—in his own words, "fit for ocht."

It was through his mother's influence that Ainslie was early smit with the love of song.   Like Agnes Brown, the mother of Robert Burns, she had a teeming repertory (as it is now called) of ancient ditties and legends, both humorous and pathetic, which she sang with great tenderness and vivacity, and the boy was never tired of listening to her.   He had a most sensitive and accurate ear for rhythm, and as the works of Ramsay, Fergusson, and Burns were in the small collection of his father's books, he very soon devoured them all.   They set him to rhyming, and though he could not extract much of lyric spirit from the ill-starred and marvellous boy's graphic delineations of humble city life, he drew on Ramsay and Burns for what he wanted of that spirit, which he supplemented by importing into his simple songs an infusion of the racy and well-nigh uncatchable reckless jollity and curious felicity of phrase which are Fergusson's distinguishing characteristics.   To a great extent he did in the end manage to attain it; and to this is attributable the subtle and irresistible charm that all feel and so few understand, but which pervades most of our poet's verse.

At this juncture Sir Hew, whose estates were extensive but not very productive, fell into the hands of a "Mr.

Capability Brown "—nay, we believe his name was White—who had a repute for transforming peat-bogs into prairies of pleasantness, and barren sandy knowes into succulent Goshens; and there came in Mr. White's wake a crowd, or as it would now be called, a *gang* of sturdy Englishmen, fully provided with pick-axe and shovel for the *improvement* of the Baronet's arid and worthless domain. Our embryo poet, with his usual docility and zeal, was, among others, tempted to go into the Goshen-creating business, and contrived to pick up considerable information about planting and floral culture. It is to be hoped that Sir Hew, when the terrestrial hubbub ceased, after three years' tremendous exertions, managed to escape, less damaged than Sir Arthur Wardour did from the clutches of Herr Dowsterswivel.

In the intervals of labour young Ainslie had many opportunities of going out a-boating on that wild coast, forming acquaintance with nondescripts, half-sailor, half-smuggler, to be utilized afterwards with splendid effect in that most vigorous and graphic of marine lyrics, "The Rover of Lochryan," every line of which is redolent of "the saut sea-faem." The following smuggling reminiscences from Ainslie's own pen will be read with interest:

When, with some other boys from Girvan side, I attended the parochial school of Ballantrae, there was still a considerable remnant of those bold smugglers alive, altho' most of them were on the veteran list; and it is not to be wondered at that their wild yarns more stirred our blood than the quiet sober ploughman and shepherd tales we had listened to at home. Sorry indeed were we to learn that the cursed "King's Cutters" and the "Lubberly Land Sharks" had destroyed the noble occupation of the braw Free Traders, taming them down into sober fishermen, or giving them berths in his Majesty's men o' war.

The most interesting to us boys, of those mariners, was auld Rab Forgie. Rob had, in the gude auld times, kept an ale-house by the

Bennane Craig, where he had long officiated in the double capacity of landlord and sentinel for the "Boys o' Ballantrae" or the "Lads o' Lendalfit," hoisting a sheet by daylight, or blazing a whin bush by night, if any of the sharks were about.

One gallant crew of seven brethren, the big Coultars, seemed to have been his especial pet, and much he told us of their wild and reckless exploits. One of them occurred in his own howff.

They had, he said, made a fine clean run, had got all the goods snugly stowed away, and dreading no danger, were taking a refreshing booze, and, of course, "getting fu an' unco happy." Rob too, who ought to have been on the watch, had, in the joy of his heart, joined the social corps, when lo! as the night was near its deepest and the seven brethren were near their highest, the house was suddenly surrounded by a press-gang of thirteen men, and the Boys summoned to surrender.

This was a stunner; and what made the matter still worse, they had lent the Lintowers all their defensive weapons. "Surrender," however, was no word for a living Coultar to obey. A brief council of war was held, and Rob was sent to inform the captain of the gang, that if he wanted the Boys, he must come in and carry them out, as, "puir lads, they war owre far gaen to stagger ayont the hallan." Meantime Hughie, the tallest, stoutest, and coolest of crew, had ordered his brethren and Rob to squat down on the floor and trip and choke the men as they staggered in, while he, seizing the big cake griddle for a shield, and a brandy bottle for a weapon, stationed himself near the entrance. The door by the captain's order was soon forced, and the first two that entered abreast were floored or rather crushed to the ground by blows from the bottom of the bottle, which, worked by the ponderous arm of Hughie, fell upon them like a sledge-hammer. On, on they came, staggering and reeling in the dark over their fallen companions, not one of them, however, escaping a flooring and a taste from Hughie's bottle. All but the captain had now entered, and had been properly secured by the brethren; and he, seeing how matters went, stood hesitating at a little distance from the door, when Hughie, who could throw a missile with the precision of a pistol-shot, hurled the bottle at his head and brought him down like a bullock.

"Sic a sight as this," cried old Rob, "was never seen afore or since at the Bennane Craigs. Thirteen big men o' war tied up on my change-house floor, like sheep going to be smeared. O Hughie, Hughie, ye're a braw boy!"

As there were no lives lost, although considerable blood had been spilt, the affair ended much more pleasantly than could have been expected. The wounded were washed and salved, while the stupified and stunned were revived and refreshed with brandy. Indeed, according to Rob's account, most of them, and particularly the captain of the gang, suffered as much from the internal application of the bottle as from the external.

In the morning, our brave Captain Hugh and his brethren, without ransom, shipped their prisoners for the King's Cutter, which was lying in the offing, expecting no doubt a good haul from Rob's howff. Hugh at the same time sent a note to their Captain, in which he thanked him kindly for the very respectable and gallant delegation he had honoured him with ; stated that he had given the gang a night's lodging and entertainment, and treated them to a *bottle* apiece ; and concluded by trusting they might ever continue to be a credit to him and an honour to their country.

But, besides boating, there were other diversions to enliven the trenching, torturing and general bedevilment of the patrimonial acres. The young Southrons, in addition to shovel and pick-axe, had brought with them theatrical propensities—easily carried. Securing a large granary, they had it fitted up as a theatre. The "shows" proposed to be given to "the nobility, gentry, etc.," of the neighbourhood were the tragedy of "Douglas," and Ramsay's "Gentle Shepherd," and in due time Ainslie, to use his own words, was found to his great joy, "tall enough, lassie-looking enough, and flippant enough to take the part of the pert Jenny." "The first relish," he adds, "I got for anything like sentimental song was from learning and singing the songs in that pastoral—auld ballads that my mother sang (and she sang many and sang them well) having been all the poetry I cared for." He had also to "make up" for the part of "Anna," the waiting-maid and confidante in "Douglas." Monsieur Worth, as then, was not, and for that and probably other reasons, he did not send to Paris for robes, but was fain to borrow such habiliments as the country lasses willingly spared him for his *debut*. Hew was wont with infinite zest to recur to this episode in his life. A *soupcon* of carmine was tenderly bestowed on his cheeks through the medium of a rabbit's foot—a corset of generous proportions was forthcoming—earrings, curls, 'kerchiefs, and many nameless "tittivations" were strenuously insisted on—all the anatomical proprieties rigidly observed, amid much sly quizzing and repressed merriment, until the unblushing proposal of planting two small tea-cups on the sunken region just below his attenuated thorax, broke up the fountains of his patience, and "roused the lion in his den," as he burst forth with a vehemence that only provoked inextinguishable bursts of laughter, "I will dress no more!" These perhaps were Hew's happiest days.

> "O happy hours, so soon to cease
> For cares that bite and burn!
> O gowden days of perfect peace
> That never can return!"

How the Englishmen (not one of whom could pronounce "Auchtermuchty" for his life) got along with the "Gentle Shepherd"—who murdered "Bauldy" and who botched "Patie"—on these points history is silent. Let us take it for granted that "the nobility, gentry, etc.," were all hugely delighted, and gave the well-developed "Jenny" a most vociferous *plaudite!*

In 1809 (Hew being then seventeen) the *improvements* were pronounced complete, and Mr. Capability White, with his regiment of Southrons, shaking the dust from their boots, folded their tents and departed. For what reason we know not, Hew's father, who had been in the Laird's service for many years, also made his exodus, removing with his family to Roslin, about six miles

from Edinburgh.   Between one of the sisters—
"dear, sweetest Eleanora"—and her reflecting but
not ungentle brother, there sprang up an affec-
tion, almost motherly on her side, akin to that between
Mary and Charles Lamb, or between the wild-eyed
Dorothy and William Wordsworth, bound with ties that
only death could break.   She was of quiet and medita-
tive disposition, extremely fond and proud of the hand-
some, delicate boy, who even then gave token of his
coming power.   It was she who, in their rambles around
Roslin's mouldering tower, among the crypts of the
classic and beautiful chapel, the grandest relic in Scot-
land, by the banks of the Esk and the Muse's Hawthorn-
den, first opened his eyes to the beauties of Nature and
of mediæval art.   It was not written in the book of Fate
that our poet should sing—

> "The Blessing of *my later years*
> Was with me when a Boy"—

but he could truly say of this amiable and intelligent
girl—

> "She gave me eyes, she gave me ears,
> And humble cares and delicate fears;
> A heart, the fountain of sweet tears,
> And love, and thought, and joy."

After spending a few weeks luxuriating among the
lovely and romantic scenery of Roslin, Hew was
sent to Glasgow, where he was engaged to study law
with a relative.   He found the task, however, dry and
forbidding; so, within a short period, he rejoined his
parents, his next move being to a situation procured for
him in the Register House, Edinburgh.   His hand-
writing was even then singularly elegant, and his position
was merely that of a copyist—wretched drudgery, while

the remuneration was pitifully small.   Yet he remained
in this House of Bondage (except for a brief inter-
val) until 1822, having in 1812 ventured on the
bold step of taking unto himself a wife, in the per-
son of his cousin, Janet Ainslie, whose eldest brother,
John, was married about the same time to Hew
Ainslie's sister, Eleanora.   Hew's companions in the de-
partment to which he was attached were Alexander
Campbell, known as Editor of " Albyn's Anthology,"
to which Sir Walter Scott made some contributions ;
Robert Jamieson, translator of various Scandinavian
poems and sagas ; and Thomas Pringle, author of " Farewell
to Bonnie Teviotdale," and many years afterwards of
" Afar in the Desert I love to ride."   Pringle was a man
of considerable ability.   He was very lame and had with
a Mr. Robert Cleghorn, also lame, started a Magazine, of
which William Blackwood was publisher.   But it did not
pay, and after a short and unsatisfactory struggle, an ar-
rangement was entered into whereby Mr. Blackwood
took the concern into his own hands, relieved the gentle-
men of their duties, changed the name to " Blackwood's
Edinburgh Magazine," and became his own Editor.   It
never had any Editor but a Blackwood, notwithstanding
the fact that Professor Wilson and Mr. William E. Aytoun
were very generally credited with that dignity.   They
were simply contributors, advisers it may be in a way,
but they did not control the Magazine.   Of this there is
no doubt.   John Leyden was at this time in Auld Reekie,
helping Sir Walter with all his energy—and it was tire-
less—to gather material for " The Minstrelsy of the Scot-
tish Border."   Ainslie does not seem to have fraternized
very cordially with any of these men, but he certainly
never quarrelled with them.   If they stood aloof on ac-
count of a little brusqueness in his manners, Ainslie was

just the man to let them "gang their ain gait," and never
heed them.   He had in him that proud humility which
is so noble—even if it be occasionally an inconvenient—
trait in so many fine Scots whom I have known.   As a
man of genius,—a true and original poet,—he was worth
all the four men I have named rolled together.   His
name will live when theirs are forgotten, for he alone of
the five has dowered his country with creations that the
world will not willingly let die.

There was one, however, whom we may be very sure
he did not shun, and that was James Hogg, whose peri-
odical visits to Edinburgh were always hailed by every
admirer of the poetic gift.   It was Hogg's custom to take
up his quarters (free) at the White Hart Inn in the Grass-
market, sail round for a few days making calls on his
numerous cronies, and the day before his return to
Altrive invite them all to that ancient hostelry for a
"kift owre a chappin."   The summons was always
faithfully responded to.   A grand splore, beginning per-
haps at eight or nine and never concluding until two or
three in the morning, during which the "Shepherd" was
in the seventh heaven of inspiration, was the result.
Gills, mutchkins, and chappins, at the call of the visitors
and of the entertainer, most surely, appeared and disap-
peared with marvellous celerity.   Towards three A.M.,
mounting a chair, glass in hand, the author of "When
the Kye comes Hame" thanked the company collec-
tively and individually for the honour they had done
him, bowed himself out, and in two minutes was beneath
the blankets, leaving his guests, who all understood the
joke, to settle the *lawin'* with mine host of the White
Hart.   Of course Hew could not fail to pay fealty at
such a shrine.

Edinburgh was a terrible place for forgeries—literary

forgeries—in those days.   Dick Surtees, a near relative
of Lord Chancellor Eldon, managed to impose on Sir
Walter ; Allan Cunningham passed off as an antique
" The wee, wee German Lairdie," which indeed it would
have been dangerous then to have owned.   He bam-
boozled Cromek with scores of pieces which he pre-
tended to have jotted down from the recitals of certain
old wives and which were published in a volume entitled
" Remains of Nithsdale and Galloway Song," until the
bubble was pricked by Sir Walter ; Hogg himself aided
and abetted in the concoction of the far-famed "Chaldee
Manuscript," which set the town in a ferment and woke
up a tornado of indignation ; Lockhart scribbled articles
by the score in prose and verse, signed Hogg's name to
them, and when they appeared in Maga and the unfor-
tunate Shepherd was twitted about the authorship, his
hopeless and utter bewilderment,—for he had never seen
one of them—was pitiable to behold.   Nay, so audacious
did Lockhart become that he dumped into the Magazine
reams of stuff to which he affixed the name of one J.
Scott, a timid and very gentle dentist in Glasgow, going
so far as to advertise a two-volume collection of the
works of the great and only Odontist, who had never
penned a stanza in his life, gulling the public so that
when the innocent Extractor of Molars proceeded to
Liverpool on a small matter of business, he was pounced
on by the literary quidnuncs and fairly badgered into
accepting an invitation to a public dinner !   Miss
Clementina Stirling Graham had the felicity of making
Lord Jeffrey her butt.   In short, meet twenty people as-
sembled, and you might take your affidavit that nineteen
at least were unconscionable liars.   Sir Walter, as we
have said, was at this time preparing for the press his
" Minstrelsy," and it was the darling wish of scores of

poetasters to foist off their drivel on him as precious relics of the past.   Ainslie fell in with the general humour.   He wrote a few legends, some of them by no means unworthy of a place in such a repository, and, unless the writer be greatly mistaken, one or two were really accepted and printed in that invaluable publication.   Robert Chambers too was glad to accept some of them for his " Scottish Ballads."

Owing to his clear and rapid penmanship, Ainslie was recommended to Professor Dugald Stewart, then residing at Kinneil Castle, as a fitting amanuensis for works he was preparing for the press, and obtaining a short leave of absence from the Register House, proceeded to enter on his new duties.   His greeting by the Professor and his accomplished lady, Helen D'Arcy Cranstoun, sister of lawyer George Cranstoun, afterwards Lord Corehouse, was marked by great urbanity.   Mrs. Stewart was author of at least one song that will keep its place, for Burns added to it a verse and procured its insertion with music in Thomson's " National Melodies."   In a luxurious library, richly curtained with brocade and furnished with fauteuils, which the poet afterwards described as veritable "Sleepy Hollows," sat the dignified philosopher in the most imposing of the easy chairs.   So had he sat many years before in an Ayrshire mansion ponderously fishing for those metaphysical minnows which admiring satellites were wont to hail as forty-pound salmon, while at that moment in the cock-loft of a stable a few miles away, on a rough deal table, with the coarsest of paper and the stubbiest of pens, a tall swarthy lad, with stooping shoulders and great glowing black eyes, was, in an interval snatched from severe toil, reeling off those grim satires and delicious lyrics which were soon to confer on him an unlooked-for immortality.   To work went the twain (the philosopher and Hew), the one all head, the other but a whilom delver's horny hand.   Apparently so, but appearances are sometimes deceiving.   The Aristotelian and Baconian systems were passed in review, the brilliant theories of Condorcet exploded, the soap bubble vortices of Descartes blown into the air, the Monads of Leibnitz mercilessly ridiculed, the fallacies of Hobbes and Mallebranche exposed, Free Will and Necessity, the eternal Yea and the everlasting No put into the crucible and weighed.   Poor Hew's ideas began suddenly to expand.   He had received a new light and was impressed with an awe and respect for this venerable teacher that he never lost to his dying day.   It would have been the height of cruelty to suggest to the enthusiastic neophyte that possibly this august personality of Kinneil Castle might "kythe" as but "a little tin god upon wheels" after all.   Cruelty !   It would have been anathema maranatha—flat blasphemy—audacious sacrilege.   When Hew's "stent" was finished it was gall and wormwood to him to find next morning his flowing caligraphy mangled and destroyed by the Doctor's fastidious changes and interlineations.   In the morning too he would sometimes discover that Helen D'Arcy, under the midnight oil, had been toiling through the long watches to assist at the birth of some great idea, for numerous pages in her delicate Italian hand remained as mementoes of her wifely co-operation.

Returning to his desk in the Register House, ruminating on his cheerless position and increasing family, it occurred to him that there were other lands besides Scotland, and though it wrung him to the quick to sever the ties that bound him to his "cauf grund," he finally resolved that it was best for him and those dear to him, that transplantation, and that speedily, should be ef-

fected.   It was settled that America was to be their des-
tination.

In the Summer of 1820, during his sojourn in Edin-
burgh, he had contrived to take a brief scamper through
localities in Ayrshire connected with our national poet's
career, and the results of this trip were embodied in a
small work, enriched with some fine lyrics, and christened
"A Pilgrimage to the Land of Burns."   So it was to
Hew Ainslie that the Scottish and English-speaking
world is indebted for the proverbial phrase now on every
lip, of which fact he was not a little proud.   The entire
work (copies of which are now exceedingly scarce) is re-
printed in the present volume.   This original edition is a
12mo of 271 pages.   The following is a transcript of the
title page : " A Pilgrimage to the Land of Burns, con-
taining anecdotes of the bard and of the characters he im-
mortalised, with numerous pieces of poetry, original and
selected.   'We have no dearer aim than to make leisurely
pilgrimages through Caledonia, to sit on the fields of her
battles, to wander on the romantic banks of her rivers,
and to muse by the stately towers or venerable ruins
once the honoured abodes of her heroes.'—*Burns*.
Deptford: Printed for the author by W. Brown, and sold
by Sherwood, Keely & Jones, Paternoster Row, London.
1822." William Brown was a friend of the author's :
hence the publication in Deptford.

It has in many quarters been assumed that Hew Ainslie
ventured into the recesses of Ayrshire a doughty, single-
handed Paladin, and that " The Lang Linker," " Jingling
Jock," and "Edie Ochiltree" (a name borrowed from Scott's
"Antiquary "), were purely fictitious—myths taken for
the nonce.   It was not so.   Two companions, dear
cronies and bosom friends, accompanied him on his
tour of discovery, and all that is described actually

happened. He did not wish it to appear as if he, "The Lang Linker," actually turned out all the lyrics himself, and so attributes now this and now that to one or other of "the three merry boys." "Jingling Jock," or the "Jingler," was John Gibson, then a clerk in Edinburgh, afterwards holding the position of janitor and professor of physical training to the boys in Dollar Academy, at that time presided over by the well-known William Tennant, author of "Anster Fair." Gibson was a man outwardly exceedingly grave and dignified, given to philosophical conundrums, but at bottom ready to enjoy the most boisterous and roaring joke that could be perpetrated. Tennant, in his secret soul, was precisely of John's kidney, with a kind of placid and amiable "offishness" that strove to repel familiarity from those not admitted to his literary adytum. The consequences of these peculiarities may be imagined. It is quite improbable that the "Jingler" ever stood revealed to the unapproachable Hebraist, or that the learned Pundit did ever unbend in the society of the professor of gymnastics, with whose saltatory movements, poor man, he could have no sympathy.

The third, "Edie Ochiltree," was of a very different stamp. His name was James Wellstood, of the Society of Friends, and a shawl manufacturer on South Bridge, Edinburgh. To admirable temper, courteous manners, and far-reaching sagacity that fitted him for the conduct of great enterprises, he added a kindliness, warmth of heart and generosity only limited by the circumference of a purse that was not bottomless, traits which, it is pleasing to add, have been, nay, are hereditary among his numerous descendants—male and female, without exception—in America and other parts of the world. Though not a poet himself, only because lacking in the "accom-

plishment of verse," he counted among his friends and
correspondents the choice spirits and wits who maintained
the reputation of Auld Reekie as a literary centre in the
beginning of this century.—Captain Charles Gray; Patrick
Maxwell, editor of Miss Blamire's Poems; David Vedder;
etc., etc.   But for him it is more than doubtful if the
"Pilgrimage" would ever have appeared in cold type, and
it was his deft hand that furnished the illustrations.   He
also produced silhouettes of the participants, besides a
water colour miniature portrait of Hew Ainslie, which,
before the artist and the poet sailed for America, was
presented to the beloved Eleanora.   This water colour
was carefully treasured by her, and by relatives into whose
hands it passed after her death, its present possessor
being Mr. Mark Sanderson, Leith.   A copy of this minia-
ture, with the added profiles of the two other pilgrims, has,
through the kindness of Mrs. Annie Wellstood Johns,
been engraved for this volume.   A very old and re-
spected friend, James Smith, born in the same year with
Ainslie, and who died in London only three years ago,
at the great age of 97, had arranged to accompany the
three friends on their visit to the "Land of Burns," but
owing to unforeseen circumstances was unable to carry
out his intention.

Of the "Pilgrimage" it has been well observed that it
is a "prose-poetic medley of shrewd humour, quiet
observation, and fine feeling for Scottish character.   For
Ainslie was not only a poet ; he wrote also excellent
prose.   A young man's book, it is full of exuberant
spirit, but it has, beyond this, the narrative art that is
copious without being dull.   Then the Scotch that he
employed is of genuine quality.   Like the immortal
Canterbury group, these three pilgrims also beguile the
way with literary amusement ; only, instead of tales,

there are here songs and ballads. These compositions too are adapted with dramatic propriety."

A large edition was printed, and copies were liberally distributed, one to the Ettrick Shepherd, who however made no sign, as he had but little sympathy either with the pilgrims or their object. In his own edition (in conjunction with Motherwell) of Burns' works, he had the good taste and sublime audacity to pronounce the "Cottar's Saturday Night" a dull, heavy poem, filched in all its essential features from Fergusson's "Farmer's Ingle," and heaven-inspired Jamie Hogg had a perfect *scunner* at borrowing, though he graciously permitted Tommy Moore to borrow from *him !*

Another copy, but this was seven years after publication, was sent by James Wellstood, the indefatigible, to Sir Walter Scott, then near the close of his illustrious career and struggling bravely with adversity. It bore the following inscription—" To Sir Walter Scott, for the many hours of pleasure, amusement, and instruction which the subscriber has received from a perusal of the author of *Waverley's* writings, this small tribute of respect is humbly presented by his admiring friend, Edie Ochiltree." A brief letter followed the book, in which Hew's champion, after stating that the publication was a pecuniary failure and that the book had been suffered to fall into unmerited oblivion, requested Sir Walter, as a great favour, to give his opinion of its merits (not for publication, and it never was published, but that he, "the bosom friend," might carry it across the water to cheer an exiled poet's heart). Very promptly and courteously he was answered, and the great man's reply is for the first time submitted to the world.

" SIR,—I have always been in the habit of declining to give any expression of opinion either in order or intended to be con-

b

strued into any action which exposes me to more of publicity and
remark than are agreeable or convenient, still I may say this from
a respect for the friends who took part in the Pilgrimage you sent
me : It seems to be the work of a very amiable man with a feeling
for the beauties of nature and some command of language to de-
scribe them. The work has, of course, its faults, one of the greatest
of which is a want of that quality, the most necessary to eminent
distinction, I mean, originality. The author appears rather to have
written as he thought Allan Ramsay or Burns would have written
in his situation, than from the stream of his own thoughts. I shall
be sorry if I have given you pain by ranking your friend's talents
something lower than they probably stand in your friendly estima-
tion, but no person can be better aware, than one of your
communion, that an opinion, to be of any value, ought to be sin-
cere. I am, Sir, your obedient Servt,

(Signed)   W. Scott."

How difficult it is even for the finest intellect to
judge accurately the qualities of a contemporary. That
fatal nearness distorts and obscures the vision. Passing
by the question of originality as respects the prose por-
poems, composed in various measures—never eccentric
or crinkum-crankum, be it observed—and all distin-
guished by that artless ease and pawkiness of phrase that
tion,—making the tenderest allowance for troubles and
harassments then torturing the proud soul of this most
lovable of men,—granting that his days and nights were
so engrossed with herculean labours that he had but
little time to bestow on outside aspirants to literary hon-
ours,—still it will strike many with surprise that the keen
grey eye that could discern in Byron's feeble " Hours of
Idleness " scintillations of promise, utterly failed to see
any lines worthy of commendation or even remark in a
volume freighted with such attractive gems as " The
Ingle Side," " The Bourocks o' Bargeny," " Tam o' the
Balloch," " It's Dowie in the Hint o' Hairst," and " The
Rover of Lochryan."   All of these surely ought to have

been songs after "The Last Minstrel's" own heart. We can hardly imagine that he ever glanced at them, or saw more of the book than perhaps a sentence or two of Ainslie's scathing denunciation of the Government of the day, which for Sir Walter would be enough. But that his friend Jeffrey, coolly dissecting one of Wordsworth's three *bookies* containing the Yarrow poems, "Rob Roy's Grave," and the unapproachable "Ode to Immortality," in very loftiness of scorn could wave them aside and relegate them to the trunkmaker or the fat scullion for the singeing of chickens, is equally remarkable.

The author of "The Pleasures of Hope," then editor of the *New Monthly Magazine*, had clearer vision. Reviewing the "Pilgrimage" (October, 1823) although Campbell always eschewed the Scottish "dialect" in his own writings, he pronounced it "a lively and entertaining volume, with a mixture of the jocular, the serious and the sentimental, which gives it considerable piquancy and renders it an agreeable companion for an idle hour. . . . Some pieces of original poetry are also interspersed, but whether collected or original, the verses in which the volume abounds, and which, indeed, form the most valuable portion of it, are highly creditable to the taste of the pilgrims. *Some of the songs are very simple and beautiful*, and we have great pleasure in extracting the two following." "The Ingle side," and "On wi' the Tartan," are quoted in full.

Before sailing for America, an ardent but surely not strange longing seized Ainslie to revisit the scenes of his infancy and boyhood, to *daunder* once again, it might be for the last time, among the lowly "Bourocks of Bargeny" and his schoolboy haunts at Ballantrae, to tread by the stormy shore which the "Rover of Lochryan" has so dauntlessly defied and see

if the "Lads of Lendalfit" were as drouthy as of old.
He put his project into execution, and a sudden whim,
shall we call it, took hold of his fancy as he was so near
Dumfries, to extend his wanderings and pay his *devours*,
so he styled it, to Mistress Jean Armour, whom the world
has for well nigh a century persisted in calling "Bonny
Jean." Her illustrious husband never did so designate
her in his "Epistle to Davie," nor anywhere else when
she happens to be referred to. "Bonny Jean," the
heroine of the song under that name, was Jean Mac-
murdo, the beautiful daughter of the factor for the Duke
of Queensberry at Drumlanrig. I never saw her, but I
have sat a thousand times opposite the portrait of her
sister "Phillis the fair," in the habit of a shepherdess,
when for a time I resided with her widowed husband,
the late Norman Lockhart of Tarbrax and Ballageary.

On his arrival at Dumfries, Ainslie's first step was to-
wards the Gray Friar's Cemetery, where was Burns' grave,
as yet with but the most primitive of monuments. *He*,
too, had thought of emigrating "ayont the line," forced
by grinding poverty's hard behest, though he had been
saved at the eleventh hour. The coincidence could not
fail to strike the "younger brother in the Muses," and it
was in a somewhat pensive mood that he sought and en-
tered Mrs. Burns' humble cottage, where she lived in
comparative comfort and unquestioned respectability,
supported to a great extent by the bounty of Lord Pan-
mure, who, though he refused to contribute more than a
paltry pittance for the maintenance of his son and heir,
the Hon. Fox Maule, was pleased to indulge one of his
crochets by donating £100 per annum to Robert Burns'
struggling, half-destitute widow. She was overrun with
visitors, but the stranger introducing himself, she received
him in her kindly motherly way. His manner was very

winning when not oppressed by a sense of condescending patronage, and of that Jean had none. They got "unco pack an' thick thegither" in less time than it takes to tell it, and of course the dead poet formed the staple of "the twa-handed crack." She communicated to him a good deal that has now passed from a usually retentive memory. "Fowr oors" was just approaching, and the venerable dame proceeding to "mask" her tea, courteously invited him to stay and take with her a refreshing cup. They talked of relic hunters, and she professed herself utterly a-weary of them and their pertinacity. She spoke almost cheerily of the "roup" of their furniture after the great man's death and of the "awfu'" prices realized by eight-day clock, dilapidated "chairs, pans, griddles, etc." "But oh!" she said jokingly, "if they were to be sell't noo they wad bring twenty times mair." Hew wanted to take a short walk in some of the bard's haunts, and she immediately looked for a shawl to accompany him. "I'm thinkin'," remarked our young man, "that can hardly be the shawl ye got frae George Thomson." "No quite," was her simple reply, "that wad need to hae been well hained to last sae long. It's sax an' thretty years sin he made me that present." They walked together to Lincluden Abbey, I think—at any rate to a ruin—and she stood for a moment on a certain sheltered and lovely spot. "It was just here," she observed, "that my man aften paused and I believe made up mony a poem an' sang ere he cam' in to write it doun. He was never fractious—aye gude-natured and kind baith to the bairns and to me." Hew felt then, as he did long afterwards, that Jean, of all the women in the world, was the one specially fitted to be the poet's life-long companion. Clarinda had a dangerous "spunk" about her and would have stood no nonsense nor tolerated his admitted aberrations. Mary Campbell, though gentle and amiable, had yet Highland blood in her veins, and the ire of the scions of Macallum is sometimes easily roused and sometimes not so easily laid. But Jean was indulgent, patient, affectionate, gentle, good, and above all, most forgiving. She was by no means the un-tidy woman she has been represented. Her skin and complexion, even in advanced age, were fine, and she might be considered a comely, as she was unquestion-ably a pleasant, woman. When they returned from the trip, Ainslie proposed taking his immediate departure, but before leaving, grasping her hand, he said : "I wad like weel ere I gae, if ye wad permit me to kiss the cheek o' Burns' faithfu' Jean, to be a reminder to me o' this meetin' when I am far awa." She laughed, held up her face to him and said : "Aye lad, an' welcome." So he printed a kiss on her still unwithered lips and that was the last he saw of Jeanie Armour.

It was finally resolved that, leaving his wife and three children temporarily in Scotland, Hew should venture out alone to the United States and bring out his family when he had got a suitable habitation for them. Sailing from Liverpool in company with his friend James Wellstood, he landed at New York in July, 1822, being just turned of 30. Land being very cheap in Rensselaer Co., N. Y., Mr. Wellstood invested part of his money in the purchase of a farm at Hoosick, in which the poet settled and spent three laborious years. It was re-christened (need it be said who was the officiating pastor ?) THE PILGRIM'S REPOSE. A "sicht for sair een" the Lang Linker must have been at this era—6 ft. 4 in. in height, tipping the scale at 145 pounds, a mere bag of bones, in his shirt sleeves (garment unboiled), with a great straw som-brero and gauze inexpressibles, hoeing his melon patch

and pumpkin beds, he must have looked no bad repre-
sentative of the solitary of Juan Fernandez ; but for the
"Repose," alas !   Failing to make the farm pay, he
moved West and joined himself to the community recently
formed at New Harmony, Indiana, by the well-meaning
but somewhat visionary Robert Owen.   After giving this
venture a twelvemonth's trial he was compelled again
to hold up his hands, sighing that all was vanity and
vexation of spirit.   His next step was to form a partner-
ship with Price & Wood, a firm of brewers in Cincinnati,
and in 1829 he established a branch at Louisville, Ken-
tucky.   Previously to this, his family had rejoined him,
and the children were now becoming strong and hearty ;
but business misfortunes seemed to dog him.   His
brewery was swept away by an inundation of the usually
placid Ohio, and a similar establishment which with in-
finite pains he had erected in New Albany, Indiana, was
as effectually destroyed by fire.   Not discouraged by
those mishaps, for he was always of a hopeful nature, he
nevertheless determined that these should be the last
breweries he would ever build on his own account.   He
had to hustle for a living, and so it came about that for
the remaining period of his business life he sought and
found not unremunerative employment in superintending
the erection of like " institooshuns " for others.   How-
ever, he did not entirely escape the avenging Nemesis
that watches the " Worm of the Still."   How many
tumbles and falls he experienced while clambering and
treading the shaky joists and unbraced girders of the
structures he planned, how often he suffered from broken
legs and arms and collar bones—of these the annals of
brewerdom have kept no record.   Big and strong man
as he looked and was, he used to say merrily that he was
" a thing of shreds and patches," and that " Gude only

kent how he stuck thegither." He found time, however, also, to "stick thegither" a great many songs and invest all he wrote with a peculiar and inimitable charm. Converse with the Muse was a safety valve that permitted escapement of megrims that might have resulted from the constant worries and as depressing commonplaces of his exacting and laborious employment. He was wont to remark with his jovial laugh, " Had it no been for the rhymin' blethers I wad hae been but a puir miserable cretur." His sons had by this time attained to manhood and were engaged in the business of iron founding and bridge building. They attained to great eminence in this walk—their bridges over the Ohio, and other American rivers and ravines, being considered matchless in their day—and some of them are now ranked among the most prosperous and respected citizens of the " wild and woolly West."

Shortly after 1853, our poet paid a long visit to his intimate friend, Mr. Stephen Wellstood, in Jersey City. It was while he was living here that the terrible catastrophe of the steamer *Arctic* occurred.   While all were mourning the accident—the blunder rather—Hew had special cause to grieve, for on board had been James Smith, a son of his old Edinburgh chum and proposed associate of the " Pilgrimage ; " but the tears had scarcely dried when sorrow was turned into joy and the fatted calf was killed when his friend turned up alive and well, not having been doomed to go down with gentle Henry Reed and many another noble one into the dark and soundless waters.   The rescued James Smith, having emigrated to the United States, in his youth, carried on business in Mississippi from 1833 till 1855.   He then opened an establishment in Glasgow, where Mr. Stephen Wellstood was induced to join him in business in 1858, under the firm of Smith & Wellstood—a partnership attended with remarkable success. With the Smith family, as with the Wellstoods, Ainslie maintained till the end of his life the most affectionate relations, and the grandson of his old Edinburgh companion—Mr. James B. Smith of Clifford Park, Stirling—has in his possession some interesting relics of the poet. A younger brother of Mr. Stephen Wellstood's partner, who was left in charge of the Mississippi establishment—Col. R. A. Smith—was killed in the Civil War, in 1862.

While Hew Ainslie resided in the East, he was a welcome guest at many happy firesides, among which may be named those of John G. Wellstood and his brother; but perhaps his favourite howf was the residence of a charming woman, still living, Mrs. Margaret M. Wellstood Spence. To the poet she was as a daughter, and in truth he loved her well. Her children grew up around his knee, and to them and all the Wellstoods he was nothing but "Uncle Hew."

About thirty years ago, when New York was not quite so big, there were almost, at the corner of Eighth Avenue and 52nd Street, now the very centre of the American metropolis, twelve city lots, on which was a comfortable cottage occupied by Mr. Andrew Spence and his wife. There were few houses near it, as it was then counted "out of town," but the lots were neatly fenced in, and in the course of a short time a tiny *demesne*, which, if not resembling Goshen, was suggestive at least of the far-famed "Garden of Alcinöus," arose as if by magic. Flowers of exquisite hue and aromatic odours; pleached alleys in which various coloured grapes, peaches, apricots, and nectarines contended for supremacy; wisterias, laburnums, and Virginia creepers—all were there. The place was admired by tens of thousands, and often have

I stood in silent delight inhaling the fragrance and en-
joying the beauty of this oasis in the desert, totally un-
conscious of the enchanter whose spell had awoke such
floral harmonies in rude undigested Gotham.

But had I again visited the spot at the shut of some
July eve or the following morning about "the sweet hour
of prime," there might have been discovered through the
bosky vistas a spare gigantic figure passing leisurely
along the walks, caressing here a drooping rose and
dropping benediction there over a crushed lily, conspic-
uous by his "swallow-tail," his ruddy cheeks, his long
beard, white as snow, and bearing on his ample bosom
the never-failing red breast-pin—his only ornament; and
under this guise might have been recognized a form
not unlike that of Scotland's well-beloved poet—Hew
Ainslie.

In 1855 he collected his poetical works for publica-
tion. They were issued in a neat volume by Redfield,
publisher of Edgar Poe's Remains, with a fine portrait—
no likeness could be better—drawn by Mr. S. Wellstood,
and engraved by Mr. William Wellstood, a reproduction
of which is given in the present edition. The 1855
volume, which has long been out of print, contains the
following preface :

The author of the following fugitive rhymes has long been a
truant from the "laurelled walks of literature," and now, in the
autumnal gloaming of life, like Rip Van Winkle from his moun-
tain slumber, he comes once more among the haunts of men, with
antique accoutrements and forgotten phraseology, to enquire of
wondering old friends and neighbours whether this busy world
stands where it did "in his hot youth, when George the Third
was King."

To the query, "Why has the author written in the Scottish dia-
lect?" he can only reply, it is his mother tongue—the language
spoken by Scott, and sung by Burns. With its Doric music all his

earliest and dearest associations are entwined.   Its melodies lulla-
bied his infancy ; and will, he trust, contribute their share in tran-
quilizing his parting hour.   It was thus the twig was bent—thus
the tree was inclined—and thus must it eventually fall.

The fact that the author has spent the last thirty years of his life
in what was wont to be called the *far West*, will be apology enough
for the few pieces on American subjects at the close of the volume ;
and, with this simple avowal, he, in law parlance, *will rest his case.*

To the friends who on this occasion have *formed a square* around
him, what can he offer but the warm and spontaneous thanks of a
glowing heart, whose earnest wish is that they may individually
realize the pleasures their generous regard has so deeply conferred
on him.   And so

"To each and all a kind good night."

It was in 1855, while residing in New York, that I re-
ceived a very kind invitation to call on him at the Well-
stood mansion. My reception was cordial, and acquaint-
ance very quickly ripened into close intimacy.   His
personality was very striking. I have come across small
and big poets in my time. Among the first may be
reckoned Thomas Campbell and Thomas Moore, who
received my boyish advances with courtesy and kind-
ness ; also Gerald Massey, whose demeanour was on the
north side of friendly.   He had come over to America
to "abate the Christian religion " as an effete superstition,
and like Voltaire, rather flattered himself that he had
" done the business."   His audiences did'nt amount to
a corporal's guard, and of course his temper was not
improved thereby.   One of the reporters on the paper
with which I was engaged had dubbed him " a crank,"
and unaware of this, I in my innocence ventured into the
lion's den. The *finale* may be guessed—all protestations
were unavailing, and I who had braved the horrors of an
exceedingly frosty and slippery night to do the tiny
poet a service, had to take my leave in short order.

The big poets were Bayard Taylor, who has not yet gathered the laurels he deserves, and David Vedder, a Skald of such massive mould, that as Peter Still, the deaf poet observed, one required to be introduced to him at least twice—once on the north and secondly on the south side. Hew Ainslie in height towered above them all, and one look into his face sufficed—and that amply —for introduction. The impression he at the first glance made on me was recorded years afterwards, and conveys, I think, a fair idea of the man. "A truer Scotsman than Hew Ainslie never trod the heather. In person tall, stately and agile, even in advanced years, his face was the index of his character, frank, open, honest, genial and manly. He looked the personification of Wallace wight or Bruce, the warrior-statesman, and in a personal encounter he would have been a match for half-a-dozen ordinary men. Gentleness, however, was his distinguishing characteristic. His head was beautifully set on his square shoulders, his eyes were of a kindly and brilliant blue, his broad, lofty brow betokening a rare and transcendent genius."

In 1862 Ainslie's longing desire to revisit Scotland was gratified, and he took passage in an ocean steamer, a great change since the days when he crossed the Atlantic in 1822, solacing himself in the crowded steerage of the *Nestor*, with a greasy old pack of cards, as he has graphically told us. He had now much choicer fare, over which he gloats, not without reason, in that choicest and toothsomest of gastronomical effusions, "Buckwheat Cakes," a fitting pendant to which is "The Blackberries o' Bethel," a delicious little effusion addressed to Miss Katie H. Crist, then budding into womanhood, the beautiful and amiable daughter of his staunch old friend, Samuel B. Crist. He was away for a period of about three years, during the greater part of which he was the guest of his kind friend, Mr. Stephen Wellstood, at Bonnybridge, but he also enjoyed frequent rambles about Scotland, England, Ireland, and the Continent of Europe, never tiring of exploring and examining all the "ferlies at all comeatable." His reception in Edinburgh especially delighted him. He was made quite "the lion" of the hour. Professor John Stuart Blackie, a brother poet and one of the most accomplished and versatile men of genius that Scotland has produced since the days of Robert Burns, showed him much kindness, for which he was ever afterwards grateful. James Ballantine, and others of like poetical affinities, also received him with open arms.

On Ainslie's return to America, I found him but little worse of the wear. He soon departed for Louisville, the home of his children, abandoning the Muse for pursuits scarcely less congenial, the care of his eldest son's large and fine garden, surrounding his home. There, having experienced another fall, while walking through his room, serious trouble supervened, and to the great sorrow of his kindred and many friends he passed peacefully to his rest on the 11th day of March, 1878, at the patriarchial age of 86.

By way of further biographical detail, it may be mentioned that Ainslie had ten children : Jean, George, and Eleanora, born in Scotland (the last remaining with her grand-parents in Roslin until womanhood) ; William, Hew, Mary, Annie, James Wellstood, Lily and John, born in America. Of these, Hew and John were killed by accident on the street, and Annie was drowned in the Ohio, in consequence of a collision that threw her overboard. George and James Wellstood Ainslie achieved

honourable success in business as members of the firm
of Ainslie, Cochran & Co., Louisville Foundry.

On the occasion of the poet's Centenary, an enthusiastic
meeting was held, near his native place, at Girvan, when
Mr. Andrew Robertson, librarian of the M'Kechnie
Institute of that town, delivered an able and warmly
appreciative lecture on Ainslie, and several of his songs
were sung to the delight of a large audience. The pre-
sence of Mr. James B. Smith and Mr. Alex. Watt, (both
of whom had personally known the poet) and their grace-
ful tributes to his memory greatly enhanced the interest
of the proceedings.

It is not difficult to estimate Hew Ainslie's contribu-
tions to Scottish Song, and we are spared the trouble of
forecasting the place he is to hold in the National
Valhalla. For two generations his admiring countrymen
and countrywomen have seen to this, and their well-nigh
unanimous verdict can scarcely fail to be ratified by the
generations to come. The following extract from an
article on the genius of our well-beloved bard, which
recently appeared in the columns of the *Scotsman*, will be
accepted by most as a fairly balanced, judicial, and yet
generous summing up of his literary character :—

"Not many Scottish poets of minor rank come so
near the absolute gracefulness of the master singers. He
has rare sweep of vision, while compactness and point
distinguish his execution and his language. He sees
also with singular truth. The personality of the writer
gives additional charm to his work. Of broad and
masculine yet genial temperament, Ainslie appears to
have ever attracted esteem. In the land of his adoption,
as well as in Scotland, he gained friendships peculiarly
strong. . . . The late Principal Shairp, who had

much liking for Ainslie's verse, divided it into three classes—vigorously descriptive, sentimental and pathetic, and the love song proper.   If we remember that the first-mentioned section is pervaded by a true vein of humour, the classification may be deemed apt.   Perhaps the poet never wrote anything better than the melodious and impressive 'Dowie in the Hint o' Hairst,' but in the 'Bourocks o' Bargeny' his power is also well manifested. . . .   These lines afford a good instance of his delicacy of touch, in addition to his firm conception of a song :—

> " I left ye 'mang the leaves sae green,
>   In rustic weed befittin' ;
> I've found ye buskit like a queen,
>   In painted chaumer sittin' ;
> Ye're fairer, statelier, I can see,
>   Ye're wiser, nae doubt, Jeanie,
> But oh ! I'd rather met wi' thee
>   'Mang the Bourocks o' Bargeny ! "

The grief of absence gives him special room for his pathetic turn, prominent in 'The Last Look of Home' and other pieces.   But, unlike nine-tenths of the minor bards of the present hour, Ainslie was withal a cheerful thinker; and in such a stave as 'I'm Livin' Yet' there sounds a sort of Horatian satisfaction with fate."

In addressing "an old flame," in the "Pilgrimage," what a quaint, original and delightful turn does he give to the artless and lively lyric when, after avowing

> " There's an ember in us yet
>   That might kindle were it fit,"

he says or sings :—

> " Then fare-ye-weel, my fair ane,
>   An' fare-ye-weel, my rare ane,
> I ance thocht, my bonny leddy,
>   Thy bairns would ca't me daddy ;

But that braw day's gane by ;
Sae, happy may ye lie,
An' canty may ye be
Wi' the man that should been me."

His own favourite among his songs had always been
that by which he was best known.   Singular, was it not,
that he, like "the homeless bard who sang of home"
(Howard Payne), knew for so many years so little of his
own "Ingle Side."   We were talking of it one day and I
hazarded the assertion that the gem of his collection was
the "Bourocks o' Bargeny."   He looked a little sur-
prised when I ventured this remark.   I said that the
theme had been taken up by Robert Chambers in
"Young Randal," and later by Robert Nicoll in "Bonny
Bessie Lee," but that, *me judice*, it had not been handled
by either with such delicacy and power as had been
evinced in his own simple lines.   After some considera-
tion he seemed inclined to defer to my opinion.

On another occasion, when we touched upon the in-
spiriting power some poems possessed, I happened to
remark that while I was a "laddie" in Scotland there
were three brief "heart-heezers" that always recurred to
me in moments of depression.   The first was uttered by
Tom Campbell :—

" Yea, even the name we have worshipp'd in vain
  Shall awake not the sigh of remembrance again ;
  To bear, is to conquer our fate."

The second was from Longfellow :—

" O fear not in a world like this
  And thou shalt know ere long,—
  Know how sublime a thing it is
  To suffer and be strong."

The third was taken from the wallet of a poor nameless "gude-for-naething," of whom the less said the better :—

> " Gie her sail, gie her sail, till she buries her wale,
>   Gie her sail, boys, while it may sit,
>   *She has roared thro' a heavier sea before*
>   *And she'll roar thro' a heavier yet.*"

I should have liked some one to have seen Hew's face as I rang out these noble lines.

Of course, like all poets, Ainslie was keenly sensitive to appreciation of his merits. He was particularly pleased one day when I handed him a copy of "Wee Davie," by Dr. Norman Macleod, in which that man of fine genius and noble heart paid him one of the highest compliments my good old friend had ever received, on some lines in that exquisite poem, "It's dowie in the hint o' Hairst." The little book from that time was carefully treasured in the Louisville Library.

There is a peculiar and delightful raciness in his poetry. His conversation in our first talk fully developed this quality, and later still I was to find the identical trait in every letter he penned. A copy of Burns's Poems was on the table open at the page containing "Lines to a Mountain Daisy." "Look there noo," remarked Hew, "Mountain Daisy!—Mountain Daisy! Hech, wow! but the callant was in a creel to ca' it by siccan a term, and that after he had already kirsened it by its ain name, 'a gowan.' What Scotsman or Scotswoman or Scots bairn ever heard o't or kent it by sic a title? Mountain daisy! poof! That was ane o' the whim-whams o' Doctor Gregory. I wonder the Doctor didna persuade him to ca' his 'Mousie' a—rodent! Let's see how that wad hitch in rhyme :—

> " ' But *rodent*, thou art no alane.'

> " ' The best laid schemes o' *rodents* an' rogues
>   Gang aft agley.' "

And here a series of hearty guffaws followed his quizzi-cal commentary.   He added, " It wad hae been a long time ere the author o' ' Braid Claith ' and 'Leith Races ' wad hae stooped to ca' the gowan o' the green swaird, a —mountain daisy ! "   His contempt for everything that savoured of affectation or over-refinement, sheltered under any authority, however august, especially where the Scottish language, which he would never permit to be called a *dialect*, was concerned was always pronounced.

First, last, and all the time, Ainslie's burning love of his fatherland was conspicuous in all he said and did. Although always loyal to the land of his adoption, which upon the whole had been kinder to him than the country he left, and though at rare intervals in his poems may be found such lines as :—

> " That land where honour's more than name,
>   Where honesty's renown,
>   Where the *Eagle* made the *Lion* tame,
>   And the *Cap* has cowed the *Crown*,"

this quatrain is more than offset by his truthful though somewhat lugubrious picture of toilers amid the dismal swamps too prevalent on his own " dark and bloody ground "—e'en old Kentuck—and the transient "swither-ing " is completely neutralized by the freshly natural and joyous outburst :—

> " There's brawer countries on the map
>   An' richer, too, in kine an' crap,
>   But while this heart contains the sap
>   O' life, by jing !
>   Auld Scotland maun stan' at the tap
>   O' a' the bing."

Why does Scotland allow such men as Hew Ainslie to leave her ? She has not profited one iota by the lesson she received in 1786, when, had it not been for the prescience of a *blind* clergyman, (for ever blessed be the name of Thomas Blacklock) the greatest genius that ever conferred glory upon her and upon all humanity, would have been lost to her for good and all—shipped off to Antigua, and there held as a bondsman until the price of his passage was defrayed. Only think of it : the most illustrious son of whom she can boast,—not to put too fine a point on it—a slave, liable to be put on the auction block and sold to the highest bidder, if the ransoming shekels had not been forthcoming !

And now beloved old Hew Ainslie—last friend I had remaining who could call me " my dear Tom,"—farewell ! I drop—not offending thy *manes* by calling it " mountain-daisy "—a GOWAN of the green swaird upon thy honoured grave.

A Pilgrimage to the Land of Burns

THE PILGRIMS:
WELLSTOOD—GIBSON—AINSLIE.

LAND OF BURNS.

There were three carles in the east,
  Three carles of credit fair,
And they ha'e vow'd a solemn vow
  To see the shire of Ayr.

They went not forth like cadgers,
  A hotching upon brutes;
They went not forth like gaugers,
  A yanking on their cloots.

But frae the sta' they've ta'en a steed,
  And they've bun him to a whisk,
Syne awa' they flew, like the great Jehu,
  Or Willie o' the wisp.*

IN presenting the public with a Pilgrimage to the Land of Burns, we feel sufficiently assured that no apology is required for the subject. It were well if as little might serve for its matter and execution. Without, however, attempting any, we beg leave briefly to state the motives

---

* In *Scottish Songs, Ballads and Poems*, by HEW AINSLIE, published in New York in 1855, the pieces which had appeared in the *Pilgrimage*, are prefaced by the following note: "Before leaving Scotland for America, in 1822, the writer published, as a souvenir for his friends, a small volume entitled *A Pilgrimage to*

that led to, and what was proposed by, such an under-
taking.

Although in the poems of Robert Burns the humour,
pathos, and passion are all of the first order of excellence,
yet it is unquestionably his admirable talent at catching
"the manners living as they rise," of overhauling char-
acter, and the boldness and freedom with which he
ranges through the human breast, which give to his
writings that sort of electricity which makes every bosom
feel the shock, and every spirit a conductor ; which sent
them through his native land like lightning, and es-
tablished them therein as the necessaries of life. It is
this universal charm that makes his pages glitter in the
library of the lord, and lie in the winnock bunker of the
labourer, even more honourably thumbed than his vener-
able co-mates, Boston and Bunyan. It is, moreover, no
less owing to this, and to the closeness of his observation
and the truth with which he delineated, that the vicinity
of his birth-place is more interesting than that of almost
any other poet—as the land he lived in was ever the
scenery, and the beings he lived with always the subject
of his song.   .

Thus believing, the intended pilgrims, though. fully
aware that the industry and research of Mr. Cromek
had gleaned the gross of what the profusion of Burns'

the Land of Burns. Assuming from Scott's _Antiquary_ the
names of _Edie Ochiltree, Jinglin Jock_, and the _Lang Linker_, the
three ' Jolly Beggars ' set off from the City of Edinburgh for the
purpose of visiting the scenes which have been consecrated by the
genius of Burns, and of collecting any fragments of national songs
that might fall in their way. Two of the pilgrims, however, had a
double interest in the visit ; they were natives of the shire of Ayr.
The incidents of travel were all sufficiently real. The songs and
rhymes were made for the nonce ! "

genius had scattered, still were no less aware that "Auld
Coila's plains and fells," those noble volumes from which
he studied Nature in "'a' her shows an' forms," were still
fresh and unsullied as when he read them : nor did they
despair of finding (not, however, in such good preser-
vation) a quantity of that living material out of which he
built so imperishable a fame.   By rough draughts of the
one, and sketches of the other, they hoped to amuse
their friends ; as their prospect of amusing then, and even
until lately, had "that extent, no more."

It must, however, be acknowledged that although this
was the ultimate object of the pilgrimage, yet its origin
might be traced to the natural ripening of that affection
which we have for an author whose writings peculiarly
interest us.   We have, beyond all question, mental as
well as material relatives ; and in the world of Poetry and
Fiction there are kindred and tribes as certainly as in the
world of flesh and blood.   Nor is it less true that the
bard who speaks most familiarly and tenderly to those
passions and feelings that possess us most entirely will
ever stand, topping the list of all those to whom our
spirits are affianced.   Our admiration of his genius, in
the first instance, prompts us to peruse all he hath written
or said : our love and interest in the man next sets us in
search of all that has been said or written concerning him.
And, lastly, when love and admiration have in a regular
way begot enthusiasm, we long to see the land that gave
him birth, the rivers by which he roamed, the woods in
which he sang, the walls that kept him warm ; yea, even
our devotion extendeth to the old roof tree that strode
betwixt him and Heaven.

The spirits with which our three representatives of im-
mortal mendicity, Edie Ochiltree, Jinglin Jock, and the
Lang Linker, bad adieu to Edina, Scotia's darling seat,

can only be rightly appreciated by those whose senses
have been long familiarised to the smoke, sound, and
scent of a city, but to which their spirits stubbornly refuse
ever to naturalise, from an inborn love of Nature, or per-
haps from the circumstance of having spent their most
susceptible days where

> " Wild woods grow and rivers row,
>   Wi' mony a hill between."

The general appearance which our pilgrims exhibited,
both as to equipage and equipment, on the 23rd June,
1820, as at daybreak they bore away into the high road
that leads to Lanark, though it had little in common with
the dashing of modern tourists, seemed to a considerable
extent to wear the uniform of their purpose.   Their ve-
hicle, a machine of the curricle family, more notable for
its capacity and convenience than for the flourish of its
trappings or the freshness of its fancy, was kept rapidly
and steadily in motion by a noble " aiver " that had fre-
quently, with more lumber behind him, run fifty miles
beneath one sun.   It moreover contained, besides great
sufficiency of bottom room, a large cavity or cellarage,
which, being stowed with the most approved sorts of
wayfaring victualling, and accompanied with almost an
exciseable stock of liquors, put their appetites quite at
ease as to bad inns, while the large tartan cloaks in which
they were severally swaddled, and the manner in which
the whole man was so properly roofed in with the
ancient Kilmarnock bonnet, seemed a sufficient vouch
for the security of their skins.

The morning, at their outset, assumed rather a watery
look, the hills retaining too long their misty nightcaps,
which, when weighed with the clouds that lay, white and
swollen, bundled up in the west, certainly made it appear

considerably under the attachment of that old Scotch
saw, which warns us—

> " When the cluds are dim as daigh,
>   When the swallow flitters laigh,
>   When the haur hings on the hill,
>   When the leaf is lying still,
>   Gif ye'd keep dry, in back and wame,
>   Hap ye weel, or haud at hame."

In the face, however, of ancient wisdom it broke
pleasantly up, and to their long town-tempered senses the
country began to get delightful.   There is, indeed, some-
thing peculiarly delicious in the firstlings of a summer
morn, when the earth seems as it were in the unlimited
possession of bird and beast, and they sing and gambol
away fearlessly, ere man comes like a tyrant from his
haunt and drives them to their nests and coverts.

The Jingler, when they had passed all symptoms of the
city, fell into a sort of reverie, his countenance working
considerably, and his eye flying from object to object,
like a swallow catching flies, till with a sudden jerk his
jaws burst asunder, and forth came the following in a
whirlwind of din :—

THE JINGLER'S MORNING SONG.

> Give ear unto me, Linker,
>   And listen, Ochiltree,
> For I ha'e na seen a blyther day
>   Thae twenty years an' three.
> O ! my tongue it winna lie, my lads,
>   This bonny morn o' June :
> My words they come in rhyme, lads,
>   My breath comes in a tune.

Chorus—
And hurrah, and hurrah,
    And hurrah, my merry men,
I wadna gi'e a June day
    For a' the days I ken.

It's braw to see the blythe sun
    Come blinkin' o'er the lea ;
It's sweet to hear the cock-bird
    A singin' on the tree :
A singin' on the tree, my lads,
    An' whistlin' in the lift,
O ! it pits the heart o' Jinglin Jock
    Into an unco tift.

And hurrah, and hurrah,
    And hurrah, my merry men,
I wadna gi'e the lintie's sang
    For a' the sangs I ken.

We'll tak' it canny up the braes,
    Syne gi'e the beastie head ;
An' when we fin' a bonny howe
    We'll sit us down and feed.
Our kebbock an' our cakes, lads,
    Will mak' our meal a treat,
An' a wee drap o' Jock Barleycorn
    Will mak' the burnies sweet.

And hurrah, and hurrah,
    And hurrah, my merry men,
I wadna gi'e Jock Barleycorn
    For a' the jokes I ken.

At a good inn upon the confines of that extensive
moor that stretches with little interruption from the

village of Little Vintage to the town of Lanark, they
made their first baiting halt ; and though the outside ap-
pearance of the inn—a lone, wind-withered, ancient
house—promised little, the inside pleasantly belied the
promise, as an excellent breakfast was served with con-
siderable despatch, and despatched with a corresponding
degree of activity. By the time they were again ready
to resume their way, the wind had freshened seriously
from the west, and the sky had almost thickened to a
storm grey. They mounted, however, without any loss
of spirits, and with their tartans high buttoned, their
bonnets lowered, and their tongues busy, they sported
merrily away some fourteen miles of Scotland's very
barest earth. Carnwath Moor, with its south and north
connections, has with great propriety been called the
backbone of the country. It is, indeed, a bare highland,
up to which the softness of summer cannot creep ; and
though the heath may wave abroad its bloom, and the
marsh-bent its white downy banner, it is more to declare
that Summer is in the land than that it is there. Among
their other moorland amusements a tollman was, by
Edie's dexterity, manufactured into a good laughing
stock. He was a lean, hard, withered-looking thing—
seemingly nearly related to the heather and thistles
among which he had grown. Edie, catching his char-
acter, drew out an old foreign coin, and offered it for pay-
ment of the toll dues. The old moorcock, on "sighting
baith sides o' the shilling," declared "they could na win
through his yett for sic like siller." Edie, assuming a
foreign accent, asked him—"Vats de matter wid de
mony ?" "Because it disna wear the King's image o'
this kintra," replied the old boy, "sae canna pass my
purse neck." "It's van great pity you can't take my
coin, but you may as vell stop me for speaking de foreign

tongue as carrying de foreign mony." "Na, na," re-
turned the bar-man, getting hot, "that's anither tale—
it's nae concern o' mine, tho' ye had nae tongue at a'—
but Goth, gif ye ride on Scotch roads, ye maun pay
Scotch siller for them ; I'll learn ye that, Monshur Pick-
the-puddock." By this time he had put himself into a
violent passion, and his auditors into a violent fit of
laughter—so throwing him a coin to his mind, they drove
on to enjoy it.

About noon they reached Carnwath, rather a tolerable
looking village, from which they had a fine view of Tinto
Hill, and truly it was a grand sight to see its huge pin-
nacle tearing in twain the dark clouds that came sailing
heavily from the west.

When inspecting the village in search of "uncas," they
discovered an old woman sitting spinning in a cottage
door, and singing an old Jacobitical jingle, which, as they
had not seen it in Hogg's collection, they thought proper
to extract, as the record seemed hurrying fast out of the
reach of compilers. She had it, she said, from her father,
who was out in the '45, who sang it as long as he was
able, then she sang it to him, and during his last illness,
she declared, the sound of it lightened him more than
even the singing of the psalms.

THE GOUD UPON CHARLIE.

AIR—"*Owre the Water to Charlie.*"

If ye'd drink yill, and be canty still,
  Sin' the breeks has bang'd the kiltie,
Wale out the lads wore the white cockades,
  And delight in a Jacobite liltie.

Chorus.

Then up wi' the lads wore the white cockades,
    Altho' they be scattered right sairly,
There's a sough in the land, there's a heart an' a hand,
    That may yet put the goud upon Charlie !

Tho' a poor German daw's got the crap o' the wa'
    And our ain bonny doo it has pookit ;
We've guid falconers still, and when they get their will
    They'll put the right doo in the dookit.
Then up, etc.

Then keep your blue bonnet a wee ere ye don it,
    And keep your claymore frae the stouring ;
Ye may yet hear a horn on a braw simmer morn,
    That may thank ye weel for the scouring.
Then up, etc.

Tho' base hireling swords an' cauld-blooded words,
    Hae yirded the pride o' the thistle ;
Tho' the bouk's in the grun, yet the saul's in a son
    That may yet gar auld Hanover fistle.
Then up, etc.

The country that lies beyond Carnwath is merely a continuation of the moor that precedes it. Cultivation in some spots had commenced a sort of battle with Nature, but it was a losing one, the poor, stinted trees that were doomed to this banishment seeming to say to the passengers, " We are frae hame."

"Stuffing keeps out storming," says the same wisdom that prognosticated the storm by the sky dress of the dawn, and well it was for our wanderers to the west that they believed implicitly in both, for scarcely had they cleared the village when Tinto began to let down the bowels of the clouds upon them, which, assisted with a stiff, cold breeze and the surrounding scenery, gave a summer shower all the appearance of a winter blast. Indeed, it seemed hardly possible for wind and rain to have singled out a fitter spot for exhibiting their fury to advantage—a bare unhedged road, winding through a dusky ocean of heath, here and there broken with those grim sepulchres of a former world—peat mosses ; while at intervals, amid the dash and howl of the performers, the pewet threw in his weeping note with all the effect of a big O ! in a tragic speech.

A little before they reached Lanark, however, the day broke up, when a new heaven and a new earth opened upon them. Passing the town they gave their vehicle to the care of a boy, and turned into a footpath that leads down the river Clyde to the fall of Stonebyers. They had not proceeded far till they were surrounded by a covey of clamorous little boys that seemed to hover about the cataract like a flight of gad flies, preying upon passengers. They had picked up a quantity of large flashy words that former visitors no doubt had dropt, and though at first our pilgrims were not over fond of such an extensive cry of service, they soon got reconciled to them from the amusing and laughable way in which they speckled their boyish chatter with the big words they had caught. As every hoard hath its head, this little band of harpies had likewise theirs. His superiority, however, did not consist in exterior. He was a small, thin, yellow, ill-clad thing ; but there was an alertness in his movements, a spark in his eye, a certain gallantry in the manner in which he set even his rags a fluttering and bore himself in the midst thereof, that at once distinguished him as the " Triton of the minnows." When they came in sight of the fall he exclaimed, with all his dignity mustered—" You are particularly fortunate in visiting the fall to-day. The recent rains have, you see, swollen the river lip full, and dyed the foaming flood a rich brown. If you step down there, gentlemen, until your eye clear the impending sprays of that mountain ash, you will then have the whole volume before you at once." Then, turning to one of his mates, he proceeded in the same breath, though in a different tone and tongue —" I say, Tammy, man, I kent a whittie's nest in at the root o' yon rowen tree. I faun'd when it was wi' egg, an' I tell'd Johnny Brown o't ; an' the vile nigger harried it when the young cam' out, just bare gorbs, to gi'e to his brither's howlet ; but I gied him something 'ill learn him to harry my nest again, the dasht thief." Returning to his former tone, he went on—" Now, gentlemen, had the state of those bank steps allowed you to reach the margin of the linn below, the sight would have fully compensated your toil, as the whole cataract is there seen as it were awfully tumbling above you, but the path to-day is too slippery for the attempt. (Ye're a big liar, Will Harp, I never drew your set line but ance, an' there was naething at it but a black eel. It was Johnny Brown that cutted aff the heuks, sae was't, as sure's death—I may never steer.) The height of the fall, gentlemen, perpendicularly is 84 feet, according to the latest survey, and from the smooth water above to the smooth water below it measures in all 120. It is by all allowed, gentlemen, to be one of the first cataracts in the kingdom." There was something in this urchin's facility of change and distinctness of utterance that faintly reminded them of Matthew's " Bartholemew Fair," and it was not without reluctance that they paid off this clever little epitome of elder men, who can speak both coarsely and rashly to their inferiors and equals, but who have picked up pretty words for their superiors or those they look to gain by.

They had not long resumed their seats when a most unanimous cry arose among them for dinner, and as they had the materials for satisfying such craving in the gig, their business was to find a proper spot for the scene of action. This, luckily for the state of their stomachs, soon occurred, for having perceived on the roadside an opening that led into a wood, Edie, the Jehu of the party, drove fearlessly in, as if it had been a pendicle and pertinent of his own manor, until they reached a beautiful green spot, where they lighted, tied the animal to a bush in such a manner that he might enjoy the herbs, and with great activity and address discharged the gig of its savoury contents, lodging them, by the direction of Edie, under the shade of a most ponderous and venerable oak—one, in fact, that seemed the very Adam of the whole forest, where, in short space, and with little ceremony, an incredible quantity of pork ham, roast lamb, cheese, bread, and whisky disappeared. After this labour was accomplished—we say labour, for had anybody seen the long-bodied son of the west, Jingling Jock, digging with his large jockteleg into the fat flank of the Westphalia, quarrying out portions like rubble work for the purpose of building up the empty stances or vacancies that twenty miles' ride had created in their food repositories, he would have declared it labour, and hard labour too—they began to consider where they were seated, and finding they were in the vicinity of the Cartlan Craigs, famous on account of Wallace, and as the apparent antiquity of the tree they sat under seemed to warrant the supposition that he might have honoured it with his presence, their Scotch blood warmed within them. Patriotic toasts were roared abroad as if they wished the whole of Clydesdale should hear them, and at last, with a voice that made a trifle of the waterfall, they sang, " Scots wha hae wi' Wallace bled," and tossed up their bonnets in the air as if they meant to part with them.   There is no calculating when their mirth would have let them leave the oak, had not a cow which was grazing in the neighbourhood, instigated perhaps by the melody, begun to bellow, and, from the indistinct manner in which the sound was heard at first amid the other noise, made the Jingler believe it was the voice of the proprietor coming to pound, fine, or prosecute the party for their trespasses.   A cold sweat came upon him, his under jaw broke away from its upper brother, and he sat fixed and immovable, as if the strain of the cow had conjured him to a stone.   Another tune from the same minstrel satisfied them regarding the author, but the Jingler's harmony was gone, and they were obliged to leave their royal canopy, to humour the fears of this unfortunate victim of brutality.

Their ride was now for about seven miles down the rich banks of the Clyde, where at intervals were seen, through trees luxuriantly stuck over with infant fruit, the wide-gushing stream, pleasant corn fields, fenced in with woods and orchards, with many a fair mansion and neat cottage, giving life and interest to scenes as fair, when seen by the soft light of a summer evening, as any that, our pilgrims jointly declared, ever extorted praise.   The very human beings of these regions seemed distinct from their moorland neighbours, for instead of the cold hankering look that accompanied the answers of the latter, they had free replies to their queries from stout, merry-looking men, and plump, smiling lasses, affording matter of vaunt to the Linker, who had his favourite theory thereby countenanced, viz., that the mind and manners are greatly moulded by locality.

About five o'clock they halted at a country inn adjoining the village of Dalserf, pleasantly settled in the corner of an orchard. The landlord was a happy-looking young man, and apparently fast filling with that sort of intelligence which so well becomes a red nose and a round belly—the first of which, by the bye, seemed a promising bud, and the latter was evidently putting forth. In the course of some discourse they had with him he happened to repeat a few lines of Blind Harry's "Wallace." This was sufficient to send our pilgrims full cry through all the corners and covers of his intellectual domain, and though they found nothing but the common vermin of love ditties and garlands, he informed them that an old woman presently employed upon his potato field had, he believed, some eight days' singing of old songs, among which were some concerning his "country's saviour." Had this man of corks spoken of a gold mine in his field it could hardly have called forth the fervour with which they demanded where this land lay. The landlord, with a ready ale-selling civility, conducted them incontinently to the field, where half-a-dozen of the fair sex (fye upon't !) were beating with hoes the weeds from the young crop. The group was composed of personages of divers ages, from cherry-cheeked fifteen up to the old beldam with her yellow haffet pinched and puckered with the finger of Time like a quilted petticoat.

A few words from the landlord were sufficient to bring the party from the middle of the field. "Here's three gallant gentlemen, Girzy," said he, addressing the oldest, "wha wud fain hear ye croon ower ane o' your auld rants." The old woman modestly wished they might not think their time mis-spent, and without further ceremony they all doubled themselves down either upon the headridge or edge of the ditch. The younger ones bundled up themselves to smirk and titter, the older to enjoy a blast "o' the lunting pipe." Edie settled in front of the "auld wifie" to catch her song at the purest, while Jock and the Linker, mixed with the red-cheeked part of the company, kept filling up the pauses with laughter, produced from sundry queer questions they put privately to their partners.

The ancient songstress had certainly at that date lost both her beauty and her voice, yet there was the look of a contented spirit wrought in among her wan furrows, and a complaisance and a wish to please woven into her broken tones, that far more than compensated for the absence of both. It is, indeed, something truly heart-aching to see the old and stricken in years throw lightly aside the recollection of their frailty and furrows and cheerfully attempt to amuse the young. The spirit that can taunt at such efforts, or scan the doing without glancing at the intent, should have been born among the Kaffirs of the Cape, and remained there.

Circumstances and situation give, no doubt, the same sauce to mental that health and appetite give to culinary treats. It is, therefore, partly owing to this sauce of circumstance that the following old song was so loudly cheered, which, had it come from the press of John Moren, Last Speech and Ballad Printer to the Black-guards of a certain City, had possibly been held expensive "at the small charge of one penny," even in company with three or four other "Excellent New Songs," furnished in front with a decent cut of the Devil :—

THE KNIGHT OF ELLERSLIE.

A CLYDESDALE DITTY.

The Southern loun's wrought meikle skaith
　　Unto our west countrie ;
He has ta'en the gear, but he's got the wrath
　　O' the Knight o' Ellerslie.

Sir William's ta'en his sword in hand,
　　It was weel proved an' good—
Three waps o't roun' his buirdly breast
　　Has cleared a Scottish rood.

Upon his lip there is a vow,
　　Upon his brow a ban ;
He'll teach his faemen their ain march,
　　If it may be learn'd by man.

To see him in his weed o' peace,
　　Wi' the dimple on his chin,
O, stood there e're a fairer Knight
　　A lady's love to win.

To see him in his shell o' steel,
　　Wi' his braidsword by his thie—
O stood there e'er a braver Knight
　　To redd a hail countrie ?

Step out, step out, my gallant Knight,
　　By thysel' thou shanna' stride,
Tho' white the lock lie on my brow,
　　An' my shirt o' mail hings wide.

Blaw up, there's gallant hearts in Kyle,
  An' the upper ward o' Clyde ;
Blaw up, blaw up, a thousand spears
  Will glitter by thy side !

There's mony bow to goud, I trow,
  There's mae that bow thro' dread ;
But blaw a blast, thou wight Wallace,
  An' luik for man an' steed.

Oh ! wha could stick by pleugh an' spade
  When a Southern's in the land ;
O, wha wud lag whan Wallace wight
  Has ta'en his sword in hand !

To him that dares a righteous deed,
  A righteous strength is given ;
An' he that fights for Liberty
  Will be free in earth, or Heaven.

From Dalserf they took across the country for
Strathaven.

After a most disagreeable ride, for about eight miles,
upon a wretched up and down parish road, made or
rather unmade, as Edie observed, for the purpose of
killing horses and making men curse, they reached the
town of Strathaven, where, in an excellent inn, and over
an excellent supper, they laughed over the pleasures, and
talked over the aches, that forty-six miles' riding had
bequeathed to them. For, although such talk would
have made the man merry who is one half of his life out,
and the other half in the saddle ; yet, to our pilgrims,
whose habits were rather sedentary, and who might be
said to journey through life on their bottoms, such stirring
and jolting was new, and new habits of any kind require

use to make them fit.   It is not, therefore, to be
wondered at, as they stretched out their limbs to the fire
and their hands to the glass, that Edie's thoughts and
voice wandered into the following old chaunt; or
that the spirits of his brethren rolled sweetly up with it
in chorus, spinning and twining it away like a three-twist
cord.

THE INGLE SIDE.

It's rare to see the morning bleeze,
    Like a bonfire frae the sea;
It's fair to see the burnie kiss
    The lip o' the flowery lea;
An' fine it is on green hill side,
    When hums the hinny bee;
But rarer, fairer, finer far,
    Is the ingle side to me.

Glens may be gilt wi' gowans rare,
    The birds may fill the tree,
An' haughs hae a' the scented ware
    That simmer's growth can gie;
But the canty hearth where cronies meet,
    An' the darling o' our e'e—
That makes to us a warl' complete,
    O, the ingle side for me!

Next morning our pilgrims, in spite of yesterday's
fatigues, and eke the tempting softness of their couches,
had inspected the town and vicinity of Strathaven, ere
the hand of the hired labourer had lifted his tools; and,
shortly after, they were to be seen snugly seated in their
travelling machine, upon that extensive moor, famous

and notable as the scene of the memorable struggle of Drumclog.   The Jingler, who pretended acquaintance with the spot, began to enlarge upon the battle, and seeing here and there in the fields several large columns of rough granite set up, he, with the full consent and concurrence of the other pilgrims, immediately rated and reckoned them as the memorials and death-stances of some great men on that fearful day.   Just as this opinion was settled, and severally attested, they overtook a countryman, going forth, spade in hand, to the moss-digging.   After saluting him, according to custom, they, with a look of shrewd discovery, asked him what memorable incident in the engagement did that stone mark, pointing to one of these erections.   The man, turning up a puzzled countenance, as if he had been questioned by a foreigner, replied, " What's your wull, sir ? "   " I mean," said the Jingler, " to what particular in the battle of Drumclog does that monument point ? " "The battle o' Drumclog ! " returned the clown, " I canna say onything anent that ; but the way that thae stanes are staunin' there, gif it's them ye mean, is just to let the laird's kye claw themselves on, as ye see there's nae trees in the parks."   Luckily for our pilgrims, this son of the soil had no spice of quizzery in him ; on the contrary, so much were they taken with his good-natured bluntness, that they dismounted, and by the side of a rill, which tempered their " gude Scotch drink," they drank with him their morning dram.

They were now within a few miles of the shire of Ayr, upon a fine, gentle, sloping highway, and keeping up a spirited march to the tune of the merry larks, of which Edie thought the sky in this quarter had an extra supply, longing and ready for an extraordinary burst whenever they entered that far-famed shire.   This the stone on the

road had no sooner announced than each pilgrim, to the
extent of the crying ability in his possession, set up an
"All hail!" to the Land of Burns, flourishing, at the
same time, their "Kilmarnocks" manfully round their
heads, even until their throats and arms were severally
fatigued.   After a refreshing pause, they burst into
"Ayrshire Lasses," at which they continued steadily
until they reached a farm house, where, upon the grass
plot of its "kail yard," a "sonsy hizzy" was spreading
clothes. The Jingler, whose spirits were in a spring-
tide to-day, accosted her with "Gude morning to ye,
my bonnie lassie, and mony a fair stitch may ye wash
as white—aye, as the lily hand that rubs them."
"Thanks to ye, sir," said the girl, "for your mony wally
words; but, I doubt, gif I dinna mak' my claes a wee
thing whiter than my han's, the gude wife will think they
hae gotten little gude o' the sapples." "Weel then,"
returned the Jingler, drawing largely upon his stock of
gallantry, "I'm a seceder from the gude wife, altho'
aiblins she be a woman o' nae sma' rummelgumshon, for
onything that has a likeness to a fair creature like thee is
far dearer to me than gif it shamed the lily o' the valley,
the goud o' Ophir, or the cedars o' Lebanon." She
replied, laughing, that if he keepit ay in that mind it
would be a bra business to hae his arle penny in her
pouch.   "But I'm feared," she continued, "gif ye hired
at Beltan, there would be ither words amang your win'
afore auld Halla'-day, for ye ken, it's a bonnie burn that's
aye clear and sweet lips that are aye dear."   "By the
Land o' Robin," cried the Jingler, in great heat, "thou'rt
a canty queen. I could hae sworn it was Ayrshire we were
in by the blink o' that blue e'e; and the smirk o' that
sweet mou' might wile e'en Mess John frae the pulpit, far
less a daft chiel frae a whisk. Tak' care, lads, till I light."

So saying, he made an effort to leave the gig, which Edie observing, applied the whip, and drove him, growling and kissing his hand, away from the tempter.

About eight o'clock, they came in sight of the pleasant village of D——l,* in the vicinity of which the Pilgrim John had sown his wild oats—that unshackled, that pure portion of our existence when, like the colt, we kick and scamper about as the spirit bids, ere the world hath taken us (like the horse jockey) and broken us into dull posting and laborious uses.   His heart waxing fuller and fuller at the sight of the hills and valleys of his native shire, he was at last under the necessity of venting it a little in

A HAMEWARD HYMN.

Each whirl o' the wheel,
　　Each step brings me nearer
The hame o' my youth—
　　Every object grows dearer.

Thae hills an' thae huts,
　　An' the trees on that green ;
Losh ! they glour in my face
　　Like some kindly auld frien'.

E'en the brutes they look social
　　As gif they would crack,
An' the sang o' the bird
　　Seems to welcome me back.

O ! dear to the heart
　　Is the hand that first fed us,
And dear is the land
　　And the cottage that bred us,

* Darvel.

An' dear are the comrades
  Wi' whom we once sported ;
But dearer the maiden
  Whose love we first courted.

Joy's image may perish,
  E'en grief die away ;
But the scenes o' our youth
  Are recorded for aye.

In passing through the village John was recognised by a number of his former schoolmates, who soon brought to and boarded the curricle ; attacking him at all quarters, with "Eh, man, is this you?" "Dear sirs, how's a' wi' ye?" "Gude save us, man, how hae ye been?" etc., etc., to which he kept up a sort of running reply of "Very weel, thank ye," at the same time thrusting out his hand amongst them, which they shook with friendly and almost dangerous violence.

It is with a mixed sort of feeling that we meet, after a lapse of years, with those early frends whose portraits we have treasured up in the inner chambers of our hearts. We smile, perhaps, on seeing one whom we parted with in beauty's bud, blown into full flower ; but we sigh as the eye wanders over the pale cheek of her we left in the bloom, and fret at the spoiler Time "who mows the rose away and sets the lily there."

With some difficulty they got the Jingler and his first friends disengaged, when half a mile's further riding brought them to W—hs, the residence of his father.   A welcome needs something more than words to speak its sincerity ; but there is a certain brightening of the eye, and a squeeze of the hand, as if the heart pulled the nerves, that admits of no dispute.   Such symptoms may always be depended on as genuine, and such it was our pilgrim's bliss to meet on " Bonny Irvine's side."

The forenoon was mostly spent in visiting some beautiful and classic spots—"Galston Moor," o'er which the " glorious sun " looks upon the " Mauchline belles," being quite at the door; while "Loudon's bonny woods and braes," together with " Patie's Mill," are their near neighbours.   Indeed, the whole surrounding scenery was full of strong poetical provocatives, being generally in that half wild, half cultivated state, where neither the broad, rich meadow gives monotony, nor the bare, bleak mountain disgust.   Here the Jingler was literally at home, and a pleasant sight it was to see him take old friends by the hand, and give and receive histories of what had happened since their last meeting.   In stumbling upon spots that had felt him with a lighter foot, he broke away into long rhapsodies on the pleasure of play-days, and coming to a wood he had seen—nay helped to plant —some twenty years ago, he could talk in prose no longer, so forth came

A JINGLE TO A TREE.

Look, neighbours, do ye see
That giant o' a tree?
Would ye think that I had seen
That stately tent o' green,
A finger-length o' timber—
A thing so light and limber,
That a crow, intent to bigg,
Micht hae ta'en it for a twig
An' wove it among straws,
Such a trifle then it was—
Tho' now ye see the crows
Might hatch upon its boughs.

Thae trees, that hale plantation
Hauds the glen in occupation ;
Faith, I hae seen the day,
For all their grand array,
When wi' little stress I could
Hae carried the hale wood ;
Tho' the smallest now, ye see,
Might be my gallows tree !
Lord hae mercy upon me !

The idea that concluded the Jingler's " Tale," attract-
ing and involving so many *violent* and *painful* reflections,
obstructed their mirth for a time, and they moved on,
solemnly musing upon these apparent and frightening
facts—that a man may not only " cut a stick to break
his own head," but that he may likewise plant a tree with
his hands that may come to hurt his throat.   These
unpleasant, though *exalted* reflections, were pleasantly
interrupted by meeting a fair dame, to whom the Jingler
flew lovingly, and was as lovingly received.   Sweet con-
verse and kind enquiries ensued, until, " like a summer's
cloud," the dame's matrimonial engagements came across
his recollections, and then, with the valour of a man who
makes inclination the vassal of honour, he stiffened his
talk into cold ceremony and bade her adieu.   He
thought proper, however, as the incident sat a consider-
able time on his recollection, to commemorate it in
rhyme, whereof the tenor follows :

TO AN OLD FLAME.

It was you, Kirsty, you,
First warm'd this heart, I trow,
Took my stomach frae my food,
Put the devil in my blood,

Made my doings out o' season,
Made my thinkings out o' reason,
It was you, Kirsty lass,
Brought the Jingler to this pass.

But when amaist dementit,
My sair heart got ventit;
O, what happy days we'd then,
'Mang the hazels o' yon glen!
Aft by bonny Irvine side
We hae lain, row'd in a plaid,
Frae the settle o' the night
To the income o' the light.

An' Kirsty, lass, I see
By the twinkle o' thy e'e,
An' Kirsty, faith, I fin'
By a something here within,
That tho' ye've ta'en anither,
An' tho' ye be a mither,
There's an ember in us yet
That might kindle—were it fit.

Then fair-ye-weel, my fair ane,
An' fare-ye-weel, my rare ane.
I ance thought, my bonny leddy,
Thy bairns would ca't me daddy.
But that braw day's gane by;
Sae, happy may ye lie,
An' canty may ye be,
Wi' the *man* that sou'd been *me*.

After dinner, they revisited the village, where some fine specimens of Scottish kindness were presented to them, and there, likewise, they had the pleasure of encountering the ancient Ayrshire tea-drinking, or "four hours," as it is there termed—toasted cheese upon cakes being presented to the first cup ; wheat bread and butter to the second ; and to the third, or even fourth, if pressing can effect it, a rousing glass of whisky. This meal met with the unqualified praise of our pilgrims in all its parts, but they seemed particularly *intoxicated* with the *spirit* of its termination. The village being a manufacturing one, after tea they went through a number of their workshops, where they saw at work several female weavers. This sort of probationary state, they were told, most of the mothers in the village had gone through, but on marrying they generally gave up the "box and babbins" for a "baby and a blanket." In general they seemed stout, healthy-looking girls; still their situation seemed a very unseemly one ; and though, in Homer's days, Penelope might look a highly poetical and interesting figure at the loom, yet in the days of Edie Ochiltree, Jinglin' Jock, and the Lang Linker, so "dowy and dowdy " did the she weavers of D——l appear, that even Jock, flaming as he was, could not afford them a couplet. Indeed, he signified his regret, "that a bonny Ayrshire lassie should, instead o' handling the inwork o' a house, or tripping amang the green grass, be condemned to mak' her bread by such unluesomelike thumping and kicking."

Before sunset, they again reached W—hs, when Edie, who was always in search of antiques, discovered a choice collection of old ballads, dream books, mole books, jest books, etc., etc., compiled, as is frequently done in the country, by purchasing, now and then, from passing pedlars a pennyworth of their verse or prose, and stitching it to their former stock, which often occasions most amusing combinations, such as "George Buchanan," or "Paddy from Cork," lying like brothers with "The

Cloud o' Witnesses," and " Wise Willy and Witty Eppie,"
in the arms of " Alexander Peden." The present pile
was huge, seeing it was fifty years since its foundation
was laid, and some of its songs they considered scarce,
among which may be reckoned the following, entitled—

THE WAESOME DEATH O' CHRISTY FORD.

TUNE—*Tamlane.*

It was nae Hallowday, I trow,
   It was nae Beltane tide ;
But winter winds owre baudly blew,
   For feckless folk to bide.

The lee-light that December gi'es
   Was lairing in the wast,
Whan Christy, wi' her orra claes,
   Was boun' to dree the blast :

Waesuck ! for wight, on sic a night,
   That's far frae hauld or hame :
But, O ! waes me for them that flit
   Ere term tide's fully gane.

An' wae war some in Gentree ha'
   Whan Christy took her plaid ;
An' sair the bonny bairnies grat,
   An' hecht her aye to bide.

She kissed them ance, she kissed them twice,
   Wi' heart owre grit to speak ;
But heavy, heavy, were the tears
   That drappit frae her cheek.

Out owre the buirdit burn she gat,
    Out owre the bourtree slap;
An' slowly wan she thro' the broom,
    For steerless was her stap.

Aye, lightly may ye loup, maidens,
    Wha's hearts nae sorrows ga',
An' lightly, lightly, may ye loup
    Wha's waists are jimp an' sma'.

I wou'd nae ban the wily thief
    Wha steals to fen' his need;
Nor yet wou'd I the wight that's wrang'd,
    Wha strikes his wranger dead.

But, Rab o' Barnton, thou boots
    A heavier ban than mine—
An' gin we meet on yird, that spot
    Shall kep my blood or thine.

Now dark and grusome grew the night,
    As 'twould be the death o' a',
For first there cam the slushy sleet,
    An' syne the drifting snaw.

She's waigled owre Knockgirron Moor
    Owrecome wi' cauld and care;
But when she gat to Gariloup,
    Her legs they dow nae mair.

O! had I found thee, Christy, there,
    When yet thy lip was red,
Afore the last o' mony a tear
    Was frozen on thy e'elid,

Afore the low an' heavy moan
   That loosed thy soul for heaven,
I'd gripped thee to my breast bane,
   An' a' that's bye forgiven.

The snaw was now her bed sae white,
   The deep drift was her sheet,
The wild wind sung her last baloo,
   An' soun', soun' was her sleep.

The morning raise on banks an' braes,
   On fields an' forests fair ;
It wauken'd burdies frae the bough,
   An' outlyers frae their lair ;
But she that lies in Gariloup
   Nae morn can wauken mair.

An auld wife wins by Girvan side,
   Was a mither ere yestreen,
Now waesuck ! she maun bairnless dee,
   Altho' she dee or e'en.

For villains there's a gallow tree
   Wha kill by gash or stab,
But wherefore does it pass the rogue
   That kills like Barnton's Rab ?

The hour had now arrived when their worthy and
venerable entertainer proceeded, as was his wont, to
finish and wind up the duties of the day, after the fashion
so feelingly described in the " Cottar's Saturday Night."
Any one who has witnessed, in the true spirit of grateful
holiness, " the Priest-like father read the sacred page,"
must have, with the immortal bard, exclaimed—

" Compar'd with this, how poor Religion's pride,
    In all the pomp of method, and of art,
  When men display to congregations wide,
    Devotion's every grace, except the *heart!* "

Pompous display and refined composition may assist in keeping us awake in our Sunday seats ; the eye may be pleased with the orator, and the ear with the oration ; still, our immortal part is left untouched, to commune at will with the earth.   But it is not so when true heart-bred piety bends before his Maker, and in the unpolished language of his fathers, pours out his gratitude and praise.   He employs no earthly trickery to catch the ear of the creature, he seems to be aware of no presence but that of the Creator, and, should the pious worshipper be heavy with years, leaning as it were over the awful edge of eternity, the pouring forth of his soul seems like the out-goings of Noah's dove in search of a place where the worn and weary spirit may at last repose in peace.

This evening devotion, independent of its eternal utility, appeared to our pilgrims as an admirable partition betwixt the day and night ; the quiet solemn thoughts which it is calculated to produce being a far better and surer guarantee for a sound and dreamless sleep than when the anxious thoughts or noisy merriment of the day follow us up to our pillow.   This idea was no doubt suggested by the profound sleep with which our pilgrims separated the second from the third day of their journey.

The ensuing day being Sunday, our pilgrims, from the absence of that common bustle which distinguishes a country life, were allowed to sleep deeper into the day than they intended.   Indeed, in all well-regulated families of the West, those labours or duties of a noisy nature are either executed on Saturday night or reprieved until Monday, so that, as no rude stroke was heard at the building of the house of the Lord, none may disturb the solemn repose of His Sabbath. The kitchen, in particular, undergoes a complete change; instead of being filled, as on other days, with all sorts of sounds, from the chirp of the infant chick, up to the boom of the big wheel, you hear only the clatter of your shoe on the sanded floor, the hum of flies, or the buzz of a captive wasp upon the window.

Without, all undergoes a corresponding change; "the mattock and the hoes" rest by either side of the door, the plough sticks up to the shoulders in the furrow, and the cart stands in the court with its shafts reverentially pointed to heaven. Even the lower animals seem, in some degree, tempered to the day. The old watch-dog, having no visitors to announce, no beggars to bark at, lays aside not a little of his every day din; while pussy, purring unmolested by the fire, seems for a time to have forgot her week day wickedness. The "feathered throng," from the removal of those rural sounds that generally mingle with their notes, appear to have a Sabbath song; the cock crows in a more solemn key; and even the hen, as she tells on the dunghill what she has done in the loft, seems to have a Sunday cackle.

Then may be seen the labouring man, his step slow and broken, with his brawny hands folded up and reposing in his pockets, as he

> " Walketh forth to view the corn,
> An' sniff the caller air."

He hath sold the strength of his arm, and the sweat of his brow, during six days, but on this he hath no tasker but his own taste, no master but his Maker; he washes away the soil of the hireling, and puts on, with his Sunday coat, a look of reverence and independence.

After breakfast, our pilgrims soon convinced them-
selves that the low, monotonous sounds that prevailed
within, keeping up a lulling tattoo upon the drum of the
ear, were likely soon to lay them asleep; to avoid which,
they stept out into the fresh fields, and in a little settled
themselves on a shady spot by the river side that com-
manded a view of a kirk gate.   John, however, whose
thoughts, when let loose, like the carrier pigeon, were
always flying back to the lady of his love, crept away
from the rest into a more retired nook, evidently big with
something that struggled for utterance.   He had not
long absented himself, when the church path began to
take on its load.   First came the aged and infirm,
obliged to take the road earliest, as stiffness and corns
obliged them to be longest upon it; then followed in
little bands, the sober, careful-looking family man, with
his wife and children; and lastly came the young men
and maidens, light of step and light of heart, little think-
ing that as they were fast gaining ground on their elders
they were likewise fast making up to their cares and
their corns.

Few men who have passed, or are passing, the green
years of courtship, need be told that a fair creature in a
grove, her gentle ankle toying with the wood flower and
her fair arms with the tender spray, is an object superior,
beyond all reckoning, to the smart gaudy thing that wan-
tonly dances over the flags and glitters against painted
walls; to the one, the hand and heart are tasked at a
salute, and, How do ye do? while to the other the
bosom opens like a church-door and the arms spread
abroad like the boughs of a wall tree.   To our pilgrims,
therefore, who had both been extensive practitioners of
woodland courtship, the feminine part of this last group,
as they fluttered their white muslin and ribbons down

the winding lane against the deep green foliage, were particularly interesting, and as they disappeared amidst the trees and bushes, at its further extremity, they shook themselves up with a sigh, as one does on the vanishing of a pleasant dream.

" Can you tell me, Mr. Lang," said Edie, as the procession closed, he having observed that though most of the lasses "were in the fashion shining," yet, monstrous!

> " Their coats were kilted, which did plainly shaw,
>   Their straight, bare legs, that whiter were than snaw "—

" Can you tell me the meaning of this strange nakedness on the land ? "   The Linker held it to be merely a piece of rural economy, obtaining most in the West of Scotland on account of frequent rains rendering the paths oftener bad ; and it being also, as a matter of health, better to have the feet dry when in church than comfortable when coming, as he declared they had always shoes and stockings in their possession, carried generally in their laps, but used like their Bibles, only when engaged in worship.   Edie, however, on the contrary, thought he perceived a vestige of Popery in it, as walking barefooted in Catholic countries, on flinty roads, is a very common mode of doing penance, and consequently deemed it a relic of the " great whore " that had skulked amongst them since the Reformation.

While they were thus attempting to hunt down this barefooted custom by conjectures—loitering carelessly amongst the flower-bearing herbs, and enjoying the cool river breeze that came wandering through the bushes to their bower—John re-appeared with

> " Fire in his eye, and paper in his hand."

" In the name o' the Nine," cried Edie, " what sort of

3

a brain-web is this you have been weaving? Is't a sonnet to a bumbee, or a monody to a dead mush-room?" "No, Edie," he replied, "it neither touches upon insect nor fungus, so should not affect either you or your brother; it's nothing less than a pretty half-yard o' tenderness to my darling in Duneddin." "Truly it's a pleasant joke," said the Linker, "to hear one speak o' a particular darling who measures out bales o' love to everything he meets under forty years of age and a bonnet. Your love letters, Jock, should be like State letters—printed circulars."

"What a black interpretation to put upon my fair, general loving-kindness for Nature's 'noblest works.' Why, lads, ye seem not to understand that a right built heart ought to be like a stately mansion, where, though it be under tack to one particular tenant, is still room enough to take in a stranger now and then, aye, and entertain him nobly too, without at all infringing on the lease of the legal occupier. O, confound your sma' scrimped butt-and-ben hearts that barely ha'e accommo-dation for one lodger; give me the man whose door and whose heart stand ever open to honest men an' bonny lassies; for, in the words of the gallant Sterne, I declare sternly, 'that he who hath not a love for the whole sex cannot have it for one.' But listen, and be converted"—

JINGLIN' JOCK'S EPISTLE TO JEAN.

"DEAR JEAN,

> Here, while the ither twa are lying
> Ahint a buss, and eident spying
> The kintra bodies, kirkward hieing
>   To furm or pew,
> I wi' my head and hand am trying
>   A verse to you.

An' tho' the Irvine by me flows,
A stream weel lik'd, ye may suppose;
An' tho' my e'en, an' lug, an' nose
          Are feasted fine,
Still backward to Auld Reekie goes
          The rovin' min'.

In truth, we're queer, inconstant craft,
Whyles harden'd, when we should be saft;
Whyles dowie when we should be daft,
          Against the grain;
An' when we look for pleasure, aft
          We meet wi' pain.

But, Jeanie, lass, I maun admit,
Up to the date that here I sit,
We've met wi' nought but pleasure yet—
          The very best;
An' faith we're e'en a canty kit
          As ere draive west.

Slee, wily Edie, an' the ither—
That creature like a greyhun's brither—
Hae been sae wud, my honest mither
          Thought they'd the vapours,
An' wiser folk had ta'en a swither—
          Seein' their capers.

As for mysel'—but that's a theme
I'd aiblins better let alane—
Faith, I've been naether 'lag nor lame'
          To play a stick;
Altho' in naething had the name
          O' blackguard trick.

It aften seems to me surprising,
(Ye'll ferly at my moralizing),
That chiels wi' right afore them rising,
        As plain as parritch—
Will listen to the deil's advising
        An' scorn their carritch.

A lad may gi'e an antrin sten',
Ayont the prudent scores o' men ;
But when he maks mischief his en'
        Wi' spirit willin'—
It's then the thoughtless fool ye ken
        Frae settled villain.

Some folk are high an' low by fits,
An' some are mean to fill their guts,
But gif a deed o' mine e'er pits
        Rogue to my name ;
Say, then, the Jingler's tint his wits,
        His reason's gane.

Now, Jean, I would na think it queer
Gif ye should ax yoursel' just here,
What's set the Jingler thus to clear
        His gaits to me ;
As I had ony right to speer
        What they may be.

The truth is, Jeanie, lass, I fin',
That in this wicked warl' there's ane,
That gif she lays nae wilfu' sin
        Upon my back,
I dinna care a puddin' pin
        Hoo ithers crack.

But fareweel, lass, for faith the sun
Ayont the crap o' Heaven has run,
An's westward hitching to the grun,
      Sae we maun in,
Wi' spoon an' plate, right belly fun,
      To stent our skin.

Ance mair fareweel, and min' this, Jean—
Tell ilka kin' enquiring frien',
That in the land o' pastures green
      An' flower an' flud,
Our feeding like our fun has been
      Baith great an' gude.

An' fare-ye-weel again.   Like twa
Are sweirt to part, but maun awa'—
I turn to say, that like a wa',
      Or as a rock,
Ye hae a frien'—aye, worth them a'—
      In Jinglin' Jock."

Having dined, the inmates of the house, and by their example, our pilgrims, dispersed themselves about the apartment, each with their Bible, or "gude buik," to study apart, until, in the face of conviction, inclination, and conscience, the majority of the party read themselves asleep. The heaviest, dullest part of a long sunny summer day is, without doubt, the afternoon ; the very birds then take a sort of refreshing drowse to prepare them for the exertions of the evening ; the delicate flowers—even the hardy " Mountain Daisy "—look languishing to the west for the dewy breeze of eve. The Jingler, who occupied a snug berth within " rax o' the ingle lug," was among the first to " steek " his book and eye. His vicinity to the simmering of the tea-kettle certainly considerably assisted the author in gaining this victory over the spirit.   He had, however, commenced, when awake, a sonnet to the tea-kettle, which he continued to prosecute when in the " dead thraw " between sleeping and waking; even some of it, he thinks, was composed when " clean awa'."   Indeed, it bears internal evidence of this, for to say the least of it, it is a very sleepy piece.

LINES TO A TEA KETTLE.

Tho' to me it is a feast,
Whan the morning leaves the east,
To hear ilk merry thing
That can whistle, chirp, or sing,
Be its belly on the fluds,
Be its seat upon the wuds,
Or its wing among the cluds,
Cry out, wi' a' its might,
A welcome to the light.

Yet on drowsy afternoon
There is naething like the croon
Or curmurrin' o' the kettle,
Be it tin or copper metal,
When wi' glancin' han' an' pow
It sits clockin' owre the lowe,
Oh! the goudspink on the timmer
Is naething to its simmer !

The very sweetest strain
Aften speaks o' days are gane ;
Sae, whatever bliss it brag,
In the hinny there's a jag ;

But thee—thy saddest hum
Still talks o' joys to come,
And thy wildest minstrelsie
Cries for butter, toast, and tea.
Thou'rt an instrument, I wot,
Without ae gloomy note.

I declare, as I'm a sinner,
It's a cordial after dinner,
On an easy chair to sit,
Wi' the fender 'neath your fit,
While in the deafening ear
Thy drowsy hum we hear,
Till it steals us clean awa'
Like a baby's hushy-ba ;
Syne we're aff, in visions sweet,
To where flowers lie in the weet
Or Beltane lammies bleat.

Syne to wauken frae our dream,
As the sugar or the cream
Plays plout into the cup—
Hech, how happy we luik up
To the frien's are smirking o'er us
An' the food that reeks afore us.
O, by Jingo ! it's exceeding—
'Tis the Paradise o' feeding.

In fetching a walk at the dew-fall of the day, our trio
fell in with a fine canny cracky body. He had been
born in the neighbourhood ; bred a weaver ; had listed ;
fought through the late war ; and again returned to his
native water-side and weaving. With somewhat of a
philosophical eye, he had marked the change that war,

and the increase of manufactures, had wrought upon his native shire; as the high price of corn, and the large bounties offered for recruits, had changed both the green mantle of the fields, and the grey jackets of its cultivators, to red. And now, though the land was again putting on its green, and the hind his grey, it was not with equal benefit to both; the former had lost a quantity of its broom and briars, which was "gaining a loss," the latter had lost his rude gait and rough honesty—a loss ill supplied by the polish of a guard-room.

The old veteran, they found, was quite a depot of anecdote, civil and military; but his 'prenticeship recollections, as they lay in the warmest corner of his heart, and lay, to boot, upon the sacred land of Burns, had, to our pilgrims, a very superior interest. His memory stretched back into those good trusty old times when borrowings and lendings were unattended with the formality of bond or obligation; when an "auld gudeman" would cry, on a pinch, over the burn to his neighbour, for a "claut o' siller," and on the instant it was heaved across, stowed in a stocking foot. A dispute, he told them, once arose betwixt two such, as to the extent of the sum lent; the borrower thought he had got fifty guineas, while the lender was dead certain it could only be forty, because he "had them lying bye in a bit sma' baggie that only could tie tightly owre twa score." In strong contrast with this ancient honesty and unlimited trust, he stated that a modern drover, being met lately on his way to a court of justice, was asked by an acquaintance, "whar' he was gaun." "I'm on a braw errand the day," said he; "I'm gaun to win a plea." "Win a plea!" said the other; "how do ye ken that?" "O, that's easy kent," he replied, with a knowing wink; "the case is referred to my oath!"

It was late ere our pilgrims could persuade themselves
to part with this amusing old man, and, as they intended
being "early at the gate" next morning, they were ex-
cused, by particular dispensation, from attending upon
the "buiks." So, taking farewell of their hospitable en-
tertainers, and making a few arrangements for the mor-
row, they hurried to bed, and were all, in a twinkling, as
"soun's bats at Yule."

As they had planned—like men in the important heat
of a mission—our pilgrims took Monday at such an ex-
tremity that the villages of Newmilns and Galston were
passed ere the smoke was visible from a "lum head,"
and they drove at a fine "han canter" down the Kyle
Stewart as the "herd callan" was going whistling forth
with his charge to those deep green pastures from
whence is extracted, by the handsomest of all horned
cattle, the Kyle cow, that cheese which, under the desig-
nation of "Dunlop," has so many lovers in the land.
We intended spending a few words in prose upon it, but
the Jingler has anticipated us in his

CROON TO A KYLE COW.

My bonny brockit leddy,
I can see that Kyle has bred ye,
Wi' your snawy face an' fit,
An' your riggin' like a nit.
I can guess, even by your fleck,
Or your genty nose and neck—
In fact, your very tail
Declares ye seldom fail
To sen' hame a reaming bowie,
Three times a day, my cowie.

Thy bulk is no uncouth,
Like the monster o' the south ;
Nor hae ye ony trace
O' that hairy Hielan' race
That come south frae hills an' bogs,
Like droves o' horned dogs ;
No, thou'rt the queen o' brutes
That moveth upon cloots !

I protest there's no a man
In the borders o' this lan'—
Nor a beast, if ye haud aff
The canny sucking calf—
That delights so much as I
In what is ta'en frae kye ;
For here let it be tauld,
That be it warm, or be it cauld,
Be it cream'd, be it kirn'd,
Be it lappert, be it yearned,
Be it sour in croak or pig,
Be it crappit whey or whig,
Be it blinkit, be it broke,
It's welcome aye to Jock.

But whan, as fat as grease,
It comes forth in name o' cheese,
As rich and yellow's brimstone,
An' as big's my father's grunstone—
What e'e is no ta'en captive,
What jaw is then inactive,
When the gudewife cries, " Fa' on ! "
To the wally whangs an' scone ?

When a drouthy chiel or twa
Tak' a scour o' usquebah,

Gin about the hour o' ten
The browster wife bring ben
A stow o' cheese, made nice
Wi' a stouring o' the spice
Fra the ingle, fat an' fryin',
An' on cakes sae crumpy lyin',
Gif the lads be in a plight
To ken the day fra night,
It's an unco pleasant sight.

O ! to see on simmer morn,
When the craik's amang the corn
An' the gowan's 'mang the grass,
A sonsy kintra lass
Rin scuddin' thro' the dew,
An' cow'r down aneath her coo,
Syne wi' canty sang an' glee
Stroan the leglin to the e'e,
Sic a sight has gart me swither
Atween the taen an' tither—
That is, her lip sae sweet,
An' the bowie 'tween her feet.

Having gained an eminence on the left bank of that
valley in which the Irvine flows, our pilgrims found
spread before them, all within eye reach,

" . . . . That place o' Scotland's isle
That bears the name o' auld King Coil,"

which contains almost the whole earthly materials of the
"Vision." Before them, "low, in a sandy valley," sat
the "ancient burgh" by the edge of the blue frith,
building slowly into the quiet air its morning smoke; a
little to the left the " hermit Ayr staw thro' his woods ;"

beyond which the woody tract of "Bonnie Doon" was
seen hemming brown Carrick hill with green; while,
here and there, castle steading and cot glistened amongst
the trees like "gowans 'mang the grass." Summer that
morn seemed to have done her utmost for the scene.
Heaven and earth mingled beautifully their green and
gold, and the drowsy breeze loitered on the land as if
afraid to disturb their union; the fields on every hand
spread forth their blossoms to dry; the broom shook out
its gilt tassels; and the gallant brier, bridegroom-like,
mounted its blushing cockade. Birds choired it loudly
in the brake, while their merry leader, the lark, "in
pride of song," buried himself in the blue of heaven.
When they came to a halt, by the mere arrest of sense
and soul, John, who had been in training for this fair
show, drawing off his bonnet, and stretching out his
hand towards "auld canty Kyle," gave utterance to

A MORNING "ALL HAIL TO COILA."

Huzza! to the land of our minstrel's birth,
  The green fields that wav'd in his eye,
The echoes that rang to his woe, or his mirth,
  · And the mountains that bounded his sky!

It spreads on the sense like a beautiful dream,
  'Tis the mantle that Coila wore;
Bedropp'd with the forest, enstrip'd with the stream,
  And fring'd with the fret of the shore.

Yet had Winter been here, with his heaviest sigh,
  Had the sea rolled his heaviest wave;
And the stem of that flower, which now gladdens the
      eye,
  Stood a monument over its grave;

It had still been the land of our heart, the sweet spot
  That stands in our fancy the first,
And symbol'd more truly the desolate lot
  Of the ill-fated spirit it nurs'd.

Ye sweet birds of Summer that sing from the brakes,
  Ye larks that the blue vaulting skim,
How the bound o' the heart to your melody wakes ;
  'Twas your sires that gave music to him.

What spirits have warm'd wi' his melody, oft
  To be quench'd in the chill o' the world !
Or hoisted a banner of manhood aloft,
  That necessity's mandate has furl'd !

But here let us vow that, whatever may come,
  However our fortunes be starr'd,
Our precepts shall be those that have hallowed thee,
  Fair Land of the Patriot and Bard !

No worldly-wise man could believe in the quantity of
spirit that rose from the gig on this occasion. The
pleasure and delight received from poetry does not
always correspond with its excellence ; but when the
bosom is warmed, and the faggots of the feelings, as it
were, all heaped together, it is a poor piece indeed that
cannot light the pile.

In the village of Monkton they halted to "corn the
naig," at a neat-looking inn, embellished with the effigies
of the gallant Black Bull.   On summoning the house, a
bonny Ayrshire lassie appeared, whom they discovered
to be the landlord's daughter, and named Bessy Ballan-
teen.   She was clad in the maidenly habit of her country
—short gown and coat, which even elegantly became a

tall, shapely figure, such as a hot fancy may raise, but
that seldom appears "in animated dust," more especially
to the ringing of an ale-house bell.   Her face was a
sweet one.   And none might look upon it—saving, per-
haps, a few of those natural eunuchs called bachelors—
without wishing blessings on her "bonny blue e'e," and
a long summer to the red rose that bloomed beneath it.
John, who had convinced himself that although her eye
glistened sweetly with the soft blue of feeling, it likewise
contained a pretty spark of roguish wit, began, on her re-
appearing with a beverage they had bespoke, to recom-
mend his long friend to her as a suitor, announcing him
as one whose heart had been hurt by a jilt.   She re-
plied, with a merry readiness, that though she would
gladly put a sa' to any poor bodie's sair, yet matters were
not come to that pass with her that she needed to take
another lassie's leavings.   Edie was then recommended
as a brent new body, hale in lith and limb, wi' a heart as
soun's a bell, saving the crack that she had given it.
"But what's wrang wi' yoursel'," said she, looking arch,
"that ye're sae fond to ha'e your frien's fit in a tether,
an' yer ain out?   O, may be 'ye're saird an' set by?"
He was as free to the full as the rest of his friends, he
said, and it was nothing but downright modesty that kept
him from being the first offerer.   "Na, na," she replied,
"that tale 'ill no tell, for the lad that can offer his lass to
his frien' may mak' a big brag o' his frien'ship, but for
gudesake let him never speak o' his love."   "Weel, my
bonny Bessie," he rejoined, "tho' ye lightly my love ye'll
may be tak' twa words o' my advice just as a kin' o' keep-
sake."   "Wi' a' my heart, and be thankfu' to the mense,
but let it be short, for lang counsels are like Cameronian
sermons, no easily minded."   "O, as for that," said he,

"ye may sew't in your sampler.   It's a bit o' an auld
sang, but I hae forgotten the tune.

> " ' Dinna tak' a fat man,
>   For he's a lazy loon ;
> Dinna tak' a lean man,
>   For he's soon broken doun ;
> But a gude half an' half man,
>   Just neither young nor auld,
> O that's the man to comfort ye
>   An' keep ye frae the cauld.' "

"An' Bessy," he continued, "be gude to the honest
woman's son whase blessed bosom ye mak' your nest in,
for gif ye dinna live in harmony, whan under the un-
slipping bauns o' matrimony, it were better for ye that your
bridal hap were a mortclaith, an' the coverlit o' your bed
sax fit thick."   "Mony braw thanks to ye, reverend sir,"
said the girl, laughing, "I didna ken wha I was talkin'
wi', but gif I kent whar ye're to preach niest Sunday I
wou'd hear ye, though it sou'd cost me aught miles' tramp
an' a bawbee to the broad, especially sou'd ye tak' for
your text ' Be not unequally yoked.'   Ha ! ha ! "

By this time the gig stood at the door.   "Son of the
West," said Edie to John, as they stept into it, "the
charms o' that fair maid o' Monkton ought to be sung."
"And they shall be sung," said he in a great heat, "be-
fore I feed, though I should fast till Friday."   Ere they
reached "Auld Ayr, whom ne'er a town surpasses," he
redeemed his right to breakfast by producing

BONNY BESSY BALLANTEEN.

AIR—" *Green grow the Rashes, O.*"

Gif ye're a lad that langs to see
    The fairest face that e'er was seen,

Gae down to Kyle—it's worth your while—
An' speer for Bessy Ballanteen.

CHORUS.

Bonny Bessy Ballanteen,
Bonny Bessy Ballanteen ;
Mony a bonny lass I've seen,
But nane like Bessy Ballanteen.

Altho' your lassie ha'e nae faut,
  Altho' you've sworn her Beauty's Queen,
I'll wad a plack, ye change yer crack,
  Gif ye saw Bessy Ballanteen.

Bonny Bessy Ballanteen,
Bonny Bessy Ballanteen,
Mony hearts for you 'ill green,
My Bonny Bessy Ballanteen.

Yet gif ye're tether'd to a stake—
  Gif ye're a married man, I mean,
For fear ye'd rue your marriage vow,
  Beware o' Bessy Ballanteen.

Bonny Bessy Ballanteen,
Bonny Bessy Ballanteen,
Your wedded love's no worth a preen,
Gif ye saw Bessy Ballanteen.

But gif ye're free as man may be,
  A canty birkie swank an' clean,
Gae try your luck, my hearty buck,
  The prize is Bessy Ballanteen.

Bonny Bessy Ballanteen,
Lovely Bessy Ballanteen ;
He is in heaven wha is at e'en
Wi' bonny Bessy Ballanteen.

As the "dreary dungeon clock" was chiming nine they entered the town of Ayr—and dreary, we doubt not, it hath often sounded to those poor wretches that have been doomed to shiver in its black cellarage; yet, to our pilgrims, it rang like a greeting peal, while the measured quantum of its strokes raised up pleasant bread and butter scenes—prospects that twenty miles' riding had sufficiently endeared. It was their hap to light at an excellent inn, about half-way up the High Street, kept by Mr. M'Culloch, and they feel it "writ down in their duty" to recommend all future wanderers in the West to search it out, as they would search for happiness, though with them it commenced rather equi- vocally; for, on reaching the breakfast room, John, who had caught the barmaid's name in passing the kitchen, with the familiar swing of an old acquaintance turned upon her with, "Dear me, Peggy, hoo's a' wi' ye? I dare say I hae not seen ye this forty year." Peggy, who was rather upon the outposts of maidenhood, and con- sequently not very well pleased with the alleged date of their former acquaintance, replied tartly, "Then gif ye hae nae seen me this forty year ye never saw me." John saw he had touched on a sore, so drawing off and directing his jokes to a more invulnerable quarter, they soon began bantering, as friendly as if their acquaintance had really been of the supposed standing.

Having breakfasted and repaired their travelling ap- pearance a little, they proceeded to muse over the im- mortal mason-work of the burgh and gaze on the habits of its inhabitants—pleasant pastimes both. To those, indeed, who have had their spirits deeply refreshed at the pure founts of Nature, the active, muddy, noise and bustle of their fellows is, for a time, an amusing spec- tacle; and it is not till we have mingled in the mass,

4

and the spirit grown society-sick, that we begin again to thirst for those renovating springs. Ayr, too, is a neat, fair, little town ; not one of those thick-set podges of man and matter in which one feels buried like a leaf in a forest, but a distinct clump that eye and mind can take up at once and inspect without confusion.

The first object that interested our pilgrims was the "Wallace Tower." It is certainly a most questionable display of the art Masonic ; and the artist seems more than once in its erection to have been in a "queer swither," the bottom being pure barn work, the middle dove-cote, and the top steeple presenting *in toto* somewhat the appearance of a willow grafted on a squat thorn. "The Auld Brig" next stood before them, striding sulkily "above the broo ; " frowning so sternly at the gaudy upstart below that the very waters change colour as they pass on to their new friend, who enlivens them with his white cheek, and throws down all his "virls and whirligigums" on their breast. Then came the "Ratten Quay," a landing-place a little below the "New Brig," for wherries, skiffs, and fishing-boats, and a depository for fish offal and other orts of the town. Rats, finding there a decent livelihood and good lodging in the embankment, have procreated to a famous extent.

After circumventing, intersecting, and re-intersecting the town—after feasting their eyes with the ancient fort, the "Barns o' Ayr," and the house that Wallace was thrown from, they finished their town tour by calling upon a fair female friend of the Linker's. She had assisted largely in sweetening his childish days on the banks of the Girvan, and consequently with her name and girlish look many pleasant feelings were associated. Ten years, however, had wrought changes upon both, and although, when our hearts are allowed to continue on in their natural growth, we still show, at whatever after period, the same with enlargements ; yet Fashion, that vile forester, often prunes, cuts, and twists our most prominent shoots and grafts anew, so that although the trunk may be the same the fruit is not.   The uninterested pilgrims enjoyed this meeting much, and it was even pretended that a few lines were found in the Linker's possession that evening to the following effect :—

THE BOUROCKS O' BARGENY.

I left ye, Jeanie, blooming fair,
　'Mang the bourocks o' Bargeny;
I've found ye on the banks o' Ayr,
　But sair ye're altered, Jeanie.

I left ye 'mang the woods sae green,
　In rustic weed befitting ;
I've found ye buskit like a queen,
　In painted chaumers sitting.

I left ye like the wanton lamb
　That plays 'mang hadyeds heather ;
I've found ye noo a sober dame,
　A wife and eke a mither.

Ye're fairer, statelier, I can see,
　Ye're wiser, nae dou't, Jeanie ;
But ah, I'd rather met wi' thee
　'Mang the bourocks o' Bargeny.

It was a portion of their poetical creed that a fragment of rhyme found upon the banks of the Ayr or Doon was as sacred and valuable to the sons of song as a fragment of sculpture found near the Tiber or Nile is to the connoiseurs in stone—for why? songs prior to the date of Burns they esteemed as the fuel or food that fed his mighty mind, while posterior productions were interesting as having their spirit (if any) infused into them by that immortal renovator of Scottish song. In pursuance of this belief forth went our wanderers a song-hunting, Edie, much unlike his prototype, heading the pack with his "pocket book and keelyvine pen" drawn and ready for action.

In the vennel or lane in which the facetious "Souter Johnny" once lived and "tauld his queerest stories," and from whence the world knows he was only recently removed, they found, burrowed in dark huts, an extensive warren of old women who had settled down around the Souter from mere sympathy and family feeling. It is, of a truth, into lanes and cots and into the centre of rags that the literature and feelings of our fathers have been stowed like rubbish, and he who would re-gather them must bear with the husk to come at the kernel. The following are samples of what they picked from this rich nest of the muse of Coila. The first, a modern Scotch composition, is supposed by some to refer to Burns' unfortunate amour with his dear Highland Mary. The second speaks pure English, though of Scotch birth and parentage, and is merely interesting on account of its independence in wooing—one of Burns' most prominent characteristics, both as a lover and a man.* The last is evidently the mere head and feet of an old ballad; should the body be afterwards found it will be given, that a union of members may be effected.

---

* This piece, not being Ainslie's own composition, is omitted.—*Ed.*

"ITS DOWIE IN THE HINT O' HAIRST."

It's dowie in the hint o' hairst,
　　At the wa'-gang o' the swallow,
When the wind grows cauld an' the burns grow bauld,
　　An' the wuds are hingin' yellow ;
But, oh ! it's dowier far to see
　　The wa'-gang o' her the heart gangs wi'—
The deid-set o' a shining e'e
　　That darkens the weary warld on thee.

There was muckle love atween us twa—
　　Oh ! twa could ne'er been fonder ;
An' the thing on yird was never made
　　That could ha'e gart us sunder.
But the way of Heaven's aboon a' ken,
　　And we maun bear what it likes to sen'—
It's comfort, though, to weary men,
　　That the warst o' this warld's waes maun en'.

There's mony things that come and gae,
　　Just kent and syne forgotten ;
The flow'rs that busk a bonnie brae
　　Gin anither year lie rotten.
But the last look o' that lovin' e'e,
　　An' the dying grip she gied to me,
They're settled like eternitie—
　　Oh ! Mary that I were wi' thee !

*　　　*　　　*　　　*　　　*　　　*

WILLY AND HELEN: A BALLAD.

" Wharefore sou'd ye talk o' love,
    Unless it be to pain us ?
Wharefore sou'd ye talk o' love
    Whan ye say the sea maun twain us ? "

" It's no because my love is light,
    Nor for your angry deddy,
It's a' to buy ye pearlins bright,
    An' to busk ye like a leddy."

" O, Willy ! I can caird an' spin,
    Sae ne'er can want for cleeding;
An' gin I ha'e my Willy's heart,
    I ha'e a' the pearls I'm heedin'.

" Will it be time to praise this cheek
    Whan years an' tears ha'e blench't it?
Will it be time to talk o' love
    Whan cauld an' care ha'e quench't it ? "

He's laid ae han' aboot her waist,
    The ither's held to heaven ;
An' his luik was like the luik o' man
    Wha's heart in twa is riven.

The auld laird o' Knockdon is dead :
    There's few for him will sorrow ;
For Willy's steppit in his stead,
    But an' his comely marrow.

There's a cosy bield at yon burn fit,
    Wi' a bourtree at the en' o't ;

O, mony a day may it see yet
   Ere care or canker ken o't !

The lily leans out owre the brae,
   An' the rose leans owre the lily :
An' there the bonny twasome lay—
   Fair Helen an' her Willy.

As our wanderers had engaged themselves to dine in the churchyard of Alloway Kirk (the gig having been properly victualled and watered for that purpose), they found it expedient, about three o'clock, to get into the path that honest Tam o' Shanter cantered upon, that never to be forgotten night when Ayrshire's infernals had a ball and the devil turned piper.

"There are a few lines that come to my recollection," said the Linker, when they cleared the town, "that are said to have been written by Burns, on his revisiting the Doon after he had gone to reside at Mossgiel." "Every good article hath its counterfeits," said Edie, "and I dare say this is one of them : but let's hear't, Linker— sma' fish are better than nane." The Linker complied by repeating

DOON REVISITED.

I ha'e frien's on Irvine's side,
   An' my heart's in Mauchline town,
Yet my spirit hath a pride
   In the bonny Banks o' Doon.

Tho' the weary wark o' time
   Has altered a' I see,
An' the hame that ance was mine
   Is a fremmit house to me ;

Tho' mony a heart lies cauld
  Would ha'e warm'd to meet me here ;
Still thy murmuring, sweet Doon,
  Melts wi' pleasure in mine ear.

O ! it brings the fields an' flowers,
  Where my spirit's growth began ;
An' all the joyous hours
  That built me into man.

It brings the e'enings mild
  An' my soul's serenity,
Ere my heart's blood started wild
  To the glance o' woman's e'e.

Thy charms are written down
  On a page that will not blot :
O ! I'll mind thee, bonny Doon,
  Till all but heaven's forgot.

As the Linker had just completed the last line of the
above, they hove in sight of the snug, comfortable, white-
washed cottage, which announces to the reading passen-
ger, from a board stuck on the right side of the door,
that the poet Burns was born under its roof.

Equipping themselves properly in their Scottish
habulziement, they dismounted, entering the cottage
procession wise.   Having enquired for the landlord by
the name of Miller Goudie, and also the apartment con-
taining the portrait of the Bard, they were informed by
the Miller's marrow, a civil, decent-looking woman, that
the Miller was "butt the house in the room they war
wanting, wi' a wheen young folk," and that they might
"just step awa' in among the lave."

Striding away, by Mrs. Goudie's direction, they entered upon the "spence," where, opposite to the door, upon an old-fashioned chest of wainscot drawers, sat an indifferent picture of the Poet, executed upon wood. The rest of the apartment's furniture consisted of a few chairs, two forms, and a table, all in a respectable state of cleanliness, and at present almost completely occupied by the foresaid "young folk."

Miller Goudie—an oldish, liquorish-looking man, evidently deeply imbued with that valour which makes us "face the devil"—a courage which, they understood, he frequently enjoyed—at the entrance of our pilgrims made himself conspicuous by saluting them with: "Come your wa's, gentlemen; ye'll be come, nae doubt, to see the house that Robin was born in. Leuk, there he sits in paint and timmer, that I hae aften seen sit in flesh and blood. But will ye take a side an' taste wi' us? Thir young folk are just gaun out to the yaird to hae a bit ploy o' curds and cream."

The pilgrims having returned the salute, had barely seated themselves and called for something to match the Miller's kindness, when, as he had prognosticated, the young folk retired to the garden, leaving them in the undisturbed possession of the Miller.

"Ye seem, Miller," said Edie, as soon as the coast was clear, "to have seen that great man, Robert Burns, in your day." "Seen him!" replied the Miller, in an elevated tone, while helping himself to a glass, "seen him! Whe, man, I kent him as weel's I do that gill stoup, an' that's a wide word. Eh, mony a lang winter night I hae seen yankit by wi' his glib gab, when I made meal and sell'd drink at Doon mills.

> 'An' ilka melder wi' the Miller,
> Thou sat as lang as thou had siller.'

Man, that's me he cracks o'. Ken him! Od, that's a speak." "Did he mak' himsel' unca canty wi' ye?" enquired Edie, curious to discover how Burns relished such companions. "Whyles, only whyles, I maun say," remarked the Miller cautiously, "just as his nain de'el bade him. I hae seen him sit amang us wi' his head on his han', this gate, an' no speak a word for hours, mair than he'd been sittin' amang dumb brutes." "So, that was strange," said Edie, though he thought otherwise. "But what," he continued, anxious to know how the boors among whom he was doomed to dwell accepted him, "What did you an' the folk hereabouts think o' him in thae days?" "Trouth, I thought nae mair o' him then than I do o' you or ony ither body I see and crack wi'," said the penetrating Miller. "He had, nae doubt, a pour o' unca clever turns about him when he likit. But, to gie ye a word in yer lug—there war' some folk here awa that thought he was na owre right in the head." Edie, keeping his temper to admiration, that he might not injure his purpose, enquired, "When and where did you see Burns last?" "Let me think," returned the old drunken multure and knaveship man; "aye, it was just that simmer after he gaed to Dumfries; him and his brither Gilbert war owre seeing their auld frien's at Doonside; I drank the share o' three gills wi' them that day down at the mills. Gilbert, honest man, was unca free an' cracky, but Robin, I min', was in ane o' his auld barleyhoods. I was in han's wi' the Laird at that very time for a tack o' his house. Hech! little did I jelouse that day I was to hae sae mony ca'ers on his accoont. But there's nae saying what folk may come to. There's Souter Johnny, the weary body, whatna sang was made about him the ither day; an' I'm sure I hae drucken an' spoken wi' Robin ten times for his ance."

The Miller now got quite unmanageable, answering Edie's queries with a word or two in a sort of parenthetical manner, and driving away at his own history and hopes as the main subject. Convinced, therefore, that nothing more could be made of him at that sitting, Edie and John, his respective querist and auditor, were preparing to depart, when their attention was demanded to that part of the room to which the Linker had retired almost at entering, for the purpose of studying—being a sort of draughtsman—the Bard's picture, and where he now sat, with his eyes shut and his arms folded across his breast, evidently asleep, or in a most profound state of mental abstraction.

After they had gazed for some time on the inanimate trunk of the long lad, John proposed that means should be instantly resorted to for his restoration, and drawing forth his ram's horn, spoke of effecting it by a snuff ; so, catching most dexterously the exact moment when the Linker's lungs were at the extreme ebb of respiration, he applied to his nose a large quantity of very dry macuba, when suddenly, with a sweep and current, it went snoring up like dust in a whirlwind, and almost instantaneously, or in the relationship of the flash of a pistol to its report, the Linker awoke with a sneeze that made the "riggin' rair."

On arriving at his average state of sensibility he nevertheless continued to speak to his companions like a gifted man, protesting he had been in a trance and in a vision. No sooner, therefore, had they got out of the drouthy Miller's hands, properly re-seated and in motion, than he proceeded to relate :—

THE LINKER'S VISION IN BURNS' COTTAGE.

"After having planted myself comfortably before the picture," he began, "a swarm of sweet and pleasant recollections came buzzing and humming into my mind, from the knowledge of having my seat under the roof where our favourite Bard was born, and where his mighty soul first began to burn and boil out of its earthly tabernacle. During this while I was gazing upon his dark, penetrating eye and broad forehead, which gradually appeared to swell from the board, and lowering my eye to mark if the whole man was undergoing a reciprocal swelling and detachment from the wall, I perceived at the extremity of his broad striped vest a pair of buckskin breeches about to shoot, which, as my eye dropped, seemed to terminate in top boots—the Bard thus appearing before me in his full market-day dress, seated in rather an obscure corner of the room, and evidently employed both in musing and remarking. Directing my eye to where he was apparently looking, I discovered a considerable number of males, seated in a straggling manner about the fireside and table, drinking beer out of quegh caups. They seemed to have been attending a country roup and farm stocking, etc., and had dropped into the ale-house on their way home for a refreshment.

"I now began to scrutinize the company more leisurely, and soon convinced myself that the small, grey-eyed personage on the right of the fire, with the large look of hypocritical reverence, could be none else than Holy Willy. I was the more grounded in this belief when the ale-quegh reached him, for, hanging his bonnet on his knee, he drew his hand slowly over his brow and eyes, as in mental devotion, before tasting the liquor. Wiping his mouth, replacing his bonnet, and putting the quegh into circulation, he lifted up his countenance, and said to a person sitting beside him, 'There's bra' wather, John, for the barley seed, thanks be to heaven for a' its mercies ; tho' there's mony a ane taks a' they get as thanklessly as gif the Almighty was bun by missives o' tack to gi'e them seed-time an' harvest, whether they deserve it or no.' 'Owre true, William, owre true,' said John, with a look of conviction, 'but it's nane the least o' the mercies that there are yet some strong praps in the kintra to haud the Almighty's wrath aff our poor sinfu' heads.' Then lightening his tone a little, he asked: 'How do ye think the sale gaed the day?' 'Truly John,' said the holy man, 'I saw nae wanworths gaun either in the outsight or insight plenishin', sae I coft naething.— 'Hech,' continued he, belching ; 'I daresay I've eaten ower muckle o' yon fat haggis ; I'm fonder o' it than it's o' me, an' I'll gar the bouk o' a black pea o' either sybo or leek thank me for the feck o' twa days.' 'That proceeds, William,' replied the aforesaid John, squeezing as much scientific skill and importance into his face as it would admit of, 'from the superabundance of the bile, as Buchan says, or an impotency in the digestive organs for the discharge of their functions ; but gif ye was steppin' into my house the nicht, I cou'd gie ye a pickle pills for a trifle that would help to keep your rift sweet.' I was now at no loss to know my man ; 'Jock Hornbook o' the Clachan' was shown as plainly from his speech as if he had carried his sign-board on his breast.

"My attention was now withdrawn from these two worthies by a young man coming round to our Bard, who accosted him familiarly by the name of Davie Sillars, while Davie, with the same familiarity, enquired 'What are ye doing there, sitting cowering in the neuk like a wulcat glowering at a buss fu' o' birds?'

"'Indeed, Davie,' said the Bard, 'it's neither because I'm sour nor ill-set. But there's twa or three among ye there that I like better to luk at than speak to, for I'm sometimes provoked from their balderdash nonsense, to say things I should not say, far less they hear. But if you'd step roun' an' gie Willy and Tam yonner a wink into another room, I'll let you hear a blether I've been stringing up on twa o' these wechty personages.' Davie Sillers, with the springing step of a man whose heart is in his errand, went round to collect the chosen few among whom I flattered myself I was to be included ; so was rising hastily up to retire to 'the feast of reason and the flow of soul,' when Jock's confounded application of snuff to my snout blew up the whole concern."·

"Sorrow be in't ; " said Edie, "snuff was never ony great favourite or pouch companion o' mine, but I'll like it waur now than ever when I think that the best dream that ever the Linker dreamed, or is likely to dream, was blawn to bits by a snuff o' tobacco. O ! wae be on't, its makers and takers baith."

While Edie was delivering, with his teeth set, this anathema against the staple of Virginia, the eastern or bell gable of " Kirk Alloway " burst upon them, and at one glance bound up for ever in the manufacturing cells of John's mentals, a spirited and excellent defence of black rappee; seeing he was a considerable destroyer thereof, and conceiving not improperly that the sweeping cause of Edie's edict rather took him by the nose. He had, however, this consolation in being so stopped, that he was not the first man that the Kirk o' Scotland had silenced.

In the outset of an excursion, when a scene demanding our admiration, lies freshly spread before us, we can, at the uncomplicated impulse, give vent readily to the feeling it raises ; but when scene upon scene, and pleasure upon pleasure, accumulate around us rapidly, the mind grows into such a wild and entangled thicket of ideas and sensations—such a precious but unutterable podge of pleasant musings—that words for a while get worthless, until the judgment, labouring upon the mass, like agitated particles, at last settles and throws up the most prominent object to the top, for the eye to rest exclusively upon and admire.

Our pilgrims found themselves pretty much in this unspeakable mood on reaching "Kirk Alloway"—the very core of their pilgrimage. They saw the "far fetch'd" Doon pouring a' her floods thro' her bonny banks and braes, grandly o'erstrode with that ancient "brig," containing the notable and devil-defeating "key stane ;" while brown Carrick hill, gilt and garnished with all its golden broom, and purple heath, burst proudly up behind, bounding the whole, and running at its full size and strength bodily into the frith, as if its further extremity had once leaned upon the opposite shore, but that the stormy and powerful Atlantic, in thrusting his huge arm sheer up through the dry land, had cut it in twain.

Unyoking their instrument of conveyance by the side of a cottage that stands by the bridge and contains a most kindly and complaisant old ditcher and his dame, our wayfaring men so far mastered their distraction as to recollect their dining engagement in the Kirkyard. Loading themselves, therefore, with the contents of their portable larder, they entered by a stile upon the "dead man's lee," and soon settled or hived upon a broad "throcht stane," that sat most conveniently on the south of the Kirk, pleasantly shaded by a young plane tree, now beginning, as kindly Youth does to Age, to throw its sheltering arms over the reverend pile.

The dinner was devoured almost in silence, each pilgrim seeming, from the vacant eye they let fall even upon their food, to be inwardly engaged in composing something they conceived the occasion demanded.

Their joctelegs being wiped, "faulded," and lodged in their pockets, and the fragments of the feast gathered up, Edie drew forth and planted on the stone a little brown jar, or "grey beard," filled with the noble spirits of the north, and by its side, in excellent harmony and keeping, a small drinking horn.

"We are now," said Edie, filling the horn and casting his mind's eye upon the page he had composed, "seated upon the very 'key stane,' I may say, of that scenery to which the yearning of our hearts has so long and steadily pointed—with a clear blue Heaven above us and a green smiling earth around us—while the glorious summer-day, sliding and mellowing sweetly into eve, seasons our spirits into that mild frame of hallowed enjoyment that certainly ought to characterise this most solemn and singular scene of festivity." Then, gathering himself more into a speech-making position, he proceeded :

"Friends of the Bard, and beloved brother pilgrims ; it fills my heart with joy this day to think that the tide of envy, malice, and misrepresentation, which bore our gallant Bard to the earth which buried him, and even then in coward wickedness boiled and dashed over his grave, is now fast ebbing and drying up ; and the world now condescends to discover that an honest man may rightly serve his God without tampering with bigotry, winking at hypocrisy, or damning all parties but his own.

"Another charge, however, has of late years been pre-ferred against him, by a tribe of men who hate all great-

ALLOWAY KIRK.

Reproduced from the original edition of the " Pilgrimage," 1822.

ness, unless it be born, and deprecate all genius, unless
it be filtered through a university. This charge is no less
than the cant of independence! I should have thought
if there was one trait in his manly character more suffi-
ciently vouched by his conduct than another, it was the
contrary. When the purse-proud things that surround
him, I would ask, thought proper at a time to lower them
to his presence, was it cant that made him meet them as
equals, aye, and erect his proud spirit amongst them like
a spire amidst village cottages? Was it cant that kept
him from dog-like fawning and yelping himself into pen-
sion or place? Or was it cant that instigated him, when
necessity chased him into the excise, to lift up his voice,
' uncaring consequences?' Pitiful quibblers! The soul
that cannot discern, in almost every effusion of Coila's
son, independence and manly liberty shoot up like a
grenadier amid the battalion of his other principles, is a
sorry thing, jaundiced by envy and wrapped up in pride.

"It is right pleasant, though, my friends, to turn from
the growl of bigots and the puling of party, to glance at
his achievements amongst the liberal and the good.
What honest mind hath he not enlarged? What free
spirit hath he not whetted? And what kind bosom hath
he not warmed? The description of Scott may, chariot-
like, whirl the spirit through battle and through blood;
Byron may make us shudder; and Southey—that poor
Treasury purchase—may make us *weep;* but, it is the
Ayrshire ploughman, my boys, that leads us to the house
of our fathers, the trysting tree, and the social board. It
was he, my friends, that brought us here, and to his im-
mortal name we shall dedicate this horn."

No sooner had Edie ended, and the horn gone round
in silence, than the Linker—turning up his eyes to ob-

5

viate all external diversion—began complimenting the speaker on his performance and toast.

"But, Edie," he continued, "happy would it have made the living contents of this Kirkyard—aye, and thousands out of it—had your toast been a health instead of a memory, as well it might have been.

"There is an inherent, a native diffidence and delicacy always accompanying true genius, that, as a cloud, keeps it sometimes long out of notice; and, though like the sun in a misty morning, it ultimately bursts through all impediments, yet, the kind, encouraging hand of discerning friendship is an admirable aid (like the ushering breeze of the dawn) to help the young trembling spirit forth. Such a friend and encourager was Gilbert Burns to his brother, and, as such, he has certainly strong claims upon our sympathy and regard. I, therefore, propose this horn to the health and increasing prosperity of Gilbert Burns, the beloved brother, the first, best, and most befitting friend of the Bard."

This being drunk with an amazing enthusiasm, the Linker proceeded with—

"Amid the mass that people this earth, the majority are possessed of such dull and untouchable spirits as allow the flesh to fatten under any circumstances; while there are others of such a high-toned and delicate temperament, so tremblingly alive to all around them, and so peculiarly constituted, that the life-giving heat of their imaginations is for ever growing simple griefs into compound miseries, or common joys into rapturous delights. Thus, the evil that in the world preponderates, in union with 'man's inhumanity to man,' raises in such spirits a tumult—a turmoil, that holds the indignant blood in a perpetual fever, and shakes and shatters down a goodly frame long ere its day. Such a susceptible soul had our lamented Bard—a soul that under the crush and cumber of his circumstances would have wasted down half a dozen common trunks in the period a dull sober-souled mortal would have worn one.

"In visiting the birth-place of the most of those mighty men who have made the world their debtors, we are generally occupied with the reflection that the man whose 'immortal essence' either instructed, amused, or enraptured us, opened his young eye, tottered his first step, and lisped his first word amid such scenes. But here these are only inconsiderable items in the sum of our feelings. All around —the mountains, rivers, forests, and floods—cry loudly of him, for he spoke of them. *There* lies the living library that stored his mind, and the pages from which he faithfully copied. His soul gushed forth in the brawl of the Bonny Doon, melted into melody at the song of these leafy woods, or mounted into Heaven with the wing of the morning lark. Nature, in a word, was his nurse, and while she lives, will be his monument.

"To keep my feelings from running over upon the enchanting ground that Edie has travelled, I shall content myself with a protestation—one which I have no hesitation in taking jointly without your mandate—that the man whose heart is not tuned, and whose soul is not touched with the tender and patriotic strains of Coila's Bard can never have the love or friendship of a pilgrim to the Land of Burns.

> "'Awa ye selfish warly race
> Wha think that heaven's sense an' grace,
> E'en love and friendship sou'd gie place
>   To catch the plack,
> I dinna like to see your face
>   Nor hear your crack.'"

The blast with which they acceded to the Linker's

protestation being "blawn by," Jinglin Jock, settling his
good Scottish countenance with great dignity upon his
broad manly shoulders, opened upon his attentive
brethren with—

"Lads, I hae been 'pleased to the nine,' no to speak
o' edification, wi' the weel-worded win' ye hae baith let
lowse on this memorable an' heart-kittlin' occasion. Yet,
wi' a' manner o' deference to our majority acting in the
contrair, it's finally the award o' my judgment that a
Scottish Bard ought to be spoken o' by Scotsmen in
'plain braid Lallans.' I, therefore, crave leave to eik,
in that belief, twa three words as a kin o' codicil to your
joint testimony. An' truly, callans, it seems to me a
thing weel worth the blawing aboot, that we are a'
related in a most endearing degree to that sweetest
songster in the world, viz : that we were a', like him, born
in a Scottish cottage, and were nursed and nurtured also
amang Scotlan's mensfu', gash and honest kintra folk.

"O, there's nane, but the like o' us lads, can ken what
it is to hae the lumber room, the girnal I may ca't, o'
our bairnly recollections ryped and rummaged up wi' the
canty tricks o' a 'Halloween,' or the merry glee o' 'that
happy day the year begins.' They carry us back, an'
that on the hotching shouthers o' right humour, to thae
'enviable early days' when the limbs were green an' the
heart was light.

"This advantage, this bit birthright I may ca't o' ours,
lets us deeper into the real saul o' Robin than a
Southern, or town-born body, can ever win, let them ser'
what 'prenticeship they like; and it is my pride in this
birthright, marrowing wi' my birthplace—whilk is jimply
a mile frae this spot—that gars me sit sae lightly, this
day, on a headstane, and drink, wi' my bonnet doffed,
to the memory of those Patriots, whether Warrior or

Bard, who have made the shire of Ayr the pride and glory of Scotland."

The horn having gone round, John was about to re-open upon them, with strong symptoms of much matter, when Edie, who knew he was like the widow's cruse when his breath was set abroad on such a subject, reminded him the day "was couring into the West, an' they had a gey bit to gang afore bed time."

"Aweel," said Jock, "gif ye canna afford me a mouthfu' mair o' prose to toom my saul wi', ye'll surely let me rhyme owre a verse or twa I've cleckt on the auld Kirk." Taking their silence for a warrant, he delivered with great emphasis his

ADDRESS TO ALLOWAY KIRK.

Behold, ye wa's o' Alloway,
　　This curn o' canty carlies,
Wha've driven thro' Cunningham an' Kyle
　　In search o' fun an' ferlies.

It's no 'cause mony a great divine
　　Their holy words here wair'd,
That we respect your stane an' lime,
　　An' dinner in your yaird.

But Alloway, that night ye were
　　Hell's place o' recreation,
Baith heezed an' dignified ye mair
　　Than a' your consecration.

The bit whaur fornicators sat,
　　To bide their pastor's bang,
Is now forgotten for the spot
　　Whaur Nanny lap an' flang.

The pu'pit whaur the gude Mess John
  His wig did weekly wag,
Is lightlied for the bunker seat
  Whaur Satan blew his bag.

An' what's the ferlie ? Priests an' fools
  Are gear we've aye a clag o';
But Coila's son, now in the mools,
  Eternity 'ill brag o'.

The roar with which John concluded his address
rang from "bank to brae" as the dinner party, in "im-
measurable content," strode solemnly from the festive
stone.   Passing the kirkyard stile, however, the hour of
evening, crying, " Quick march," called them into more
active service ; so, putting forth all their knowledge and
abilities as ostlers, and, with the assistance of the afore-
said kindly cottager, they soon got their "brute grippet
an' the graith on."

While the yoking operation was going forward, Edie
took occasion to enquire of the old ditcher if he recol-
lected of any timber being about the Kirk.   "O ay,"
said he, "it's no sae lang syne that there were a gey twa
three o' the auld kipples, an' ither kin' o' lowse riggin'
lying in her guts ; an' trouth, mony a year they lay as
unsteered as the throcht stanes ; but just a' at a brainge,
the folk took some tirryvie, an' awa they gaed like the
break o' a storm, an' sae clean too, that aught days on
the back o't ye could jimply gotten as muckle timmer in
her as wou'd made a yerkin pin to a parritch cog."   " I'm
vext at that," said Edie, " I wou'd liket as muckle o't as
wou'd made a heft to a kail gully, or a shank to a punch
spoon.   But, I'm saying, man," continued Edie, looking
greedily at the east gable of the Kirk, " Od I'se gie ye

twenty shillings for the tongue o' yon auld bell." The honest countryman answered, smiling, that "he was sorry he durst na deal wi' him, as he could na think o' selling a thing was na his ain."

Having properly returned thanks to the cottager for the good wishes and good night he "shored" them at parting, our pilgrims, crossing the river, and taking Carrick hill as rapidly as their "gude gaun beast as e'er in tug or tow was traced" was competent to do, reached its summit, happily in time to see the glorious manufacturer of daylight, with his broad scarlet countenance, sit smilingly down, as honest labour does after a well-wrought day, upon the rugged pinnacles of Arran.

Dropping over the south-east shoulder of the hill, and "cannily ca'ing" down its breast till they again came in sight of the Doon, they at last halted, as the bats and bumclocks were getting rife, at the farm house of B——, the residence of Mr. O—— L——,* an early, much and justly esteemed friend of the Lang lad's; and, though eleven years had laboured upon them since they parted—though it had stiffened and hardened the round cheek of boyhood into man, and, moreover, garnished and planted their faces with some hundred extra black hairs, yet the same familiar spirits still looking through all the alterations, deteriorations, or improvements, etc., kept them from having the smallest symptoms of "auld frien's wi' new faces," and made them meet as lovingly as if the term of their parting had been hours instead of years.

The whole of the pilgrims soon found themselves much at home with Mr. L——. Indeed, his was one of those open, pleasant countenances that depone to the gazer

---

* Mr. Oliver Lamb, Blackbyres.

from every feature that there is a kindly, friendly heart within that joys in the joy of others; containing, likewise, far more accommodation for laughing than crying—not the dry malignant grin that laughs at human frailty, nor the quiet inward chuckle of self-sufficiency, but the broad untempered burst that echoes to innocent mirth and glee. He was, to boot, one of those tall, well-built men that delight one to see occupied in the tilling of the ground. His brawny arm seemed to declare him a true master of the soil, and that it could with ease oblige the stubborn earth to deliver up her stores.   He was still without the hallowed pale of matrimony; an amiable young woman, his sister, managed his domestic concerns.   A younger brother was likewise of the household; one in whom the ornaments of education and study were growing strongly up amidst the virtues of his elder brother.

After supper, albeit our travellers had been " asteer " some nineteen hours, and not idle ones either, in the sun and wind of Heaven, no sooner had their jovial landlord "christened " some Arran water, alias Highland whisky, " wi' reeking water," than, with the unconquerable courage of true valour, they staunchly took their ground before it, as determined on its destruction as if it had been the first attack of the day—each toast and joke of the landlord's kindling and " beeting " their mirth; till, on the out edge of reason, the Linker arose, (by the assistance of the board) and declared he would not open his mouth to another laugh until his old friend should sing them one of his good ancient drinking songs.

Mr. L——, finding, in despite of joke or jest, that the Linker kept his jaws clenched together as if they had been dovetailed, was necessitated to give in; so, after rubbing his brow a little, while glancing over the index

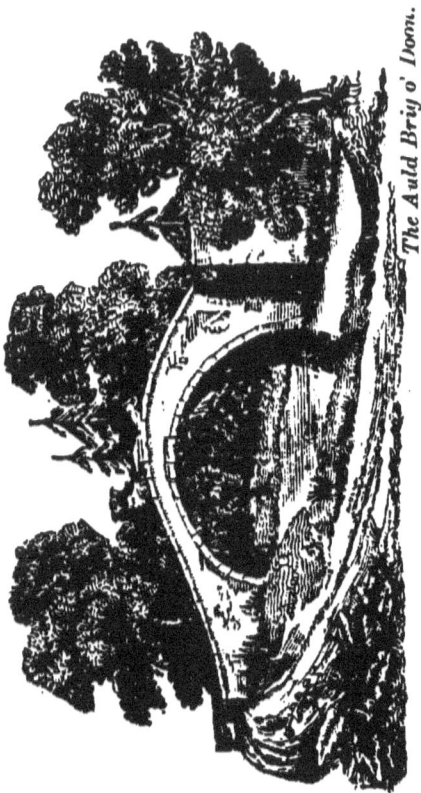

The Auld Brig o' Doon.

Now do thy speedy utmost, *Meg*, | There at them thou thy tail may toss.
And win the key-stane of the brig; | A running stream they dare na cross.

Reproduced from the original edition of the " Pilgrimage," 1822.

of his collection, he opened into " Landlady count your
Lawin'."

The din of commendation that followed the Landlord's
song being quelled, he proposed, to obviate all excuses,
etc., that the song should flow regularly round the table,
commencing at his right.

This proposal meeting with no opposition, the Jingler,
who sat next in succession, having held up the right side
of his head to the ceiling for a moment, started away into
that fine old humorous rigmarole chaunt of "Hame cam'
oor Gudeman," that all the world has heard, or ought to
hear.

This song put the party into an entire roar.   In truth,
John had a comical knack of heating up with his own
the native humour of this old rhyme to such a pitch that
none might sit quietly before it.   " Come Edie," said he,
recovering first, " come my gallant, ca' the carles ; yoke,
my boy, yoke ; its your turn now to fright the rattons."

Edie, with that alacrity which makes him so valuable
both to himself and friends, caught up that noblest strain
of honest independence that ever was worked into words :
" A Man's a Man for a' that."   It is a touchstone indeed ;
a sort of intellectual crucible, that turns out the golden
worth of honest indigence from the base dross of worth-
less nobility.

During Edie's deliverance the party seemed vegetating.
A good comfortable laugh has always a tendency to
shake one down solidly upon his seat ; but, no sooner,
from the emphatic sweep of his voice, did their souls be-
gin to stir with independence, than each backbone was
erected like a steeple, and all eyes centred in a point,
even as if the air of Edie's strain had turned their noses
on him like weather-cocks.

It was now the young lady's turn to "marry sound with

sense ;" and certainly, the stately and sober frame of mind "A Man's a Man for a' that" had put them into, was much better calculated to let them listen to a lady's song than if she had been doomed to follow Jock's merry and side-shaking jingle.   With a modesty excluding all flourish or affectation, Miss L—— sang :—

ON WI' THE TARTAN.

Do ye like, my dear lassie,
  The hills wild an' free
Where the sang o' the shepherd
  Gars a' ring wi' glee ;
Or the steep rocky glens
  Where the wild falcons bide ?—
Then on wi' the tartan,
  An' fy let us ride.

Do ye like the knowes, lassie,
  That ne'er were in riggs,
Or the bonny lowne howes
  Where the sweet robin biggs ?
Or the sang o' the lintie
  Whan wooing his bride ?—
Then on wi' the tartan,
  An' fy let us ride.

Do ye like the burn, lassie,
  That loups amang linns,
Or the bonny green holms
  Where it cannily rins ;
Wi' a canty bit housie
  Sae snug by its side ?—
Then on wi' the tartan,
  An' fy let us ride.

The younger Mr. L——, having rather more than a suspicion of Edie's predilection towards the ancient melody of Scotia, had been searching among the old winter-night lilts he had heard and recollected, for something with at least the wrinkle of a century upon it. When his call came, he was therefore prepared to give them—

FAIR JEANIE'S BOWER.

Yestreen I tirl'd my love's window,
    When the moon on hie was hinging;
The dawning heard our parting vow
    When the birds began their singing.

She took me to the binwood bower,
    Was o' her ain han' twining;
The birken buss aboon our head
    An' saft moss for the lining.

The howlet had flown to his hole,
    The hare had left the braken,
An' sweet the laveroc i' the lift,
    Wi' singing gart me wauken.

I luckit on her bonny broo,
    And sain'd her wi' my blessing,
I glowr'd upon her comely mou',
    And wauken'd her wi' kissing.

O! sweet's the diet o' the bee
    That hives amang the heather,
But sweeter far that lip's to me
    Than ought that bee can gather.

I gat a vow frae her yestreen,
    I gat it wi' a token ;
An' gin ye break it, bonny Jean,
    This heart wi' it is broken.

The Linker (whose musical moment was now come)
had kept pace with the song, while it was "merry and
free," both in spirit and in noise, giving, moreover, a
large lift to each burden or chorus ; but, about the
middle of the lady's song, feeling himself begin to
"droop and drowse," he borrowed, as quietly as pos-
sible, the Jingler's box, with the execrated contents of
which he refreshed himself wonderfully.   The best of
remedies, however, grow ineffective from repetition ; so,
towards the termination of the foregoing "lilt"—his
nose-holes being then almost plugged up, and the brace
pulleys of his eyelids getting extremely weak and un-
serviceable—he, in a fit of nature-thwarting determina-
tion, clenched his hands, built them upon each other
before him on the table, and planting his chin atop, kept
staring, with his teeth knit, upon the bowl, as if he had
been actually holding himself awake by mere physical
force.   John, who had eyed with great pleasure the
attempts he made to prolong his diurnal existence, ob-
served that as he had been struggling so manfully to be
alive when the song reached him, they certainly might
look for something astonishing, as it was frequently re-
marked of old rogues that they could not die calmly
until their breasts were cleaned.   The Linker, whose
mouth was now made up for the music, replied not ;
but, drawing himself up to his full length, roared out
"Rab Simpson's Rant."

The glass, swilled to the health and song of the singer,
having exhausted the bowl, the landlord proceeded to

speak right eloquently concerning its renewal.   However, strange to relate, considering how the house was composed, a large majority was got against it, and Edie's motion—which, by the bye, was made with one of his eyes fairly buttoned up, and the other peering through a mere slit : "That the meeting resolve itself into resting committees"—was carried by acclamation, and ten minutes afterwards completely put in execution.

So solid and sound was the slumber in which our weary wanderers of the West were laid, that all the harbingers and heralds of day—

> " The crowing cock, the lowing cow,
>   The barking dog and grunting sow,"

and every rural sound that as an alarm bell tolls up the limbs of labour to their task, was crowed, lowed, barked, and grunted as vainly to them even as the chaunting of church music is unto a dead horse.

Yet, sooth, it was not so with their entertainer.   In fact, it seemed as if the sun and he were at strife who should have the first brush at the dewy fields, and long ere "crowdy time" he had set the machinery of his farm effectively to work, and made the rest of the day his own.

He found his guests (after he had shaken them into consciousness) all labouring under that severe, though happily not epidemic distemper known by the name of "barley fever."   Their breath came forth like steam, their eyes seemed set in coral, their mouths were dry as snuff-boxes, and their tongues rattled therein like unto scent beans.   Fresh air and water were the medicines they craved, and their landlord procured them both in delicious plenty at the south end of his dwelling.

The station they occupied, in a seeing sense, put them

in possession of a noble sweep of country.   Indeed, Mr. L—— assured them it contained a portion of nine parishes.   Immediately below lay the valley that held the Doon, at the woody extremity of which the green knolls began to swell, bearing away into ruder hillocks, and thence into stout brown hills, beyond which the blue mountains of Galloway bounced up and, like an azure frame, girt in the whole.   Amid all this variety of optical possession, however, the eyes of our pilgrims soon condescended and settled upon, as the principal messuage or manor of the heart, that spot

> " Amang the bonny winding banks
>   Where Doon rins wimplin' clear,
> Where Bruce ance rul'd the martial ranks
>   An' shook the Carrick spear."

The sun by this time had outrode about a quarter of his round ; so the dew, being still upon the rise, cased the surrounding objects in that misty haze which makes even beauty more beautiful.   Mr. L—— gazed and talked like an agriculturist; the Linker, who had a trifling turn for drawing, like an artist; while that rousing spirit of the West, Jinglin Jock, with the roar of a rhymster and soul of a true Burnsonian devotee, cried out—" Behold

> " ' Auld Coila's plains and fells,
> Her moors, red-brown wi' heather bells ;
> Her banks and braes, her dens and dells,
>   Where glorious Wallace
> Aft bore the gree, as story tells,
>   Frae Southern billies.

> At Wallace' name what Scottish blood
> But boils up in a spring-tide flood ;

Aft have our fearless fathers strode
        By Wallace' side,
Still pressing onward, red-wat shod,
        Or glorious died.

O, sweet are Coila's haughs and woods
When lintwhites chaunt amang the buds,
An' jinkin hares in amorous whids
        Their loves enjoy,
While thro' the braes the cushat croods
        Wi' wailfu' cry.' "

Notwithstanding this grand and glorious show—and, moreover, to aid it a band of Summer's sweetest musicians had formed a little brake at the bottom of the garden into a complete orchestra, and were adding music to the entertainment—we say, notwithstanding all this, Edie continued throughout quite a musing thing, a perfect monosyllable man, and about the middle of John's recitation he actually slunk away into the house "like a boasted cat frae the cream." The drag to this mystical removal proved a most nourishing morsel for conjecture. One conceived it might proceed from the state of his stomach ; another that the servant lassie might have a hand, or more properly a face in the affair ; while the third spoke of looking into an almanack as a sure way of coming at the cause. They, however, jointly agreed to this : that from the features and whole countenance of the case, there was, undoubtedly, some most confounded " whaup in the raip."

Half an hour's patience brought a solution to their riddle ; for as they were marching homeward, by the landlord's commandment, to inspect the breakfast table, they encountered the old puzzling pilgrim upon the threshold, sallying out with a letter in his hand, and chaunting to the air of Gil Morice—

> " Whaur will I get a bonny boy
> My errand for to rin,
> Will hie him to the next post town
> An' slip this letter in?"

" The fient a fit, Edie," said John, "shall boy, or man either, rin on sic an errand till we see what he's running wi'." So saying, he pounced upon the epistle, made it his prey, and marched with it in triumph to the breakfast table, observing, after he had discovered how matters stood there, that as they had the bit blink on their han' atween the masking an' outpouring, and while the ham was singing itsel' savoury, they sou'd hear on what an' on whom their billy Edie had been wairing his wit. "As I'm a yerthly creatùre," he exclaimed, opening the letter and feigning great astonishment, "of a sound and sober mind, an' in the full enjoyment of my faculties, it's a lay o' love! Take your seats, frien's; dight your noses, spit out and speak to the dogs; for there mauna be a word o' this drowned in a hoast or worried in the growl o' a collie. Attention—"

EDIE OCHILTREE'S EPISTLE TO HIS LADY LOVE.

> Dear Ann, upon this hallowed earth
> That gave the Bard of Coila birth,
>   I tak' my pen an' ink
> A loving line or twa to write,
> An' on this rhyme-inspiring site
>   It cannot miss but clink.
> Although ye ken I'm little gi'en
>   Your praises to rehearse,
> An' tho' I be as seldom seen
>   To lowse my heart in verse;

Yet here, lass, it's queer, lass—
    A thing ye'd scarce suppose—
I tell ye, an' fell me,
    I canna mak' it prose.

In wrangling wi' the warl' or when
I'm getting fun wi' funny men,
        Ye're whyles forgot a wee ;
But gi'e me half a musing hour—
Then, as a bee flees to the flower,
        So hies this heart to thee.
We a', nae doubt, are fasht wi' flaws
    That shed us frae perfection,
Tho' some wi' airts, like plaister saws,
    Can smuggle their infection.
Awa' ye, foul fa' ye,
    That wear a painted skin,
Write chapters o' raptures
    When a' is cauld within.

I winna say, in case I lee,
That ye're by far the fairest she
        That e'er was in creation ;
Nor will I say, in virtue either,
That a' that's gane was but a blether
        To thy immaculation.
But this I'll say, because it's true,
    In mind as well as make,
You've charms your Edie's heart, my doo,
    To keep as well as take.
There's mair ways, an' fair ways,
    To tak' an honest heart
Than winkin's and jinkin's
    O' beauty spic'd wi' art.

An' tho' atween us, bonny Ann,
There's waters, wuds, an' mickle lan',
     In pasture an' in vittle;
Tho' day by day I'm doom'd to see
Fair lassies wi' a pawky e'e
     Would mak' your gutcher kittle;
Yet there's a bit 'neath this breast bane,
  The dearest portion in't,
Where, framed in treasured days are gane,
  Thy image lies in print.
This shiel's me, this steels me
  'Gainst ony ither flame,
An' renders a' genders
  To me the vera same.

O Annie, lass, what would I gi'e
To catch the sparkle o' thy e'e
     Amang thae banks an' braes
Where Coila's Bard would aften rove,
Burning wi' poetry an' love,
     Or raving o'er his waes!
Then, as ye sang, his sweetest sang
  Thy voice mak's sweeter still,
I'd lay me on the sward alang
  An' drink o' joy my fill.
O! this, lass, were bliss, lass,
  But as it canna be,
Adieu, then, be true, then,
     To EDIE OCHILTREE.

Edie's enraptured lines, together with Miss L——'s
excellent entertainment, being by patience and persever-
ance respectively heard and eaten to an end—the
precious moments, too, that lie like a honeymoon on the

out edge of a pleasant repast, and which, by the bye, might not improperly be called the honey moments of masticating, having been effectually occupied by the performers in hatching a plan for the purpose of filling up the period that lay betwixt them and dinner time— they proceeded down the before-mentioned slope to meet the Doon.

The spot that formed the groundwork of this meeting was a large green holm, beautifully selvaged on the un- watered sides with woods.   At its lower extremity the river, taking a sudden bend, broadened and deepened into a wheel, on the breast of which a salmon cobble or currach swam, into which they instantly got, and almost as instantly that tenderest strain of melodious sorrow, "Ye banks and braes o' bonny Doon," arose from the well-manned cobble at a pitch that unquestionably laid the echoes of a Scotch mile under contribution, though I question if their hearers would have thought they were within cry of an opera house.   The younger Mr. L——, whose mind had a classical cast, compared them to Venetian gondoliers ; John, with his turn for the rural, to a nestfu' o' whin linties ; while Edie hazarded a fear that a grazier would have taken them for a cartfu' o' calves.

At the termination of this cobble concert, their har- monious exertions, the heat of noon, and, last and largest, the living embers of yesternight's debauch, fired them with such a craving for coolness, that, unsheathing themselves like "bedward bairns," they took the water like otters, spluttered about like frogs in a well, then landed and decked themselves again, as chatteringly happy as a gang of geese by a horse pond.

Refreshed and much inspirited, if not inspired, by their toss into "the waters under the earth," they moved

lightly up the meadow, and by the guidance of their
agricultural entertainer entered into the afore-mentioned
skirting wood, the trees of which, being tall and thick-set,
excluded, for the most part, the waylaying brier, the in-
commoding hazel, or the stubborn sloe; though here
and there, close by the river edge, the large trees stood
back, as in reverence, to allow the rose and woodbine to
entwine in all their characteristic and classical em-
brasures.

"First in a wood and last in a ford," said Edie, getting
ahead and making the boughs clang behind him.
"Thae auld proverbs are fine bits of portable philosophy
for helping a man cleverly through the world."

"Selfish, though, Edie," returned John, "like the
men they make. Indeed, I mind an auld Scottish son-
net—a sort of rhyming bunch of proverbs, that, if Burns'
'Advice to a Young Friend' may be called a mould to
make men by, with equal equity it may be titled

A RECIPE FOR MAKING A SCOTSMAN.

If you would learn the lear that mak's
  A chiel baith fier an' fell, man,
Give ear unto the redd o' ane
  Wha's dree'd the darg himsel', man.

Gie gentle words to gentlefolks,
  An' bow aye to your betters;
Keep your ain han' at your ain hank,
  Nor fash wi' fremmit matters.

In cracking wi' camstairy chiels,
  Or dealing wi' the drucken,
Ne'er wrangle at ilk crabbit word,
  Nor strike till ye be strucken.

At markets, fairs, or ony part
    Whaur roun' the yill is han'ing,
Leuk like the lave, but in your heart
    Be ye a bargain planning.

But never bargain at a word,
    For either horse or wife, man ;
Ye may rue the tane a month or mair,
    An' the tither a' your life, man.

Right canny let your cracks aye be,
    But cannier be your bode, man ;
Let caution aye be sib to thee,
    An' reason be thy road, man.

Sae will ye soon get gear, an' syne
    Ye'll soon get frien's anew, man ;
For men are like the mice, they rin
    To whaur the girnal's fu', man.

As John was ending his rhyming recipe, they came
upon the pleasantest spot of woodland they had yet seen.
The hawthorn and holly clustering together, while here
and there handfuls of sunshine squeezing through the
luxuriant foliage and dancing upon the delicate wood
flowers, formed a spot of such solitary sweetness that
the schoolboy had instinctively looked about him for the
nest of the blackbird, or straying lovers had settled upon
as a proper sanctuary for breathing tenderest vows in.
A little onward, a well of water, slumbering in crystal
purity at the root of a huge holly, interestingly com-
panioned with its narrow red line of winding footpath,
announced to our pilgrims the vicinity of a cottage, the
inhabitant of which Mr. L—— described as a most in-

genious and amusing character. A few steps brought them to its door, and a halloo from Mr. L—— soon brought its inmate before them.

He was a middle-sized man, with the look of one about half way through the world, or rather half way through life, as he had no marks of the world upon him. His features were of a Romish cut, high and thin, and each point thereof was tipt with active intelligence. Not, however, that dry critical kind of it, before which one feels the necessity of putting a bar and steelyard upon the utterance, that each word may be weighed in its passage ; but that frank, communicative knowledge before which the thoughts run rompishly loose.

They soon discovered him to be a most zealous and enthusiastic botanist. His garden or nursery seemed cut out of the bowels of the wood, like the settlement of an American backwoodsman, and his cottage stuck in the middle thereof like a large white gourd or pumpkin swelling among its green leaves. Indeed, his premises might with great propriety be called a vegetable hotel ; for there natives of all nations were seated most brotherly together, drinking of the same dews, and dancing to the piping of the same breeze.

An anecdote they had from this amiable planter is of itself sufficient to illustrate the excellent qualities of his heart. A brown beech, and one who was a chief among his tribe, had at one time thrown his arms so wantonly abroad as to shadow and injure considerably several others of a different family that grew within his reach. After deliberating upon the extent of those extending injuries, he condemned him to the axe, saying, "Why cumbereth thou the ground ?" Taking up his instrument of execution, he went forth to finish his award ; but when he came to where the noble spoiler stood waving away in all his brown majesty, like Balaam before the encampments of Israel, he had not power withal to lift his hand. Evil reports, however, thickening against this vegetable invader, he again sallied forth, and again returned as before. At last, when further forbearance had stamped him tyrant to the oppressed, he rushed forth at full speed, that his purpose might not cool, shut his eyes when he drew near, groped his way to the offender's trunk, and ere he opened them gave him a few irreparable gashes; then slowly, with a sigh to each stroke, finished the work of justice.

They found, however, that this uncommon affection for the green tribes of the earth was not incompatible with a disposition obliging and free to such an excess that to praise a plant was to put it in the praiser's offer, and to covet was most positively to possess. Accordingly they might have carried off, had their stowage and hearts allowed them, loads of his fair families. As it was, they accepted with thanks, as a most appropriate present to bear from Doonside, a young sensitive plant.

Parting from the Doonside botanist and his paradisical premises, the party bent their way towards the steading. A low inward grumbling (which, by-the-bye, is an excellent dinner bell) was their adviser to return, and a wise one it was.

During dinner, or rather at the fag end thereof, when Edie's mouth was beginning to get again into the service of his mind, in putting questions to Mr. L—— touching his personal or reported knowledge respecting the characters in those parts that Burns had dignified or damned, he elicited the following anecdote concerning the merry, mad, but immortal Tam o' Shanter. He (Thomas) was going home, or rather attempting to do so, one night from an ale-house at some distance, pretty much in that

state in which he faced the Devil. Reaching a cot-house
by the wayside, he was so o'er-mastered with drink and
drowsiness that, stowing himself into the garden hedge
as well as he could, he soon fell fast asleep.   The cot-
tager, a douce, decent Christian, coming out in a little
to where the famous Thomas lay, for the purpose of
offering up his evening petitions, had got through his
wants, together with a few of his wishes, etc., when, as
he was putting up a word anent an old sick relative, from
whose testament he had expectations, took occasion to
say "that as he had baith dreed the span an' the inch,
and moreover drunk and drained the cup to the dregs,
he might be allowed to depart."   "Never in time !"
cried Tam, half-awakened with the word depart. "Never
wi' a toom caup. Just another stoup, Lady, an' then
let's ken what we're doing."

On the light wings of "drink and daffin'" " the mo-
ments winged their way with pleasure," until our pilgrims
found it necessary to resume their progress. Every
earthly sweet, indeed, hath its sour ; the largest and
longest things, even matrimony, hath an end, and all
terrestrial rapture, like seeds—

> " Even let us keep and hoard them as we will,
> Still shoot out into sorrow."

In truth, the most of Nature's laws have much of the
determined, dogged character of the Medes and Persians
in them ; no case even of the most roaring necessity can
stay their execution, no bribery subvert their effect ; and
the only man in the long history of the world who may
be said to have got out a bill of suspension against their
operation was Joshua, the son of Nun. Seldom indeed
does the march of moments keep exact time with our
wishes—too slow for anticipation, and too quick for

enjoyment. Sadly, therefore, on the present occasion was their march out of step with the feelings of our wanderers, as their looks sufficiently witnessed. Edie, who hath one of those squat, firm-built faces that will not lengthen, twisted it a little to the one side to give it a melancholy cast; John, on the other hand, whose features are excessively portable, and equally qualified for being gathered up like a purse-mouth or spread abroad like a pillow-slip, had his spread to their most dismal extent; while the Linker, with the skin of his cheeks sucked in amongst his teeth, and his head drawn down betwixt his shoulders, gave his slip of countenance, seeing his upper garment was green, the appearance of a long rag spread upon a thorn bush. Such were the countenances through which our pilgrims sighed their farewell to the honest tacksman of B——, and the other members of his household.

Nothing worth a sentence happened, or scarcely a sentence fell from our pilgrims, till they entered the town of Maybole—mounted in their usual manner. Edie occupying the right, or whip-hand side of the gig, John the left, with the Long Lad stuck in the middle like a wedge, or a telescope betwixt two globes. " Hech," quoth the Jingler on entering the town, with that sort of half sigh that one gives when looking back upon " days that are done," " It's mony a lang day since last I saw the auld town of Minnybole (vulgarly so called). Mark that big stane bigging to the right there, lads. That's the tower whar the famous but frail Countess o' Cassillis was sae lang cavied up in, like a hen that lays awa', and thae stane countenances sticking out frae the wa' there, like as mony sheeps' heads, are said to be representatives of her fifteen tinkler paramours." " They're gruesome-like tykes," said Edie, " and unca unseemly-looking comrades for a Countess." "The lads," returned Jock, "never made ony grit brag o' their beauty, as we learn per ballad—

> 'O we were fifteen weel made men
> Altho' we werena bonny.'

But, Edie, ye sou'd ken that wi' some folk, gentle as well as semple, 'quantity often gangs afore quality.'" "I have heard a story told," said the Linker, edging his word like his body betwixt the two, " and I believe it standeth on the faith of soothfast witnesses, how that one of the late Earls of Cassillis got his mouth rather unpleasantly shut with that same Johnny Faa. One M'Queer, a fiddler in these parts (a man somewhat cunning in his art), had a daughter of such exceeding fairness that she kindled the love of an English lord to that unbearable degree that he was fain to make her his lady. Some time after this my lord and his lady, at a ball or other musical entertainment, chanced to encounter Lord Cassillis, at which time and place the latter was so completely outshone by the two former that, losing command of himself, he, in the fever-heat of his envious rage, could not help whispering to the Englishman, as the musicians were playing one of the fiddler's old airs, 'M'Queer played that tune well.' 'Yes, yes,' replied the other, with most provoking temper, 'pretty so, so, but he was most excellent at the Gipsy Laddie.'"

An angle in the road a few miles to the west of Maybole laid before our wayfaring men at one sweep the long deep valley of the Girvan. Its tall green hilly barriers, gashed with glens and patched with plantations, widening at their western extremity, let out the eye upon a considerable portion of the Firth of Clyde, in the centre of which rises the singular isolated and stupendous Craig of

Ailsa, appearing, from its circular form, the bud of a
young world bursting away from the teeming sea.

The eye of the Carrick carle having dropt into the
fair and fertile strath of his native stream, suddenly
picked up a slip of its dearest scenery, flung it into the
memory, the memory to the feelings, the feelings to the
heart ; while the heart in its wantonness, giving the ribs
a rousing thump, made its possessor bolt upright from
betwixt his brethren like a mast. Making himself fast to
the vehicle with his left hand, after the manner of a back
stay, his right, like a flag in unsettled winds, kept shift-
ing and bobbing about as he apostrophised and hailed
the darling objects of his earliest recollection.   " Bear
with me, men and brethren, bear with me," said he, as
the others were grumbling at the bumps he was bestowing
upon them at each rut in the road.   " John, ye had your
daft day on Irvine side ; ye had yours, Edie, on the
Doon ; and I maun hae mine by Girvan's fairy-haunted
stream.   We're a' birds o' ae brood, my lads, and every
dog maun hae his day.   Do ye see a steeple yonner,
spearing up frae amang the massy trees like the stately
lily frae a bed o' thyme ? "   " Ay," said John, " or rather
like the heft o' a muck fork frae a midden-stead.   But
what about steeples, Linker, for trouth wi' you, it will be
a wonner gif they're kippled wi' the kirk ? "   " John,"
said Edie, interfering, " I crave that according to the
Linker's last orthodox doctrine anent daffin', he be
allowed, till we leave this water side, to word or work
cleanly nonsense to what length, breadth, and depth he
likes.   What was't ye war gaun to say, Mr. Merryman ? "
" Merely a word or twa touching the feelings that fill us
on glowering, after lang absence, at the spots that hae a
haud o' the memory's ' benmost bore,' but Jock's vile
muck fork has ted them out o' a' gathering.   How-

somever, I daresay I min' the best feck o' a sang that
comes gey near my present estate; sae, Edie, gif ye'll
quat cracking your whip sae loud, an' if Jock will gie
owre the 'mucking o' Geordie's byre,' I'll try an' let ye
hear't :—

TO MY NATIVE STRATH.

At last there streaks my native strath
    Aneath the redd'ning light ;
O ! mony a bitter day's gane by
    Sin' last I saw this sight.

An' mony a time thy stately trees
    Hae leaf'd in the summer sun ;
As often has November's freeze
    Lowsed a' to the winter wun'.

An' mony a gallant family,
    Sin' last my howff was here,
By fortune's fell an' fickle blasts
    Been scattered far an' near.

O ! whaur are a' the bonny bairns
    I left upon the knee ?
I winna ken them frae the frem,
    Nor yet will they ken me.

The lassie that I lo'ed first,
    The young thing I lo'ed weel,
Was then a fair bud on yon bank,
    An' span at her mither's wheel.

I thought thee, Jessie, then my ain,
    Stieve trystit for gude an' a' ;
But the grapple o' our young hearts
    The warl' likes to scuff awa'.

Alas ! what stint the tear an' wear
    O' time to baith has done !
Yet still thy name comes to my ear
    Like the sough o' a pleasant tune."

By this time the sun had almost run himself aground.
"Day and night," to quote from one of Edie's un-
published essays, "like good and evil, hold alternate
noons over this earth, and though on each summer morn
the black witch and her brood (like ignorance in the
Augustan age) seem buried for ever in caves and coal
pits, yet in process of time she again ventureth forth,
peeping first from her den with a howlet's eye to mark
if her fiery enemy be gone; then she creepeth into the
hollows and glens; anon she walketh more boldly forth
to the valleys and plains; and at last, like the Goth on
the seven hills of the world's metropolis, she holds her
revels on the mountain top." A Scotch day, however,
under the influence of the dog-star, cannot with truth be
said to be much pestered with the black witch. Her
domain seems then under the regency of her gentle
daughter—a sort of cross-breed betwixt her and Day; a
mild kind of Mulatto ; a sweet girl of colour, that has al-
most as many lovers as her father.

"As light," according to Shakespeare, "began to
thicken," or, according to Edie, as the witch began to
peep from her pit, they drove into the village of Dailly.
The Linker, not willing at that hour to make himself
known to the familiars of his father's house, lowered him-
self down into his former berth, and drew his bonnet
over his eyes in a way that he might spy the natives
without their recognising the spyer. Swarms of children
(an ingredient as common and necessary to a village as
barley to Scotch broth) were occupying the play-ground

of the Linker's childhood—as much strangers to him as the swarms of midges that danced around them.   It was in all likelihood their last game for the night, though actively performed as the first.   Merry little elves, like a day at the equinox, they have no drowsy twilight, but drop at once from the meridian of their mirth, often caught by sleep in the very posture of play, with the chuckle of their last fun stiffened upon their chubby cheeks.

About the middle of the village they observed a short, stuffy-looking old man, with a fishing-rod in his hand, enter a cottage.   "There," said the Linker, "goes as harmless a little spirit as ever was enclosed in clay ; although many a time Hughie has committed regicide, if the salmon, as Smollett has it, be the monarch of the flood.   His mode and manner of living are rank curiosities.   Having no property or possession on the earth, he makes pretty free with the inhabitants of the heavens above and the waters beneath.   It's well worth a pint an' a gill to hear him speak o' some o' his fishing days amang the mossy lochs that lie 'behind yon hill where Stincher flows.'   'I was owre at the loch side,' I have heard him say, 'afore ye'd kent a whittrit frae a whaup. There was a fine pirl out frae the wast, wi' a sma' smurr o' rain, an' as sure's I'm sayin' it, they set up their heads like harrow tins, louping at the very knots o' the line. Od, I wapped them out at every throw, wi' backs like taids an' wames like the yellow goud, the sma'est o' them a span, an' some o' them like your shakle bane.   Gif the win' hadna faun an' the cluds rackit, I could hae cram'd a kist wi' them afore dark.'   At a certain season he takes a voyage to the Craig of Ailsa, bringing home a precious load of sea-fowls, which he calls Ailsa cocks, ketty wakes, petties, and solan geese, the most of which he plucks and pickles by as a mart for winter use. He used to make them generally eatable with broth, to which he gave most untempered praise as the glory of eatables. In this commendation, though often pressed thereto, I could never join ; indeed, Hughie's broth day was long a fearful day to me. However, I got my nose at last to tolerate the mess, but could never get my mouth to go the same length. Poor old Hughie! God bless ye! Thou'rt a rich man, compared with many lords. Thou taught this hand to plet snoods, cast the fisher's knot, spin lines, whoop hooks, and busk flies. May thy set line ne'er be fanked wi' eels or thy cast line catch on allers ; may the cocks and ketties fa' before thy cudgel ; aye, and may they smell under pickle to thy heart's content. Blest 'be thy basket and thy store, kail and potatoes.' "

While the Linker was thus driving away at his village anecdotes, and Edie at his animal, by the time that Day had driven so completely out of Heaven that the only vestige of him visible was the dark-red heel of his morocoo slipper, flourished above the Mull of Kintyre, they came before the gates of that dwelling where the Linker, in his assurance and confidence of kindness, had quartered them for the night. It was, moreover, the identical dwelling in which he had commenced his "muling and puking." Consequently he issued, under toleration according to paction, a pretty considerable sum of hailing and apostrophising speech, checked, how-ever, about "mid volley" by the appearance and hearty welcome of the honest householder — another born brother of their Doon-side hosts, who bachelorised it, after the same fashion, with another sister. And though he might not have the picture of friendship, sociality, and loving kindness painted so strongly and broadly over the vents of the spirit as had his elder brother, it was not because he had no such lodgers within that their effigies were not set out, as the night and day they spent in his neighbourhood fully demonstrated.

The indoor part of this evening with our merry men went by without sang, though certainly not without clatter. The Linker had much to ask touching the births, bridals, and burials that had respectively gladdened, maddened, and saddened the parish since his disappearance; while his entertainers, on the other hand, had much to answer and much likewise to enquire. On the whole, this night, though less madly merry than the former, had more the appearance of a regular rejoicing, seeing that the question, answer, and narrative of the former familiars kept blazing away like right and left firing, while the broad, lusty jokes of John and Edie burst in at intervals as great guns, drowning with their roar the small arms, and making the roof and rafters quiver with their rebound.

A little on the "yaup side o' supper time" the Jingler, as was his wont, stole out upon the night to mark how the elements rested and overhaul his feelings for the day. There are, in spite of all that hath been said and written to the contrary, not a few points of resemblance betwixt the man of imagination and him of trade and traffic. As thus :—The man of money, when the day is done, generally gathers himself up a space over his books and till, to arrange the sundries that the doings of the day have thrown upon him ; after the same fashion the man of metre takes to himself a few moments at the star-lighting hour, to arrange the objects and images his mind hath purchased, and glance over the ideas and reflections that these have bred. The trader posts his transactions into the ledger, and stows his treasure into bags ; the other jots his transactions in his scrap book, and extends his sweet sensations into song.   The former, in his visions of the night, circumnavigates the globe with a tea ship, or bears down the Atlantic in the cradling of a rum brig; the latter, in the untethered sweep of his midnight soul, plays with the planets like pebbles, girdles the earth with his hand, or toasts himself a Welsh rabbit on the left limb of the sun.   There is, however, it must be allowed, a trifling disparity in the results, the day-work and dreams of the one leading to a red nose, round belly, and riches; the other to books, booksellers, bare bones, and a broken heart.   Yet—

> " O' a' the thoughtless sons o' man,
>   Commend me to the bardie clan !
>   Except it be some idle plan
>   O' rhyming clink,
>   The Devil ha'et, that I sou'd ban,
>   They ever think.
>
> Nae thought, nae view, nae scheme o' livin',
>   Nae cares to gie us joys or grievin',
>   But just the pouch to put the nieve in,
>   And while aught's there,
>   Then heltie skeltie we gae scrievin,
>   An' fash nae mair."

While Jock was watching, with heedless eye, the out-set of the great bear, a bat happened to come betwixt them, the familiar flutter of whose wing, driving the dust off some of his long laid up feelings with which its gloaming ranges were associated, made him put forth, with the assistance of three pinches of black rappee, the ensuing metrical questions, in—

7

A BALLAD TO THE BAT.

Thou queer sort o' bird—or thou beast—
    I'm a brute if I ken whilk's thy tittle—
Whaur gang ye whan morning comes east?
    Or how get ye water or vittle?

Thou hast lang been a fairlie to me,
    An' a droll ane as e'er I inspeckit;
Hoo's Nature delivered o' thee?
    I say, thing, art thou kittled or cleckit?

By my soul, it leuks right like a lee,
    For to say that without e'er a feather
A creature should offer to flee
    On twa or three inches o' leather!

The sangster that says thou art sweet,
    Or rooses thy fashion or featness,
Maun be blin' as the soles o' his feet,
    Or hae unco queer notions o' neatness.

Yet at e'en, when the flower had its fill
    O' the dew, an' was gather'd thegither,
Lying down on its leaf, saft and still,
    Like a babe on the breast o' its mither;

Then we aft hae forgether'd, I trow,
    When my back 'gainst the birk buss was leaning,
As my e'e raked the lift's deep'ning blue
    In search o' the sweet star o' e'ening.

For its glint tauld my ain kindly Kate
    That her laddie was doon in the plantin',
Sae I lo'ed thee as ane lo'es the freet
    That proffers the weather they're wantin'.

It's no aye the love warst to bear
  That sticks to the bosom the strongest;
It's no aye the gaudiest gear
  That lies in the memory the longest.

Sae, be ye a bird or a beast,
  Still wi' dearest o' days I maun mate ye;
An' yere flitter's aye welcome tae me,
  For it min's me o' langsyne an' Katie.

The constituent members of the pilgrimage being again embodied, and having supped, as "candles burnt to bedward" John proceeded to deliver his ballad. Now supper, to tell the truth of it, is pretty much to the faculties what a poultice is to the flesh. As the latter, when applied to a bodily injury, never fails, if there be an ounce of humour in the animal, to bring it to a suppuration; so the former, in a special manner, when largely applied, tendeth, if there be any drowsiness lurking about the brain, to ripen it to a slumber. It ought not, therefore, to be held as an astonisher that Edie, whose limbs were sufficiently jaded and whose senses were well soaked with poppy, should have given a sort of chorusing yawn to each stanza, and to the last a deep nose note by way of finale. Natural, nevertheless, as this in Edie could be proved to be, it did not exactly, to a decimal, please the deliverer. Indeed, though your metre makers pretend to be large and lusty admirers of Nature, they have, notwithstanding, no admiration for those who during the reading or recital of their pieces show any propensity to take their natural rest. He received, however, some crumbs o' comfort from the Carrick carle. " The ballad," said he, " to be sure, is coarse enough; but I like whiles to see the ruble work

o' the mind as weel's the ashler—just as it comes to han',
rough an' roun', tare an' tret ; though it maun be allowed,
in exoneration o' Edie, that this bulk an' block gear
canna but be heavier than the weel hammered an' handled
ware that's tightly finished." Jock briefly acceded to the
above with a grumph, and Edie with a groan, evidently
raised with much exertion and about half destroyed in
the rustle of unbuttoning and clash of raiment upon
chair or table, on the quieting of which the scene was
shut in, like an Episcopalian congregation, with a long
and loud voluntary from the wind organ.

Jock and Edie, having rather out-slept the fair infancy
of the ensuing day, were not a little surprised on awaking
to find they had actually lost a member ; not a corporal
member, but a member corporate—the Lang Linker.
On making (to their credit be it said) prompt and
diligent inquiry concerning the long loss they had
sustained, the product of their enquiries stood thus. He
had been perceived stealing from the apartment a little
after the sun had left the chambers of the east, and,
reckoning from his propensities, it was concluded that
he was likely to be found wandering by the water edge
where he first learnt to swim, catch trouts, and make
seggon boats, bourtree guns, and saugh whistles.

Bearing away by their instructions, the couple were
just clearing out from the premises when the pleasant
voice of a country girl, chaunting an " auld Scotch
sonnet," completely changed Edie's course, and moored
him beside her for the rest of the morning.

The Jingler, continuing his course, after most diligent
search found our tall traveller pondering right moodily
within the walls of a deserted cottage. It was the one in
which his teens had been exhausted, together with those
happy and honied days that even as our teens return not.

He was standing, when discovered, with his back to the wall of a small apartment, resembling considerably, both in station and look, that domestic piece of useful furniture "an aught-day clock," with his large mushroom eye turned up upon the nest of a swallow which, in the corner thereof, "had purchased a nest." John broke his musing by repeating—

> " At the silence of morning's contemplative hour
>   I have mused in a sorrowful mood
> O'er the wind shaken weeds that embosom the bower
>   Where the home of my forefathers stood."

"Ay, man, are ye there?" said the disturbed ponderer. "I dare say, Jock, ye can rin a fit like a slow-houn'. But look ye here; this is the bit where lang syne I was wont to lie an' dream o' a warl that never was, an' think on plans that never could be. Is't na a pleasant spot? See what a pretty peep ane has frae the socket o' that window—for the e'e or glass, alack, is gane—an' how prettily the sweet briar peeps in to see, as it were, its auld nurse, for it was me that set it. The swallow, too, bears testimony in favour o' the place, for Shakespeare says, who knew baith man an' beast—

> " ' This guest of Summer does approve,
>   By his loved mansionry, that the heaven's breath
>   Smells wooingly here ;
>   Where they most breed and haunt, I have observed
>   The air is delicate.' "

" Indeed, with regard to the whole winged ones," he continued, " barring always angels and insects—my knowledge not reaching the one or descending to the other—I'm bound to say that not only in the beauty of their buildings but in the choice of sites, touching neighbourhood, exposure, and general indications of healthiness, their wisdom is such that I could poise the taste o' the Robin Redbreast against the great Robert Adam, the Willie Wagtail against William Stark, and the little but laborious Ketty Wren against her immortal brother Sir Kit."

"Verily," said John, with a leer that the Linker could not at first interpret, "the instinctive good taste of the fowl frequently makes a fool of reason. Indeed, it is asserted by some Eastern travellers that they have birds' nests there composed or catered with such exquisite taste that they are absolutely eatable, ha ! ha !"

Never was the mouth of man more effectually shut up with an eatable. The replying look that John had from him, wavering betwixt smile and frown, would have made an owl laugh. On their way to the steading, although

> " The lark
> IIad drawn his little pipe from out his wing
> And sung away for heaven,"

and though each bower held a band, and each band was making music so matchless that hawks had listened and even cats purred forth praises, yet nevertheless and notwithstanding, the Linker opened not his mouth.

They found Edie up to the knuckles amid scraps of paper, covered, as he said, with excellent old songs, as "fidging fain" as an old half-starved cock would have been in the centre of a bushel of barley.

"Here wi' your lugs, my lads !" he saluted them. "See what a morning I hae made o't ! What a bunch o' 'wood notes wild !' In fact, I hae foun' a complete nest." "Do ye hear that, Linker? He's foun' a nest too," said John slyly, with a wink to his friend. "Let me see ; ay, three o' them," resumed Edie, broadening himself proudly over his scraps. "Three o' them, I think, as

the disturbers o' ancient dust and deeds say, fix with
considerable certainty their own dates.   The first evi-
dently must have been composed in the olden time, when
the lord, the chieftain, and the knight were the only
earthly beings whose loves, hates, battles, and mishaps
were deemed worthy of song.   Their vassals, clansmen,
or serfs ' aiblins might, I dinna ken,' hae names in those
days, but were never allowed to have any character, far
less feelings, save as dictated from their lord.   In fact,
they remind one much o' a modern kennel o' dogs—
either fed for hunting and fighting, or kept for show—
propagated like the cur without love for convenience, and
killed as deliberately as black cattle, the one for feasting
and the other for fun, as the auld sang says—

> " Awee ayont the dawing glint
>   Begood the bloody fun,
> But mony a clansman lang ere noon
>   Lay girning in the sun."

But I'm forgetting the sang in han'.   It's ca't

SIR ARTHUR AND LADY ANN.

Sir Arthur's foot is on the sand,
  His boat wears in the wind ;
An' he's turned him to a fair foot page
  Who was standing him behind.

"Gae hame, gae hame, my bonny boy,
  An' glad your mither's e'e ;
I hae left anew to weep an' rue,
  Sae nane maun weep for thee.

" 'Take this unto my father's ha',
    An' tell him I maun speed ;
There's fifty men in chase o' me,
    An' a price upon my head.

" An' bear this to Dunellie's towers,
    Where my love Annie's gane ;
It is a lock o' my brown hair,
    Girt wi' the diamond stane."

" Dunellie he has daughters five,
    An' some o' them are fair,
Sae, how will I ken thy true love
    Amang sae mony there ? "

" Ye'll ken her by her stately step
    As she gaes up the ha' ;
Ye'll ken her by the look o' love
    That peers out owre them a' ;

" Ye'll ken her by the braid o' goud
    That spreads owre her e'e bree ;
Ye'll ken her by the red, red cheek
    When ye name the name o' me.

" That cheek should lain on this breast-bane,
    Her hame should been my ha' ;
Our tree is bow'd—our flower is dow'd—
    Sir Arthur's an outlaw ! "

He sighed, an' turned him right about,
    Where the sea lay braid an' wide :
It's no to see his bonny boat,
    But a watery cheek to hide.

The page has doff'd his feather'd cap,
   But an' his raven hair ;
An' out there came the yellow locks,
   Like swirls o' the gouden wair.

Syne he's undone his doublet clasp,
   Was o' the grass-green hue,
When, like a lily frae its leaf,
   A lady burst in view.

" Tell out thy errand now, Sir Knight,
   Wi' thy love tokens a' ;
If I e'er rin against my will,
   'Twill be at a lover's ca'."

Sir Arthur's turned him round about,
   E'en as the lady spak' ;
An' thrice he dighted his dim e'e,
   An' thrice he steppit back.

But ae blink o' her bonny e'e,
   Outspake his Lady Ann ;
An' he's catch'd her by the waist sae sma'
   Wi' the grip o' a drowning man.

"O ! Lady Ann, thy bed's been hard,
   When I thought it the down ;
O ! Lady Ann, thy love's been deep,
   When I thought it was flown.

" I've met my love in the greenwood,
   My foe on the brown hill ;
But I ne'er met wi' aught before
   I liked sae weel, an' ill.

"O I could make a Queen o' thee,
    An' it would be my pride;
But, Lady Ann, it's no for thee
    To be an' outlaw's bride."

" Hae I left kith an' kin, Sir Knight,
    To turn about and rue?
Hae I shar'd win' an' weet wi' thee,
    That I should leave thee noo?

" There's gowd an' siller in this han'
    Will buy us mony a rigg;
There's pearlings in this other han'
    A stately tower to bigg.

" Tho' thou'rt an outlaw frae this lan',
    The warl's braid an' wide:
Make room, make room, my merry men
    For young Sir Arthur's bride!"

The next is wrought out o' mair hamely materials, and
evidently lies a lang gate nearer our ain day—when
clansmen, throwing by lots o' their foolish valour and
devotion, and riving up the auld deep-dauded tether
sticks o' their allegiance, began to grow into tacksmen,
and lords to dwindle into lairds. There is, however, I
maun say, a smell o' the auld feudal doctrine in't—viz.,
that gentlemen sou'd hae their will. [*The Tod in the
Fauld.*]

The last is one of those pure hymns of Scottish love
that our countrymen for a century past have been famous
for—the rough, rude outburst of a passion, strong as the
rock and reckless as the wave.

THE GOWAN O' THE WEST.

Gae bring to me a stoup o' wine,
    An' fill it to the e'e,
That I may drink a deep, deep health
    To her that my heart is wi' !

An' bring to me a wooer youth,
    That I, to ease my woes,
May brag my gowan o' the west
    Against his southern rose.

She may be gentle, thy true love,
    She may be fair an' fine,
But, by the heav'n aboon our head,
    She canna be like mine.

Her cheek is like the dawning's glow,
    That gars the birdies chirl;
Her e'e is like the lightning's lowe
    That makes the heart-strings dirl.

Her lips are like to cherries twin
    That grow upon ae shank ;
Her breath it beats the simmer win',
    I' the lowne o' a flow'ry bank.

Her neck is like the siller stour
    That booses frae the linn ;
Her bosom is a lily bower
    That ane would fain lie in.

Awa', awa' ye wooer youth,
    Yours may be fair an' fine,
But by the heav'n aboon our heads,
    She canna be like mine.

"There, my boys," cried Edie in triumph; "there's a
blaw for ye—a reek, I may say, o' the soul boiled out
frae the blood o' some o' our gallant forebears.   What
think ye o' thae alms, John, that I picked this morning
out o' 'Time's wallet for oblivion?'"

"It's truly wonnerfu'," replied John, attempting to
look damp, while recollecting Edie's base nasal comment
on his bat ballad.   "It's wonderfu' to see what some
men ware their wit on.   Why, Edie, man, I'se wad ye a
Duddingston dinner—an' that's a sheep head an' haggis
—that without either muse or inspiration, save an' except
a bit tasting o' toddy an' half an ounce o' black aff the
the bean, at ae sitting I'll turn ye aff three sangs will gar
yours kyth like 'dockens to a tansy.'   Excellent auld
sangs, ca' ye them!   Auld they may be, ye may take
that wi' ye, but excellent!   O, dear!—

> "'Noted men an' nice men,
>   Men o' wit an' wise men,
> Gree aft in the mite, an' aye in the main;
> But gouks hae a gab an' a gate o' their ain.'

But what say ye, Linker, to Edie's auld heart reeks, as
he calls them?   Whether, think ye, are they kin to thae
cluds that fa' in refreshing showers, or them that are
scuffed by wi' the win'—mere empty vapours?"

As the referee was putting on the guise of a sapient
oversman by lodging a few wise wrinkles in his front, and
rubbing them with his hand as if to feel how they sat,
and as Edie was boring into the silver mine of his not-
to-be-named's in search of specie to take on John's bet,
breakfast was declared ready, from which declaration
there instantly sprang another—a declaration of peace.
Indeed, we would ask—not the man, or rather brute, of
scientific stomach, whose glory lives in

> " French ragout,
> Or olio that wou'd sta' a sow,"

but the genuine man of unpolluted palate—if anything could have been more in unison with his nine o'clock cravings, or better fitted to set him at "peace with all men," than a snug, neat country parlour, lighted up by the morning sun gushing his rays through a casement, woven up with the sweet brier and the rose, and flowering the edge of a fair table-cloth that held not only all the stoneware and stores that usually stand as chartered things within the walls of the tray, but surrounded with a most extensive suburb, among which might be numbered " farles crump wi' butter," and Ayrshire's own legitimate bread, "supple scones, the wale o' food;" while at intervals, like furnace works, smoked plates of savoury ham might have smuggled another blessing from the old flesh-loving Jacob, or laid the jaws of the great trans-atlantic Ben under water. Welcomed to all with a sweet smile, helped to all with a fair hand, and pressed to all with a sweet voice—O, meat and drink, but it was wondrous fine !

As our pilgrims rambled by "Girvan's fairy haunted stream," while yet the day stood a little to the east of noon, they were, as heretofore, tempted "beyond the flowery margin of the flood," and one of their lives put in fearful jeopardy; but, as the incident is recorded in rhyme, it is unnecessary to " prose it."

THE PILGRIMS IN THE POOL.

> Ye dwellers upon Girvan side,
>   Ye men of Carrick all,
> Give ear upon an accident
>   That almost did befall.

It fell upon a Summer day,
  When woods with music rung,
When every bush laid out its bloom,
  And every dog his tongue.

So hot it proved, that a pair
  Of youths all in a stew,
When they came to a mighty pool
  Their garments off they threw.

And having thrown their garments off,
  They threw their bodies in,
As recklessly as rogues who think
  That suicide's no sin.

Away they splashed, away they dashed,
  Upon the dark deep wheel;
The one was of a codish make,
  The other like an eel.

The one he lay or scoured away,
  As nice as heart could wish ;
And wantoned with the wave as if
  His sire had been a fish.

The other of those waterwights
  More bones than beef had got ;
So, unto him 'twas greater pain
  To keep those bones afloat.

I like not well to see a thing
  Of bone compounded chief,
As little like to see a soul
  Quite buried up in beef.

But yet, in river or in sea,
   A creature like a cod
Is better off by far than he
   Made like a fishing-rod.

As they were sporting to and fro,
   With many a swash and sweep,
The lean lad took it in his head
   To plump the gloomy deep.

And down he went as plump and sheer
   As poker could have gone ;
His brother gave a heavy look,
   And passed a heavy groan.

" Alack and well-a-day," he cried,
   And would have cried much more,
Had not a head, incontinent,
   Poked up his face before.

It had the clayish look of one
   Upon the ledge of life ;
The cheeks were like a table-cloth,
   The nose was like a knife.

And squattering hard with either hand
   To keep himself afloat,
He cried, " O, lend to me your aid,
   Or I must go to pot."

Now John, although his brow is stern,
   His feelings are like silk,
And tho' his beard be black, his heart
   Is like to thicken'd milk.

So, wheeling round his heavy hulk,
  Upon the cry for help,
He seized his neighbour by the neck,
  As one would seize a whelp.

He tow'd him tightly thro' the stream,
  He bore him to the bank,
And landed him upon the shore,
  As stiff as any plank.

They rubbed him on the thorax first,
  Then on the abdomen,
And wrought on him those diverse works
  Rescuscitators ken.

It's first he lost a little wind,
  Puffed in a sort of sigh,
And then he shook his long left limb
  And oped his dexter eye.

And as they rubbed, and rubbed, and rubbed,
  He fresh'ned more and more,
Till he came to the perfect hue
  That he had been before.

Now, let this stand a large N.B.
  To you who love the deep,
To pause a little ere ye plump,
  And look before ye leap.

And should ye chance to grow so hot
  That ye your clothes must doff,
Ne'er push into a muddy pool
  That ye know nothing of.

Early in the afternoon a pretty extensive excursion was planned, and after half-an-hour's hot preparation, the pilgrims put forth in a fashion differing considerably from any heretofore described. Edie and John occupied the gig, while the Linker, aback of a little black pony, as full and round as a woolsack, looked like a long pin slightly stuck in a cushion.

Although the cavalcade broke away in the most comely order, they had not made much ground, when a quick thought seemed all at once to touch the rider, and away he pricked past the vehicle, quite at a midwife-gallop, and in a little, the heave and set of his head, above the clipt hedges, was seen far in the west, till at last it entirely disappeared amongst the tree-mixed cottages that compose the village of Old Dailly.

The more orderly brethren having counselled their well-educated animal into a sober sort of discoursing trot, John, as was his wont, began his topographic notices and anecdotes of local superstition :

"This umquhile clachan," said he ("for ye see the kirk's laid low o' auld Dailly), is connected wi' an awful prophecy, wrung from the divining spirit o' that wise man o' the west, Saunders Peden.

> "When the aishen trees in the kirkyard kiss,
> Happy are the just that that day miss,
> For the French then will come afore it's wist,
> On a morning whan the lan's in mist ;
> An' a boy that wi' three thumbs shall be born,
> Will haud three Kings' steeds on that awfu' morn ;
> An' the burn will rin sic a fearfu' flood
> That the bridle reins will dreep wi' blood !"

"During the last threat of invasion the growing affection of the trees was watched with trembling, and the thumbs of all the young squallers in the parish care-

8

fully counted.   The laird, however, partly for the love o'
timmer, and partly to lay the axe to the root o' supersti-
tion, cut them down.   This was reckoned another awful
'kill the cow,' and gave utter displeasure to a small
reversion of Covenanters that held field preachings here.
The stumps, however, in process of time putting forth,
the saplings came up like green delights to their famished
bigotry ; for much rather would they have seen the burn
flooded thumb high, as aforesaid, than seen their oracle
confuted."

A sharp elbow in the road, a little below the
umquhile clachan, as the Jingler had it, brought the long
light horseman again in sight, not bobbing up and down
as last seen, but squatted beside an old man, nose to
nose, in the ditch, while the pony standing behind at a
little distance, gave the group much the look of a black
pointer setting a brace of grouse.

"What in the name o' bedlam are ye doing there ? "
cried Edie, as they drove up behind, " Has the brute
made a gift o' ye to the dyke sheugh ?   Hae ye broken
ony banes, or lost ony skin ? for it's nae use to speer after
things ye canna hurt—flesh and blood."   " I'm obliged
to ye, Edie," replied the Linker, " for your concern, but
this is nae doing o' the brute's, but a free will offering o'
my ain.   Johnny lad," he continued, pointing to the
countenance of his ancient comrade, " ken ye the cut o'
this ? " John gazed a remembering moment, then started
from his berth, crying : "Stiff and steady ! and is the
breath o' life still current in the nostrils o' Saunders
Brackenrigg, boatman o' the Binnan ? " as he gave lusty
salutation to the old and rather singular looking man.

He was not what is called a " big man," yet, in the
stouchy settle of his trunk there were broad marks both
of pith and power, though now evidently stiffened and

lumbered by with age. He wore an old light blue, side-tailed coat, the various out-breakings of which were battered up with indifferent patches, and glittering upon the breast, cuffs, and tail with buttons which might have made pan lids. His vest was of old red plush—indeed, so old and bare-worn that it was only from little tufts here and there one gathered that the field had once been all under the same crop—winged with exceedingly long pockets that curtained about one-third of his breeches, which, certainly, with great propriety deserved the name of small clothes, as they barely covered his knee lid when standing, and, when seated, did not even condescend to bend with the limb but held their mouths stubbornly out like two pieces of cannon. His stockings were ribbed, and of the same hue with his coat, and upon his shoes there rode a pair of brass buckles which might have made saddle trees to a Highlandman's horse. His habits, thus far, were all sufficiently inland; but a hat, covered with coarse linen, and strongly pitched, seemed to point to rougher occupations, "where the stormy winds did blow," more especially when taken in fellowship with a set of features much weather-worn, and some of them evidently driven from their original position by violence. Indeed, his nose—swung to the left like a jib sail in a side wind—declared, from certain scars, that it owed its present curve to some missile, either ponderous in itself or diligently applied. His face, on the whole, when inspected for disposition, bespoke both good nature and kindly feelings, but, when searched for character, it presented two looks, arising from the still, quiet habits of a country life attempting to master the rough reckless traits of the seaman; the latter, indeed, seemed pretty well plaistered up, though, like an old wound, it threatened to break out from the least tampering or irritation.

John was largely delighted with meeting the old boat-man, though he declared he had as soon expected to see Ailsa Craig whummel'd up like a salmon cobble as the roving boatman o' the Binnan tenting a cow on the gate to Girvan. "How," said he, "might this hae come about, Saunders, without a miracle?" "Why, I hae na turned the chow in my cheek," answered Saunders, "sin' I gied your frien' here a rough guess o't, but ye'se get it a' owre again, truly, gif ye hae time to hear't whar ane may speak wi' a wat mouth. Need I tell a lad come to your time o' life what a dry craig an' a lang crack craves?" "So, so, Saunders," returned John, "I can see that tho' ye've laid by your blue jacket and harn calshes, ye hae na laid by your drowth." "We canna work wonners," said the old man lightly, "the pock maun aye saur o' the saut. And I hae e'en heard it said o' some o' your saunts, that they found it easier to lay down their life than their ill leets; sae what can ye expect from me, wha I may say, lifted my mouth frae my mither's breast to the brandy cag; me, that rocked and rowed the best feck o' forty years, wi' an anker for my bed an' a cag for my cod; me, that has seen swashes o't could a soumed ye a' like midges in a midden dub. I say, what can ye expect o' me, man, an' reckon on things possible?"

The pilgrims having acknowledged that his drought was quite natural, requested him, if he could, to conduct them where it might be quenched. This was glorious service for the old smuggler. Without uttering a word, he tied his charge to a thorn, and easing his hat a little off his brow, with an eye beaming pleasure and a cheek ripe with joy, he strode away before, bidding them follow. The Linker, however, being still intent on prosecuting his journey, started in a contrary direction, being pretty well aware where he would find them again, and in a twinkling man and horse were buried up in a cloud of their own up-kicking.

After half-a-mile's trotting (for the smuggler walked not as his face had been churchward) he halted at a break in the hedge-row, beyond which a few yards, as the sign-board declared, stood a house of entertainment. It was a snug, sheltered cottage, thatched, and almost entirely grown verdant with moss, save where a pigeon had scratched a sunny seat or an impudent sparrow burrowed to breed. The walls were low and ill-built, but white as Irish lime could make them, and the window stones, touched up with a little yellow-ochre, gave to the exterior that clean comfortable look that a Scotsman fitly expresses by the word cozzy, while the white sand that peeped beyond the threshold, and a few yards swept around the door, seemed to speak of cleanliness within.

While the pilgrims, after having disposed of their gig, tarried a little without, inspecting with curious eye the snug little baiting-house that really seemed pitched as a bait by the wayside to catch thirsty sinners, the old man had entered and was heard pretty loud and rather lovingly engaged with the hostess. There seemed, indeed, to be a good deal both of familiarity and affection in existence betwixt the two, and it no doubt had its root in a kind of reciprocity somewhat resembling that of the Moor and the fair maid of Venice—

> " He loved her for the liquor that she sold ;
> And she loved him because that he loved it."

By the time they entered, she had got a little, round, one-legged and three-footed table made firm in the middle of the room, and was, with the tail of her apron,

pretending to beat the dust—a common browster-wife
pretext for remaining until they take an order. She re-
ceived them with a neat, customer-taking smile, played
off from an old but fresh face, deeply enclosed all around
with a stiff parapet of French lawn coped with a light
railing of narrow lace. Her gown and petticoat were
composed of that stuff, called lintsy woolsy, which our
foremothers, when young, were wont to caird and spin,
and when old, to test upon as pieces almost of imperish-
able property. On the whole, the hostess and her
habitation harmonised to a fraction—clean, comfortable,
and enticing—and both, moreover, seemed to have seen
not a little of the last century.

Having seated themselves before a mutchkin stoup of
the best in the house, a quegh cap " o' reaming swats,"
and a considerable breadth of oat cake, they proceeded
to request old Saunders, the last of the smugglers (after
wetting his whistle), to narrate that part of his history
which drove him from his former to his present employ-
ment.

He began—after gathering himself compactly together,
pinching a few extra wrinkles into the nook of his eye, and
scratching the edge of his white whisker—with " Really,
lads, that's a time I never talk o' without hot blood an' a
sair heart, when I think on the dogs that did it to me an'
the rare souls that suffered wi' me. Ye'll min', I dare-
say, neighbour, afore ye gaed east, that we foreign traders
wha wont to clear out without making custom house
entries, war sair keepit down an' cow'd wi' the cutters,
an' that it was only in the dead howe o' winter that we
could rin owre a bit boatfu' o' Irish saut?" John ac-
knowledged he knew as much. " Weel, sirs, we gart
oursel's trew that at this wark a' the cutters in the king-
dom, or a' the gaugers or tide-waiters that ever saul'd

their day's ease an' night's rest to distress their neighbour, couldna touch us. But the pig gangs lang to the well yet comes hame broken at last; sae it fared wi' us. We had rigged an' reekit out a prime swanking wherry. She was o' the right Gourock bigg, syde in the rib an' strait in the beam, could hae run wi' the win' an' took the sea like a hollan' hawk; an' the lads that wrought her (though I'm ane of them that says't) their betters never floated atween the Cumbrays an' Carrick. I thought wi' mysel' at the wa-gang, an' some o' us e'en said as muckle, that the night was rather short, an' there was a bit heel o' an auld moon in the lift. Howsomever, I daresay we war mair behauden to some ill e'e an' fause heart than either short night or moonlight. But, to mak' a lang tale short, we had run owre wi' a fine tiffle o' win' frae the west, an' as the sun took the sea, an' the win' gaed wi' him, we lay babbin' in the mouth o' the loch as deep's a *wrack-duck*. But, as the tide was in our tail, an' ony waff o' win' that was lay the same airt, we streekit a' our claith, laid our best strength on the lang oars, an' slade awa up by the lan', meaning to mak' the Currerie port about the latest. We had raiket, afore gloam, wi' a gude glass, the Carrick coast an' the best feck o' the firth, but could spy naither timmer nor tackle, sae we bore awa up for the port as bauldly as gif our burden had been spring cod or Girvan coals. Just as we entered the jaws o' the port, an' war easing awa' the sail yearns, a lang boat, wi' a full crew o' the devil's dogs, cam' scouting out frae the rive in the crabcraigs an' hailed us to lye too, an' ere we gat time to throw the wherry in the win' they had their grapples in our gunnels. I needna' tell ye that they didna' board us wi' baith ease an' honour. We faught them for the feck o' ten minutes wi' broken oars, iron crows, an' bail hefts, an' had anither boat no come up we wou'd hae set them back wi' little spulzie but their ain blood. In the hettest o' the bruistle I was somehow dung overboard, an' whan I saw it was a' owre wi' the wherry, I soum'd to a black rock, an' threw a tangle owre my head, keeping my body under water; sae they searcht for me in vain. But, O, man, whan they sailed by me at last, wi' the brave bread-winner o' mony an honest woman, the deddy o' mony a bonny bairn, the comrades o' my youth an' the best blood in Carrick, tyed up in their ain boat like brutes, I thought my very breast wou'd hae bursted. I reft at the rock I hang be, an' wou'd hae gi'en a warl' to been able to lift it an' smash'd it in amang them. O! rough be their hinner-en' an' saut be their last beddin'—confound and sink. But it's nae use now. Gie's a mouthfu' o' that yill, neighbour."

Quenching his wrath with a deep pull at the quegh, and a few heavy lungful's of air, he resumed his narrative with greater temperance. "The rest o' the tale," said he, " needs nae muckle telling. For twa three days after I gaed daunering about the san's like a body gaun to mak' awa' wi' himsel'. But the news o' our awfu' antercast, wi' an account o' my dementit state, hav'in' gaen the length o' my daughter Tibby—wha, ye'll maybe min', married a ploughman up in the Colmonell han'— anger't me sae that I wou'd naither speak wi' the tane nor 'gree wi' the tither. Weel, poor thing, in the teeth o' a' my unkindness, she and her gudeman cam' owre an' gat me wiled awa' back wi' them to whar they now live, about twa gun shots frae this. He has a bit grun' that keeps a horse, whilk he works, an' I tent the cow, as ye ken. As her pasture lies feckly by the wayside, I'm aften fa'in' in wi' an auld frien' that likes a crack an' a chappin', sae my auld banes are gaun rattling down the brae mair merrily than I cou'd hae expeckit."

When he had made an end of speaking, the pilgrims expressed much pleasure at hearing that he had got his roving saltwater propensities so thoroughly bleached out, and, likewise, that his old crazed hull had, by the cables of filial affection, been towed into such a comfortable dry dock.   "And when," said the Jingler, referring to his last declaration, "did ye see onybody frae the lan' o' your daft days, Saunders ? "

"It was about the first o' the herring time, I think, that there was ane here that ye shou'd ken—auld Rab Forgie, the honest ale seller o' the Binnan."

"Aye, Saunders, I did ken that ancient prince o' publicans.   He never thought ale ony stouter o' a gauger's stick, or brandy ony better o' a permit.   He was, over and above, nae sma' frien' to free traders, Saunders."

"That I ken, as did mony mae in my line o' merchandise, for whan ony o' us war out, gif the water gleds war on the watch, he aye hoisted a blanket on his yard hedge gif it was day, and at night he set a lunt to a whin' cow.   A bit waff winlestrae thing o' a gauger, I min', ance challenged him, when a gin sloop was in the affing, for hoisting his blanket and bleezing his whun. But Rab—wha had a breast like a boat bow an' a arm like a port stoup—tauld him that thae things war his ain, an' he wou'd do wi' them as he wulled.   'An',' quo he, 'gif ye daur to touch my blanket, or offer but to spit in my lowe, by a' that's gude I'll heeze ye in the tane till ye're saft an' singe ye in the tither till ye're sair.' Aye, Rab was the lad for thae lan'-loupers, an' mony a funny sang he had on them."

Edie, whose spirit had fallen into a dull, lounging state during the fag end of the old seaman's story, sprang stiffly up at the word "sang."   "Do ye mind ony o' them Saunders ? " said he

Saunders owned that he had been crooning one of them that very morning to his young ones. And suddenly, with a voice hollow and hoarse as the enraged element of his youth, he gave them :

THE GAUGER.

Tune—"*Nancy Dawson.*"

The gauger he's gane owre the hill,
Wi' his horn an' his quill ;
Will ye wad wi' me a gill,
    The gauger he'll come back, man ?
He's houkit thraives o' Irish bags,
He's herrit coves o' brandy cags ;
There's hunners 'twixt the Loch an' Largs
    Cou'd see him on a rack, man.

He cost M'Queen a browst o' yill,
He brake Pate Simson's whisky still ;
It's awfu' an' unkent the ill,
    This warlo'kin has wrought, man.
He gars M'Master keep outowre,
His billy keeps a seventy-four ;
He's coft his killing ten times owre,
    He'll get what he has coft, man !

Nae stream can brook a constant spate,
The dourest things maun hae a date ;
An' dogs wha hae a kintra's hate,
    Sou'd redd weel wha they bark at.
Pate Simson he's begun to bann,
An' Patrick has a lang Queen Ann ;
Now, Lord hae mercy on the man
    That Patrick tak's a mark at.

During the singing of the above, the former character of the old rough, reckless, boatman of the Binnan came stronger and stronger upon him at each succeeding verse, and he ended with his hand doubled, his brow down, and his teeth set; indeed, the last verse was literally squeezed out betwixt them. When he had laid the boiling of his blood with an application to the "cap and stoup," John brought to his recollection another, touching the same line of business, which he sang with the same spirit but with more moderation.

THE LADS O' LENDALFIT.

"The boat rides south o' Ailsa Craig,
    In the doupin' o' the night;
There's thretty men at Lendalfit,
    To make her burden light.

"There's thretty naigs in Hazel-holm,
    Wi' the halter on their head;
Will cadg't this night, ayont yon height,
    If wind an' water speed.

"Fy reek ye out the pat an' spit,
    For the roast but an' the boil;
For wave-worn wight, it is nae meet,
    Spare feeding an' sair toil."

"O, Mungo, ye've a cozzy bield,
    Wi' a butt ay an' a ben;
Can ye no live a lawfu' life,
    An' ligg wi' lawfu' men?"

"Gae blaw your win' aneath your pat,
    It's blawn awa' on me ;
For bag and bark shall be my wark,
    Until the day I die.

" Maun I haud by our hameart gudes,
    An' foreign gear sae fine ?
Maun I drink at the water wan
    An' France sae rife o' wine ?

" I wou'dna wrang an honest man
    The worth o' a siller crown ;
I cou'dna hurt a yirthly thing,
    Except a gauger loun.

" I'll underlie a rightfu' law
    That pairs wi' heav'n's decree ;
But acts an' deeds o' wicked men
    Shall ne'er get grace from me.

" O, weel I like to see thee, Kate,
    Wi' the bairnie on thy knee ;
But my heart is noo wi' yon gallant crew
    That drive through the angry sea.

" The jauping weet, the stentit sheet,
    The sou'-west stiffest gowl,
On a moonless night, if the timmer's tight,
    Are the joys o' a smuggler's sowl ! "

The spirit that gleamed through the old man now was
truly astonishing, it seemed almost to surprise himself.
"There's nae kennin'," said he, " what corn an' cord can
do for an' auld beast, or caup an' stoup for an' auld

heart. Come, I'll gi'e ye anither ane, and syne, as Rab
Forgie wou'd say, ' we'll drink mair the morn, an' skail.' "

THE ROVER O' LOCHRYAN.

The Rover o' Lochryan he's gane,
    Wi' his merry men sae brave ;
Their hearts are o' the steel, an' a better keel
    Ne'er bowl'd owre the back o' a wave.

It's no when the loch lies dead in its trough,
    When naething disturbs it ava,
But the rack an' the ride o' the restless tide,
    An' the splash o' the grey sea-maw.

It's no when the yawl an' the light skiffs crawl
    Owre the breast o' the siller sea,
That I look to the west for the bark I lo'e best
    An' the Rover that's dear to me ;

But when that the clud lays its cheek to the flud,
    An' the sea lays its shouther to the shore ;
When the win' sings heigh, an' the sea whaups screigh,
    As they rise frae the deafening roar.

It's then that I look thro' the thickening rook,
    An' watch by the midnight tide ;
I ken the win' brings my Rover hame,
    An' the sea that he glories to ride.

O merry he sits 'mang his jovial crew,
    Wi' the helm heft in his hand,
An' he sings aloud, to his boys in blue,
    As his e'e's upon Galloway's land :

" Unstent an' slack each reef and tack,
    Gie her sail, boys, while it may sit ;
She has roar'd through a heavier sea before,
    An' she'll roar through a heavier yet.

" When landsmen drouse, or trembling, rouse
    To the tempest's angry moan,
We dash through the drift, an' sing to the lift
    O' the wave that heaves us on.

" It's braw, boys, to see the morn's blyth e'e,
    When the night's been dark an' drear ;
But it's better far to lie, wi' our storm locks dry,
    In the bosom o' her that is dear.

" Gi'e her sail, gi'e her sail, till she buries her wale,
    Gi'e her sail, boys, while it may sit ;
She has roar'd thro' a heavier sea afore,
    An' she'll roar thro' a heavier yet."

As the old salt water spirit finished his " Rover," the
the red sun, as about to turn in beyond the western wave,
took his eye. He started hastily at the sight, saying that
the hour was come when his daughter would be looking
for him and hawky, and as he was a sort o' toofa' upon
their kindness, it fell his part to keep their kinches.
Proffering many braw thanks for what he had got, and
many braw days to the givers, he walked off at a round
sea-faring step.

His companions, having satisfied their hostess, soon
followed him. They had not been long away when their
ears filled with the brattle of a horse at his best pace,
and on looking round they discovered the long pilgrim
and the pony, bearing up at a great rate, accompanied,

like an old Greek God, with a big cloud, and swinging
to and fro in the front thereof, like unto a supple willow
whose rootling enjoys the juices of a mass. At first they
almost went into tremblings when they saw him swing
so loosely on the top of the animal, but on narrower
inspection they found that his extensive limbs secured
him quite like roots, and that, as in the case of the plant,
his waving was all from the spring of the trunk upwards.
He was in a rich musical mood, and to their enquiries
he sang—

THE AULD FRIEN'S AN' THE NEW.

Were the come-o'-will gifts o' the heart
   E'er reckon'd wi' gear that is sauld?
Can new-fangl'd friendship impart
   The pleasures that spring frae the auld?

New frien's may hae uncos to tell,
   An' fairies to gar the lugs ring,
But the voice o' a canty auld frien'
   O' it fingers a pleasanter string.

It brings back the joys that are gane,
   Gars the sweets o' the memory start;
It blaws aff the cares gar us grane,
   An' rubs up the roots o' the heart.

The warl' grows in bunches, we see,
   Like flower knots that cluster the swaird;
Then keep by the bundle, my boys,
   'Mang whom your young spirit was rear'd.

Awa' wi' variety's praise ;
  Gie me the frien's steady an' true !
I'd rather drink swats wi' the auld
  Than wallow in wine wi' the new.

The road by which they returned led them past the
shattered remains of an ancient castle that popular belief
had tenanted with a singular sort of spectre. The castle,
it would seem from the same authority, was built by
Julius Cæsar, and the ghost, with great propriety, was a
Roman soldier girt in steel, mounted with brass, and
spoke Latin like a Professor of Humanity. He exhibited,
likewise, not a little of the stout stateliness of his nation,
and, unlike the bulk of his shadowy tribe, he could not
be said to walk the earth. It was generally on nights
when the elements were much out of sorts, and the wind
came hastily from the west, that he made his appearance
on the out edge of a turret, where a crow might barely
sit—tall, stiff, and erect as a bit of the building, except
his right hand and sword, with which he cut and swashed
away at the wind after a strange old-fashioned sort of
exercise. When he had drilled himself thus for a con-
siderable space, between the hours of twelve and two
a.m., he always finished with letting what is called a star
sticker bolt upright into the air, when slowly his arm
seemed to run up after the thrust until the whole trunk
spun itself out into a long thin thread, and then, in the
shape of a grey cloud, floated away into the east.

We have often been astonished, (and this ghostly anec-
dote enlarges our astonishment) that among that learned
backward body of men who follow the "antiquarian trade,"
ghosts and goblins of all degrees should have been entirely
disregarded or overlooked in the way of proving facts or
settling of dates, seeing few will dispute that the testimony

of a spectre is worth a score of conjectures, and the countenance of a ghost much preferable to a guess. It must, however, be allowed that even those shadowy things are liable to change, and ghosts, like their constituents, often give up the ghost. The majority, too, of those night walkers being of the feminine gender, they were, like the rest of their sex, apt to be influenced by fashion, and it is nothing new to see, or rather hear of, an old ghostess who was wont to stalk it in the costume of the good Queen Bess—her hair in a coif, earrings like onions, beads like a string of crows' eggs, a ruffle like a turkey's tail, a waist including both breast and belly, and a petticoat like a wine pipe—tripping it now in a robe of book muslin, her head in satin and her feet in coloured kid; then, instead of the long two-handed sword which might be mistaken for a boat oar stuck through her from side to side, showing like a pair of extra arms, a gentle little poniard glitters in the top of her ribs, about the size of a decent stocking-needle. Truly it is most lamentable to think that this fashionable mania should not only injure the credit of the living, but even extend to that of the dead. To the honour of male spectres, however, it must be allowed that they stick more staunchly to their ancient outward, and Ayrshire, we are proud to say, can still reckon a few who turn out to " the glimpses of the moon " in brass caps, steel vests, and iron small clothes.

But to return from shadow to substance. Our wanderers in the West had reached their destination without accident, and had wiled away, with their excellent entertainer and his amiable sister, the merry hours up to the deepest soundings of midnight, when, as they were about to withdraw to bed, one suggestion rose from the Jingler, viz : that, as he had addressed his Bonny Jean

9

from Irvine side, and as Edie had done as much to his fair Ann from Doon side, the Linker, in justice, ought to do as much to his " Jo Janet " from Girvan side.   This suggestion met with the approbation of all but the personage more immediately concerned, who declared that his judgment was jumbled and that he was not worth either as much rhyme or as much reason as the task demanded.   These objections, however, were soon over-ruled, as they hinted that a trifling shake in the judgment was a thing which could not surprise ; that if he could not rhyme it he could prose it, and, as to reason, it was the only thing that could spoil such epistles.

That the blaze of his heart might not be blown out, or injured by the wind of common table-talk, he retired to an apartment by himself, while the rest, re-settling themselves over a fresh jug, determined to await his return.

They had sat with decent patience one half-hour, with intolerable patience a second, and were even pretty deep in a third, when, their patience giving way, Edie was despatched to investigate and report touching the delay. He was not long in returning, with a strange-looking sheet of Bath post in his hand, which, when laughing allowed him, he said was found lying below the head of his exhausted friend ; and, as he seemed to have dropt upon it before it had time to dry, there was almost a complete duplicate of it upon his left cheek, so that if his love was not. graven in his heart it was printed on his face.   He then read, or pretended to read, the following podge :—

> " Dearly beloved cousin Jen,
> I splice my fingers wi' my pen,
> On purpose for to let ye ken,

"Yestreen about the hour o' ten o'clock a.m., we came to a pause upon Girvan side, with members and mentals (to slump the thing) in an uncommon state of health and happiness. Individually speaking, I cannot recollect of feeling so unearthly on any spot at any former period.

"We have been roving boys, take my word; no creatures in a crib, no horses in hapshackles—

> My saul's rare marrow to that man
> Wha stints him to a humdrum plan,
> An' keeps, like a dull, driven hack,
> His tae eternal in a track ;
> Gi'e me the man that on occasion
> Can tak' an affset o' digression,

If it were for nae mair than to let us ken he's a reasonable creature and no completely under the operation o' instinct.

"Sair am I longing to see ye, Jenny, and thae sweet wee buds o' the next generation, my second cousins, bonny dears ! how I like to set my teeth, and haud their saft, milky cheeks to mine, and fin' the waff o' their sweet breath, as if their tongues were moss roses an' their lips a pair o' pinks. It's weel for them, lovely lambs, that they're sae heart-taking, else wha would think o' bringing up a thing that aften puts us out our house an' dings us aff the earth ? An' it's weel for their mothers, Jenny, that they hae sae mony wilings and smilings an' man-melting tricks wi' them, or, guide us, whaur would be the next generation, Jenny? I tak' it the sma'-pox was a prime thing for keeping down population, not only by the quantity it took awa' but by the ugliness it left. But ye hae nane o' thae ugly cheek pits, Jenny, that drown beauty an' scaur love ; no, thy cheek is smooth as a summer lake, thy nose as a fair rock towering therein, and thy mouth is a sweet honey well at the bottom thereof. O! Jenny, Jenny, for a refreshment thereat! Farewell, my spring o' life, my aqua vitæ, it is all over with the

LINKER."

The dawn had scantily broke when Edie and John were up and had raised, or more properly speaking, had lifted their drowsy brother, who had, as is often done in the prodigal expenditure of one day's spirits, considerably mortgaged the next. He was even found unable to participate in their landlord's hearty bonnaillie, his utmost effort being to let out his eye for a few seconds to look a heavy farewell to the place of his birth and the playmates of his youth, as with a chirp and a crack of his whip Edie urged his animal into the track that doubled up the pilgrims.

The morning was far from being an exhilarating one. The broad breast of the Atlantic had over-night breathed out from the jaws of the frith a heavy, thick mist; the earth was soaked; the gentle spray hung lank with the dreeping load, and the wild brier continued to hold its rosy hands firm clenched against the unwholesome steam that smothered up the land. The birds sat moping on their roosting sprays, blowing out at intervals a few loose notes, apparently more by the way of keeping their throats in tune than on account of any present demand. The Linker, coiling himself up in his cloak, was soon shaken into a drowse; and, to say truth, even the most lively of them began to feel the influence of the fog. Indeed Heaven hath

> " No sweeter gift
> Than a pure soul : so fully weather-tuned,
> Can frown in fogs, look gloomy in the rain ;
> But then a sunny hour can make all well,
> Freshening the sluggish pulse. O, 'tis for such
> That fields have flowers, and birds have morning songs."

As the day rose, however, and the dawn breeze fell, the strength of the sun began to master the mist. First, it rose slowly and sullenly out of the hollows, and hanging a while at a considerable height, roofed in curiously the whole valley. Then it tripped more lightly up the mountain side, as if resigned and determined to anticipate its fate; and at last, to the delight of all beholders, it melted ghost-like into air. As the mist rose, so rose the song of morning, and the spirits of our waking pilgrims mounted up with both. Indeed, evils that do not go a deadly length are always valuable in the way of contrast, and as the earth had got a ducking that took the sun a good half-day's work to dry, the green thing looked the fresher for it, and the living thing delighted in that look.

John, who, like " bauld Lapraik, the king o' hearts,"

> " At either douce or merry tale,
>   Or rhymes an' sangs he'd made himsel',
>   Or witty catches,
> 'Tween Inverness and Teviotdale,
>   Had but few matches,"

kept prosing or rhyming to each known spot like a showman, as the lifting of the misty curtain disclosed it. " That deep gash in yonder hill," said he, " is called Linngston Glen—a place notorious for nuts, foxes, and fairies. It is, moreover, notable in song. Listen !

FAIR MARION O' KILKERRAN.

The bird in Linngston's deep glen
    His hindmost sang has twittered,
An' gloaming owre the western wave
    Its latest glow has glitter'd.

The elder stars are in a lowe,
  An' fast the younger follow ;
The breeze is creeping owre the knowe,
  To sleep within the hollow.

It's sweet to scent the win' at e'en,
  Whaur the wild flower makes it balmy ;
It's blythe to hear the blackbird sing
  A baloo to the lammie.

But it's a heartfu' o' delight
  To meet wi' thee, my Marion,
When the big moon ranges braid an' bright
  Owre the dark woods o' Kilkerran.

Some flit their love for kith an' kin,
  There's mae that flit for tocher ;
But the gear could lift my love frae thee
  This warl' has nae to offer.

I hae a wee hoose an' kail yard
  I' the howe ayont Knockgirran ;
An' a' my wish is to be spar'd
  To see't the hame o' Marion.

After the same fashion, when riding up the broomy
side of Carrick Hill, he introduced

THE DOGS O' DRUMACHREEN.

Yestreen I gied my duds a dight,
  An' razor rade my chin,
An' takin' aff my craig cleath,
  I turned it outside in.

Syne canty, in the dowe
  O' a bonny July e'en,
I gaed daunering doon the howe
  That leads to Drumachreen.

The last time I was owre
  I had angert sair my doo,
By fa'ing soun' asleep wi' her
  When in the barley mow.
But I thought she'd hae forgotten,
  Or else she'd hae forgi'en ;
But the di'el tak' my dear
  An' the dogs o' Drumachreen.

I blinkit by the ha' door,
  An' whistl'd 'neath the yard ;
But she never leeted after me,
  Mair than I'd been a caird.
I airted roun' the peat stack,
  An' thought to catch my quean,
But the neist sight I saw
  Was the dogs o' Drumachreen.

It's first they reft my wylie coat,
  An' then they reft my breek ;
An' syne they fasten'd on a bit
  'Bout whilk I mauna speak ;
'Bout whilk I mauna speak,
  Tho' it waters baith my e'en ;
O, the deil tak' my dear
  An' the dogs o' Drumachreen.

It being yet early day when they again reached "the
auld clay biggin'" erected by the father and immortal-

ized by the son, they hoped to find the Miller in a more discoursable state than at their last visit. They were disappointed. He had newly crept out of his bed as they entered ; but though he was as sober as he could be, he was not a jot the more sensible. All seemed off the the hinge with him—the barley bloom upon his nose looked sickly, and his pitiful rags of anecdote were rendered even more ragged by the incessant chatter of his teeth.

As this day was devoted by our pilgrims to the inspection of what might be termed the headquarters of the pilgrimage, the town of Mauchline, they merely spent so much of it in "auld Ayr" as allowed them to breakfast and purchase Water of Ayr hones, a considerable manufacture of which is carried on a little above the town, and tons annually exported to all quarters of the globe, so that the emigrant from "auld Caledonia" in the gloomy woods of the St. John, or the Ohio, often hath both his heart and labour lightened by strains and stones from the banks of the "hermit Ayr."

The highway to Mauchline winds all the way up by the side of the river, but being closely walled up with woods, and as you advance, getting deeper into the earth, it was seldom seen, though frequently heard gurgling as it "kissed its pebbled banks." A little beyond mid-day, they gained, after frying some nine miles in the sun, a most delicious furlong or two of highway, cut through a wood, and overhung from either side with tall, heavy, and broad silver or lady firs. The road was wide, as all tree-edged roads should be, and as the horse-track only occupied about the half of it, the remainder was under the pasturage of cottagers' cows, which kept it smooth as a lawn, while a red line of footpath, winding up the middle, completed its accommodation.   Fox gloves leaned from the hoary hedge; the burdock grappled with the brier; and the dark violet sparkled in the ditch by the side of his gay sweetheart, the gowan.

The pilgrims, having dismounted to enjoy the cool shadow of those lady giants, were met by an old woman, walking with a steady step and seeming ease, with a burden on her back and a basket full of delf ware upon her arm.   She was recognised by John, when at a little distance, as a personage well and long known in these parts by the name of Pig Tibby.   She was a middle-sized, pleasant-featured body, and from the appearance of Time's tear and wear upon her one would hardly have supposed her above forty, though they discovered afterwards that she was very considerably outgone the half-century.   Grief and discontent are better wrinkle-makers than Time, and one is apt sometimes to lay the doings of the former to the account of the latter; so, as the old fellow had got no assistance from either, his works upon Tibby were not in a state of forwardness at all corresponding to the period of his exertions.   Good humour seemed quite domesticated with her, and contentment no casual lodger.   Her burden lay on her like a piece of dress, and her basket, from long jolting and squeezing, had wrought itself a pretty comfortable seat upon her right haunch.

They found no difficulty in leading her into conversation, in the course of which John artfully brought himself to her recollection.   " Dear bless us ! " cried Miss Isobel M'Maister, *alias* Pig Tibby, when she recollected him, "an' are ye really the man that, when a bonny wee curly-headed callan, I was wont to see running like a whitterit about your mither's han', decent woman, when she would be pricing a plate or a porringer ?   Weel, this is my dream read.   I thought yestreen that I saw three yellow yoldrin's chittering on the tap o' a fa' dyke, an' I never dream of yites but I meet auld frien's.   But, as the say is, whaur hae ye been, an' whaur mean ye to be?"

"These are big speerings," said John, "for a gate-side greeting ; but as we are thinking about making it dinner-time, if ye could airt us to a quiet canny bit ye shall see how we live—aye, an' what's better, taste what we live on."

Tibby, after holding counsel with herself for a little, said "as their time was like to be mair precious than hers, she would gae back wi' them a bittock to where a slap in the hedge would let them and their whisk into the wood."   The opening was at no great distance ; so, entering and following by her guidance a winding wood path till they came within the murmur of the Ayr, they singled out a sweet sequestered spot, and in a little commenced their pleasant toils.

PIG TIBBY AND THE PILGRIMS—A PASTORAL.

SCENE.

A cosy corner in a wud ;
The simmer lift without a clud ;
On ae han' saughs knee deep in rashes,
Wi' carses flower'd outowre the splashes ;
The ither busket up wi' aller
An' birk, whose shade is sweet an' caller.
The brute beside them cows the carpet,
While Edie's gotten his whittle sharpit ;
The Linker gies his lips a smack,
An' Jock an' Tibby's unca pack.

Jock—My certy, Tibby, ye hae ta'en us to a noble dining-room.   Faith, this mak's a mock, a mere pantry, o' your corporation ha's an' county rooms—partitioned,

panelled, an' painted by the rich hand o' Nature, carpet-
ed by the same undertaker, an' roofed in wi' the blue
bend o' heaven.   O, Tibby lass ! sax hours ayont our
present speaking, when the gowan has gotten a grip o'
the dew, an' the birk buss an oxterfu' o' the gloam, this
will really be a bit whaur ane could court a fair creature
to great perfection.

Tibby—Aye, aye, Mr. Jingler.

Jock—Jock, if ye please, Tibby.   Just the auld butter
the auld price.

Tibby—Weel, Jock, if it maun be sae, I was gaun to
say cadgers are aye thinking on creels, an' wooers an'
beggars on barley mows an' lowne dyke sides ; sae wi'
me I would count it a better bit for an encampment o'
cairds.   Caller water, ye see, within sax striddles ; elding
there for the riving ; trouts down in the Ayr for the
taking ; an' a' kin' o' vittle, potatoes, and poultry close
by for the stealing.   But it might do bravely for baith, as
the auld tinkler sang says—

> " Merry hae I been making a cutty,
>   An' merry hae I been making a spoon,
> Merry hae I been drinking a drappy,
>   An' kissin' my lassie whan a' was done."

Edie (officiating as carver)—Come, my auld princess
o' pig wives, what bit o' the beast does your heart gi'e ye
to ?

Tibby—It's a' fish that comes in my net, neibor ; sae
just gie me a bit pick o' the first an' readiest.

Jock—Tak' your ain min' o't, Tibby, but I gie ye fair
warning that, like a tame linty, ye're to get your seed for
your singing.

Tibby—Say ye.   Aweel, frien', gif my tongue was in
as gude tift for singing as it was the first time that your

back en' braiden'd on my plaiding coat, I sou'd gie ye, not only a roaring sang, but a bab to the boot. [*The party getting speechless for a space.*]

> Suppose their feeding fairly finish'd,
> · Their ham some 3lb. trone diminished ;
> While Edie, with a smile, brings forth
> The noble spirits o' the north.

Edie—Haud that to your head, Tibby. That's the geer, lass, for synin' down a saut dinner, simmer stour, and heart sorrow.

Tibby—Weel, lads, here's to ye, an' a' connected wi' ye, either by the bosom or by blood.

Jock—Mony braw thanks to ye, my auld canty. Hech woman! it's mony a lang day sin' last I saw your grey plaid an' heard the clatter o' your pigs and whistles. An' now, when I get time to speer, how hae ye been wagging through the warl' sinsyne ?

Tibby—Just muckle after the auld fashion—cadging about the track-pats, pouries an' succar bowls ; getting bawbees for them whiles, an' whiles troaking them for auld rags, eggs, and ait meal. Though, I maun say, things hae rather bettered wi' me this whilock. Ye'll min' the bit misfortune I had wi' the laird o' Curwhang? Gude kens, I min' it weel ; it was just the saxt year afore the dear meal. Poor body! my mither died on the back o't. It was aye thought to be some inward trouble ; but I fear, I fear, my business wi' Curwhang was the headsheaf o' her yirdly dool. Aye, man, that was black weather wi' me indeed ; a dead mither, a faitherless infant—for Curwhang, ye'll min', fell frae his horse in ane o' his rides an' brack his neck—wi' the ill will o' some, an' the ill word o' a'. But it's wonnerfu' how things come roun'. It's an auld saying an' a true—

> " The darkest day has aye a glimmer,
>   An' the warst year has aye a simmer."

An' we aften see the saut shower o' sorrow grow a fairer flower than braver days could hae bred. Sae it fared wi' me. Tammy, my bairn, was aye an unca biddable, canny callant. I put him to the wright business, an' now he's faun into an unca fine way o' doing up in Eng-lan', an' sen's me hame allenerly, at hallo'-day an' beltan, as muckle's pay for my bit house an' yaird. There's a bairn to brag o'.

Jock—Success to the get o' auld Curwhang. I'm glad he swaps so little o' the deddy; though Curwhang took mony a loving ride an' stride after ye, an' it's weel kent gif he had been spared your bread was baked; an' truly, Tibby, ye were then weel worth the traiking after.

Tibby—Aye, neebor, that's a' owre now. As the auld sang says—

> " The hitching by o' time,
>   Tho' it looks to creep sae canny,
> Mak's an aik out o' a nit,
>   An' a bonny lass a granny."

Edie—Weel said, my auld bag o' ballads. Now frien's, as we're sitting within the gurgle o' the Ayr, and under "the gay green birch," if Tibby would gie us "Highland Mary" it would completely incorporate our feelings, I may say, with our seat.

Tibby—Ony thing I'm worth, ye're welcome to; yet, I daresay, I needna say that my auld crazy voice is better sorted to hameart lilts than sic fine springs. Tho' I min' the day, but that's a twenty-year-auld brag, whan I wasna fley'd for the fykiest o' them; but ye'se get it as I can gie't. (*Tibby sings.*)

Edie—Let's turn a horn to the virgin memory of Mary, the bosom bride of our Bard.

Linker—This stream, whose murmurs float around us, is one of three that Burns has doubly hallowed by his genius and residence.   Doon was his morning stream, "where first he wove the rustic sang ; " Ayr gushed the mighty waters that quired to his manhood ; while the Nith, too certainly, moans and murmurs by his untimely tomb—

> " O ! now his radiant course is run ;
>   For Burns's course was bright ;
> His soul was like the glorious sun—
>   A matchless, heavenly light."

Jock—His farewell to this stream, composed when about to embark for the West Indies, and while he was "skulking about to elude the merciless kennel of the law," seems wrung out of the bitterest drippings of sorrow. The last verse is, indeed, the retrospective history of a broken heart—

> " Farewell old Coila's hills and dales,
>   Thy heathy moors and winding vales ;
> Those scenes where wretched memory roves,
>   Pursuing past unhappy loves."

Tibby—Aye, poor fellow ! his loves were whiles gey wanchancy as was their upshot, but he never made use o' ony o' that vile hypocrisy that tries to finneir up wickedness wi' words or wally shows.   I min' when his bonny Betty was in the strae, he coft a blithemeat cheese, and carried it to her manfully thro' the town on his head, as if it had been a wheat firlot.   He tried aye to mak' a mense for his misdeeds, but never made lies to hide them.   O ! confound the loun

> " Says ' dear an' dawtie ' in the shaw,
>   But ' jade an' limmer ' in the straw."

Edie—Amen, my old gangrel! did ye aften come athort him when he sojourned in these parts?

Tibby—Aye, when his father's house was near Tarbolton. I used aften tae pap in at night-fa', when he was dauding the barn dust aff his jacket. He was aye blyth to see me, an' never held aff me for auld sangs. After him and his billy gaed up to Mossgiel, I didna see him sae often; an' ye may guess the wharfore. He was a young, roving chiel then, an' I was neither auld nor ugly, and haein' the bit slip I made ye sensible o', it would been nae scouring to his character if I had been seen traiking owre muckle about the steading. In the spring morning, tho', whan I would be takin' the gate, I hae gotten my e'e on him pannering doon by the lowne water edge about the time that the primrose comes out frae 'mang the bare busses and black dead leaves, like some comely ken't face amang colliers. The hindmost glint I got o' him was ae gae hashy day, I think about the tail o' the tawtie-lifting, as ilka waff o' win' was sending down a shower o' yellow leaves frae the aishen tree like a flight o' gouldies. Hė was stan'ing in a dyke slap, booted, wi' a staff in his han'. I gied him the time o' day, an' speered if he was gaun to lea' us, as the kintra clatter had it. "Yes," quo' he, "Tibby, I am; but it mak's a wae foy, ye ken, when the flesh flits without the heart."

Jock—Is your memory, Tibby, yet in possession o' ony o' thae auld melodies that were wont to affect him?

Tibby—I hae them a' in a sort o' stake an' ryce way. They've lain sae lang by they're a wee moth-eaten, but I'll gie ye yin as it is. (*Tibbie sings " The Fair May's Mane."*)

Jock—That's e'en a dowie ditty. Hech, but it mak's the flesh saft, and braidens the downsitting like daigh on

a dresser. Sit yont, Edie. Come, Tibby, gie's some-
thing fast an' funny, to gar the heart creep up the ribs to
the laughing bit, an' mak' us fidge on the top o' our
back·en' like a peerie.

Tibby—Whe—(let me think)—what wad ye think o'
" Ned the Thrasher " or the " Widow o' the Wast ? "
Dealers, ye ken, sou'd aye keep the goods that's ca't for,
and our kintra folk, for the maist feck, like a lilt nane the
waur o' haein', as Jean Glover said, a gude nettin' stripe
o' blue in't.

Edie—Jean Glover ; Is na that her that made " Ower
the muir amang the heather ? "

Tibby—Nane else. Aye, Jean was really a right ram-
stam ane. Nane o' yer linen cheeks, an' muslin mou's,
that sighs an' sickens owre a fu' heart ; na, truly, it was
aye leap year wi' Jean. She gaed ance doun to Ayr, I
min', to buy a waistcoat for a lad she likit. When the
shop-hauder wou'd ha'en her to tak' some new-fangled
thing, wi' a powdered grun' an' a sett flower, " Na, na,"
quo Jean, in her rough way, " nane o' your d—— cat
feet, gi'e me something like mysel', wi' a gude nettin'
stripe o' blue in't."

Edie—Truly, Jean maun hae been nae tethered thing.
Cou'd ye min' ony o' her sangs, think ye ?

Tibby—Bide a wee, let me think—Aye, here's ane o'
them—

TAM O' THE BALLOCH.

AIR—" The Campbells are coming."

In the nick o' the Balloch lived Muirlan' Tam,
Weel stentit wi' brochan an braxy ham ;
A breast like a brod, a back like a door,
Wi' a wapping wame that hung down afore.

But what's come owre ye, Muirlan' Tam,
For your leg's now grown like a wheelbarrow tram ;
Your e'e it's faun in, your nose it's faun oot,
An' the skin o' your cheek's like a dirty clout.

O, ance like a yaud ye spankit the bent,
Wi' a feckit sae fu' an' a stocking sae stent,
The strength o' a stot, the weight o' a coo—
Noo Tammy, my man, ye've grown like a grew.

I mind when the blink o' a canty quean
Could watered your mou', an' lightit your e'en;
Noo ye look like a yowe, when ye should be a ram—
O, what can be wrang wi' ye, Muirlan' Tam ?

Has some dog o' the yird set your gear abreed,
Hae they broken your heart, hae they broken your head ;
Hae they rack'd ye wi' rungs, are ye skittl'd wi' steel,
Or, Tammy, my man, hae ye seen the Deil?

Wha ance was your match at a stoup or a tale,
Wi' a voice like a sea, an' a drouth like a whale?
Noo ye peep like a pout, ye glumph an' ye gaunt—
O, Tammy, my man, are ye turn'd a saunt ?

Come, lowse your heart, ye man o' the muir,
We tell our distress ere we look for a cure ;
There's laws for a' wrang, an' sa's for a sair,
Sae, Tammy, my man, what would ye hae mair ?

" O ! neighbour, it neither was thrasher nor thief,
That deepened my e'e and lighten'd my beef ;
But the word that mak's me sae wae waefu' an' wan
Is—Tam o' the Balloch's a MARRIED MAN !

10

Jock—By the saul o' him wha's dust's in Dumfries, I
could sit in the sough o' thy sangs, Tibby, "Frae
November till October!" But look lads, it's time we
were moving towards Mauchline.

> Now glour out o' your fancies' e'en,
> And see the foursome on the green,
> As merry's birds upon the perch—
> Then mark the lads begin to march,
> An' Tibby gether up her creel,
> An' shake her tail an' say fareweel ;
> Syne see the pilgrims grup the beast,
> An' airt his brecham to the east.

It was upon one of Mauchline's profane fair days that
our pilgrims entered it, and about that hour

> " When chapman billies leave the street,
> And drouthy neibors neibors meet."

The village is seated upon the south-west side of a
high ridge of land that gradually swells up into Galston
Muir—bounded respectively by the Ayr and the Irvine.
The houses for the most part are staid, elderly-looking
pieces of stone, hooded with thatch, and edged with
slate, and are· altogether more associated with the past
than the present. It is certainly not a good heart that
loves to look where desolation is green ; neither do we
hold it a right one that loves the spots that art has lately
touched. But the "homes of other years," that Time,
as in love, hath lapped up in moss, are pleasant finger-
posts for travelling the spirit rightly into the past.
Mauchline was full of such, and our pilgrims made pretty
little tours by their pointing.

Their first task (after lodging their animal) was to
enquire out the house of Jasper, bethral and bellman
for the parish. This they soon accomplished, but Jasper

was from home. A pretty girl, daughter to old Clinkum-
bell, told them so ; but added, if they would halt till she
mounted her shawl and bonnet, she would assist them
to search him out, as he had merely stepped out with a
market-day friend. Her offer was accepted with becoming
gallantry. She was equipped in a minute, and, taking the
keys o' the kirk in her hand, tripped lightly along with
them to the known howffs of her father.

Two or three calls had proved ineffectual, when,
meeting with a young man of a genteel appearance, she
enquired if he had seen the object of their search. He
had, and with a readiness that proved her black eye had
not been idle, undertaken to relieve her of the keys and
her mission. Jasper was now found, and immediately
on learning their errand, stepped off with them and the
young man to the churchyard.

Before, however, allowing Jasper to enter upon his
anecdotes and description of the narrow and holy house,
it is becoming he should himself be described. He was
—to give him at full length—a hardy little bundle of a
man, his stature fluctuating between five feet four and
five feet six, from the circumstance of one limb exceeding
the other the intermediate inches. His face was rather
a lengthy one ; the ground colour whereof was a strong
brick red, speckled with little moulds of a richer hue.
His nose, as to size, was nothing in itself particular ;
but the great body of his face, having a noseward swell,
gave it a most prominent look, as a small tower seems
large on a hill. His eye was a quick, determined little
grey fellow ; and his mouth spoke sharp things, even
when shut. In the whole face, indeed, there sat a
wonderful degree of regardless firmness and downright
veracity, broken occasionally with the chuckle of one
who can enjoy both a bottle and a joke, and never better

than when neither were at his own expense. His apparel
was black—at least, had been; indeed his whole raiment
had rather fallen into the moult; yet his carriage was
stately, waiving the limp, and his speech was the speech
of one more accustomed to contradict than to be con-
tradicted.

When they entered the holy spot where Fun met the
Bard and helped him to lift up the lap of many a speci-
ous cloak, Jasper towered to his full height and impor-
tance.   He knew to an inch where the "tent" stood,
and could point with the same certainty the site of the
"shed" that "screen'd the country gentry;" the spot
where "Kilmarnock's wabsters" blackguarded it; the
bottom room of "the raw o' tittering jades;" and the
stance of "Racer Jess" and her "twa three——." And
he pointed with equal confidence the path by which
"Common Sense" walked off in a pet "fast, fast that
day."

The mortal parts of most of those that Burns had
immortalized in this quarter they found had their narrow
houses close by each other, forming to the south of the
church a little poetical ward.   "Daddie Auld," that
pretty specimen of Christian meekness and liberality, had
got himself snugly roofed in with a stone that told, with
flourishes, whom it sheltered.   "Nanse Tannock," the
decent Nanse, lodged a little to the south, with no hatch-
ment but what Summer had raised.   "Holy Willie's weel-
worn clay" had "ta'en up its last abode" a little beyond
Nanse, and like the Holy Father, he, too, lay stoned in
state.   And poor "Racer Jess" had likewise run her
mortal race and was a narrow householder in the same
vicinity.   There was in the doings of that reckless leveller
and notorious spencian, Death, much matter here for
moralizing; Hamlet-wise, "to grop that earthly hole in

MAUCHLINE KIRK.

Reproduced from the original edition of the "Pilgrimage," 1822.

low pursuit " and see the holy men mingling their flesh with that of the publican and sinner; to see the same flock of worms feasting on their different members and the same crop of hemlock and docks waving green with their united juices.   Such unhallowed union !   It seemed a wonder how the worthies could lie it out.

Jasper had a little history for each grassy hillock. There was nothing particular in the last acts of the priest or publican, but the manner of Willie's decease was truly characteristic.   At a country fair he had been so foully handled by his favourite, Mr. Barleycorn, that he was packed into a cart, with a number more in similar circumstances, to be carried home.   The driver, being somewhat in the same state, had driven either so hard or so badly that William was unfortunately jolted out ; and the stupid carrier, not having counted how many head of David's swine he had taken up, never recollected the holy man in setting the rest down.   Next morning he was found in the road ditch dead.   That famous piece of frailty, Jess, they found had died of the same disease. On one of Mauchline's market days she had been picked from the street and flung into a bed, in which she shortly expired.   The young man that accompanied them rather hinted that she was supposed to have been smothered among the bed-clothes; but the old knave of spades, who seemed to have had a pea in the pot, swore that though she had been a drunk duchess she could not have got fairer play for her life.

The next object that craved their attention was the kirk—as ugly an old lump of consecrated stone as ever cumbered the earth.   It seems (if one might judge from the arched lintels that attempt to peep through the rough plaster) to have been set up by Gothic hands, and, if so, Presbyterianism has really been tolerably successful in beating it into its favourite model—a barn. The interior, is, if possible, more dismal—cold, damp, dark, and dirty; looking dissolution, and smelling decay, and a fitter place one could hardly imagine for crying "tidings of damna-tion" in.   Besides the ground floor, it contains two wonderful-looking things called lofts.   One stretches from the east gable down into the body of the kirk; the other sticks out from the wall opposite the pulpit, sup-ported by two wooden pegs, which gives it quite the dangerous look of that cunning engine, a mouse-trap. Beneath this queer canopy Jasper pointed out the "cutty stool" where Burns sat when "Mess John, beyond expression, fell foul o' him."   "But," said the bellman, "though that's the bit whaur he sat, it's no the seat. It's been made into a twa-armed chair for behoof o' a Society here wha haud his birthday, an' at this hour it stands in the yill-house we left."   "Then, let us go to the ale-house," said Edie; and they left the kirk.

In passing to the inn they picked up a few old men hanging loosely about the village (being market day), who had been acquainted with the Bard.   When the chair was produced and the bowl set a-smoke, the pilgrims enacted that each man, as he related what he knew or had heard of the immortal object of their pilgrimage, should seat him on the honoured stool.   This mode of chairing, or rather stooling, the members, produced an immense heap of anecdotes from which the following are picked :—

In the summer evenings Burns used to frequent Mauchline—either on errands of business, fun, sociality, or love; and it was easily known to those he passed what passion was uppermost.   "Whan he was coming," said Jasper, who was the chairman, "to get fun wi' the young fallows, he gaed aye at a braw spanking step, his

staff in his han', an' his head heigh ; but when ought
black was in the win' his oak was in his oxter, the rim
o' his hat laigh—wi' a leuk, bless us! would turned milk.
I hae met him this gait mysel', and then, by my certy, it
would ta'en a buirdly chiel to hae said boo to him."

One night, during the time his name was "teased
about in kintra clatter," he met in the village a female
friend, for whom he entertained a high respect ; and
understanding she had some distance to walk without
any "trysted" companion, he offered to accompany her,
provided she could get another to join them; "for," said
he, "I must not be seen with you alone, as I'm looked
on just now in the country as tar—a thing that none
dare touch without being soiled."

Burns served as a Volunteer, and once when the corps
were being exercised in firing, after a few bad discharges,
the captain asked : "Is this your erratic genius, Mr.
Burns, that is spoiling our fire ? " "No," said Burns,
"it can't be me, Captain, for look ye, I have forgot my
flint ! "

Some time after he was attached to the excise a
smuggler met him one night while wandering by the
Nith, and, not aware of who it was, offered to sell him
some whisky he had in concealment. "You've lighted
on a bad merchant," said the Bard ; "I'm Robert Burns,
the gauger." The fellow stared ; but, with a smuggler's
impudence returned : "Aye, but you're likewise Robert
Burns, the poet, and I mak' sangs too ; sae ye'd surely
ne'er ruin a brither?" "Why, friend," said Burns, "the
poet in me has been sacrificed to the exciseman; so I
should like to know what superior right you have to
exemption."

When the young man, who had accompanied them
throughout, entered the sacred chair, instead of prosing

like his predecessors, he recited with considerable energy
the following verses, composed

ON BURNS' ANNIVERSARY.

We meet not here to honour one
　　To gear or grandeur born,
Nor one whose bloodiness of soul
　　Hath crowns and kingdoms torn.

No, tho' he'd honours higher far
　　Than lordly things have known,
His titles spring not from a prince,
　　His honour from a throne.

Nor needs the Bard o' Coila arts
　　His honour to prolong—
No flattery to gild his fame—
　　No record but his song.

O ! while old Scotia hath sons
　　Can feel his social mirth,
So long shall worth and honesty
　　Have brothers upon earth.

So long as lovers, with his song,
　　Can spurn at shining dust,
So long hath woman's faithful breast
　　A bosom she may trust.

And while his independent strain
　　Can make one spirit glow,
So long shall Freedom have a friend,
　　And Tyranny a foe !

Here's to the social, honest man,
　　Auld Scotland's boast and pride !
And here's to Freedom's worshippers
　　Of every tongue and tribe !

And here's to them this night that meet
　　Out owre the social bowl,
To raise to Coila's darling son
　　A Monument of Soul !

What heart hath ever match'd his flame ?
　　What spirit match'd his fire ?
Peace to the Prince of Scottish Song—
　　Lord of the Bosom's Lyre !

From this lad our wanderers procured a few small articles that had helped to compose the browster-wife establishment of Auld Nanse Tannock, and never did pilgrims to the Holy Land stare and fumble with more devotion over the thumb-bone of some half-buried saint than did our pilgrims over those relics of immortal merriment. Mauchline, indeed, was quite the Lorretta of their hearts ; the " cutty stool " was to them a shrine, and each of their ancient companions poetically canonized. They felt spiritually at home with all around them—but, alas !

　　" Nae man can tether time or tide,
　　　The hour approaches, they maun ride."

It was a close, sultry evening when they got to the street, and the casements being generally thrown open to admit air, what knots of beauty's freshest flowers peeped out ! with hair and eyes of jet, and love's luscious cheek, that flames and fades at every glance. " Verily," said

the Linker, with water in his mouth, " if these fair maids
of Mauchline are counterparts of their mothers, this truly
was a town full of temptation to one

> ' Who keenly felt the friendly glow
> And softer flame.' "

On a rising ground, a little to the east of Mauchline,
they halted to take a last look of that village and the
valley of the Ayr.   It was a sweet hour for saying Fare
thee well !   The sun had lifted his bright cloth of gold
from the dales, and hung it for a moment on the hills ;
the thrush had mounted his favourite tree to give to the
red west his last song ; and the scented breezes, floating
gently over the fields, were singing their May tribes asleep.
Edie, who had gone into musings on leaving Mauchline,
raised himself solemnly up, and in a deep prophetic voice
delivered his

FAREWELL TO THE LAND OF BURNS.

I have said Fare thee well ! before,
    As I looked, with mine eyelids wet,
Upon scenes where my heart had a store,
    And those plants of the spirit were set
That we cannot unroot or forget ;
    And I've felt as the dark mountain's brow
Had it written in letters of jet—
    " Eternity severs us now."

And I feel that " for ever " begun,
    Fair land, as I gaze upon thee ;
No more shall that " sweet setting sun "
    Illumine those valleys for me !

Yet bright may your blossoming be,
    And soft be the gush of your streams !
O ! oft in my slumbers will ye
    Be the land of my loveliest dreams.

The remembrance of thee will not wear,
    Like the mist on thy mountains, away,
Or as temples that grandeur will rear
    To glitter and glance for a day ;
But like towers embedded for aye,
    It shall stand on the top of my heart,
And o'er my fond fancy hold sway
    While Memory her pleasures impart.

When we ride (as a seaman would say) in a road where
the heart hath many anchors, the shows of the present
and charts of the past are our studies, and anticipation,
with all its motley buildings, lies scarfed up ; but when
the hour of unmooring arrives, and we are doomed to
take another stretch into the dark ocean of life, then our
light merry spirits are stowed below, and bustle and busi-
ness take the rope and rudder.   Heavily did our pilgrims
feel this changing of the watch as they bore away from
the Land of Burns.

Their eternal farewell to Ayrshire—whether it be
poetry or not—was no poetical fiction.   The feelings, in-
deed, that wrung it out were kindred to those that drew
from Burns the saddest of his songs—

> " Farewell, my friends ! Farewell, my foes !
> My peace with these, my love with those;
> The bursting tears my heart declare :
> Farewell, the bonny banks of Ayr."

Like the heart-broken Bard, two of them had resolved
on crossing the " Atlantic's roar," to seek for themselves

and friends a resting-place in the young world of the West, where those seeds of freedom and independence that " the voice of Coila " had sown in their souls might flourish and bloom, unstinted by the poisonous pruning of despots or the deadly mildew of corruption.

The Linker had, in his stolen hours, when wandering by his native stream, composed, under those feelings, a few rambling stanzas which, the others insisted, should be titled his " Last Lay; " and as John was one of those indentured to join them when, in the wilderness, they had " purchased a nest," an adieu to him was added.

THE LAST LAY OF THE LINKER.

" Who can say that fortune grieves him
When the star of hope she leaves him ? "
—*Burns.*

If there be aught on earth that can o'erule
    A settled soul, to apathy akin,
Gushing it o'er the edging of that pool
    The withering world hath dried and damm'd it in,
    It is the bowering woods, the pleasant din
Of waters where our infancy was spent,
    Ere the fresh spirit took the tint of sin,
Ere care had made a vassal of content,
But all was pure as Adam's first intent.

Ten years have deck'd and desolated thee,
    Hath shrunk thee in, or swollen thee o'er thy meads
Since last I beat thy pools, in boyhood's glee,
    Clear sleeping in thy vale, like crystal beads ;
    While the live waters, like to silver threads,

Seem'd stringing all together; yet when I
  Would think of flowers have beautified the weeds
That I have wander'd over, thou art nigh,
With all thy glories waving in mine eye.

My memory hath of thee a faithful chart,
  And, with the waning Winter, never ceas'd
To bear me, where yon hillock stands apart,
    Holding its shoulder to the cold nor'-east,
    Making the blast o'erleap its sheltering breast,
'Till April's lovely family are seen,
    Giving the weary sense its earliest feast
Of scented yellow and refreshing green,
Spring's pleasant pledge of Summer's finish'd scene.

We left thee, like the Patriarchs of old,
  A family with all our stock and store,
Hoping, as man will hope still, to behold
    A spot where we might fix and fasten more,
    A wider cable and a sheltering shore;
But there arose a tempest, and it blew
    Till our best holds were broke and overbore,
And he, the noble helmsman of the crew,
The father of our life and love it slew.

O! I have mourn'd profusely o'er the dead,
  And wish'd that they were back, or I away,
But thy departure, father, was the head,
    The chief of all my sorrows to that day;
    Thou wert my spirit's propping and its stay,
Thy path was aye the pathway of the just,
    And all thy principles so purely lay
Within the founts of honour, truth, and trust,
That I will write above thy honoured dust:

Father, if thou hast not the rest
Eternal heaven hath named the best,
There's not a living man on earth,
Who knew thy virtues and thy worth,
But what would say, with all their hearts,
" A——,* thou hast not thy deserts."

I might have been a *something* in this land,
    Nor penury on my name had put its blot,
Had roguery but been scantier, or this hand
    Held, crab-like, by the grapple that it got ;
    But I was cold, when villany was hot,
And so it went.   But with it did I throw
    The watery, wistful look that those who dote
Gift unto each at parting ?   Truly no,—
I spoke without a sigh, and bade it go.

Youth, health, and strength, were yet within the cup,
    And spirits of a height no hand might crop,
All well-priz'd items, in my summing up,
    What this world hath to give, and liar Hope
    Held to my fancy's growth her slippery prop,
And told me, with a wanton's wiling then,
    How poorer ones had struggl'd to the cope
Of this world's wealth and honours ; this was plain—
I was a man, it had been done by men.

Yet, sooth, I had no stomach for the heights,
    Those pinnacles eternal in the beam ;
My eye was on a valley spot, whose lights
    Are tatter'd with the trees, and rather seem
    A hiding place, where inward blessings teem,

---

* Ainslie.

Ranker than outward flourishing—a nest
 Where a quiet soul might hatch its harmless dream
Far from the world, whose doings at the best,
Despoil the bosom's peace, the spirit's rest.

I girt me for this travel, but alas !
 I found that there were giants in the way,
And Truth, old stubborn Truth, rose in my face,
 Telling me in the vaunt of my essay,
 " Good lad, thou art not harnessed for this fray ; "
I might have braving courage quite enough,
 But lack'd that prudence, inches day by day,
Sly sentinel Discretion, and the stuff
That plods away, regardless of rebuff,

A stubborn iron pride that could not stoop,
 And wag and wave like willow to the breath
Of those whose word is wealth—then, at a swoop
 This gave my sickly hopes a sudden death,
 Building a tall partition in my path,
That I to sap or scale was all unfit ;
 So, failures oft repeated grow to faith,
On each new struggle this old truth was writ,
" This is no world for thee, nor thou for it."

Nor stand I single, there is joy in that,
 Misrule hath sicken'd many would be free,
And curs'd Corruption, with her brood, hath sat
 A jury upon Worth, and doth decree—
 This is no land for honesty to be.
It boils the blood to see what villains dare,
 How shade by shade they darken slavery ;
But hush, there is a balm to our despair,
A word of hope—" There is a world elsewhere."

Columbia, thou refuge, thou Canaan,
 Unto our house of bondage ! Yon red light
That now is dying on our western main,
 Leaving us in the gropings of the night,
 Is gushing on thy shores a morning bright ;
No foggy glimmer, no autumnal haze,
 That looks of heaviness, and breathes of blight,
But that wide heavenful of unflecker'd blaze
That prophecies a long, long, term of glorious days.

I see thee like a giant in his teens,
 Thy ponderous sinews stiffening to a pitch
Might make the nations tremble, but thou beamst
 From eyes, in liberty and honor rich,
 A smile declares that battle's not thy itch.
Yet woe to him who maddens thee to take
 Thy sword, and leave the mattock in the ditch ;
Thy infant brawl hath made our world awake,
And thy old tyrant mother quail and quake.

Come then, ye tribe, ye clansmen o' my heart,
 Let's launch us with our souls for Freedom's shore ;
Tho' we have ties to cut, tho' we must part
 With friends will make the inmost bosom sore,
 And scenes that twine like ivy round its core ;
What ! shall a son of ours in shackles lie,
 Slave to a reptile that our souls abhor ?
Away ! while Freedom lights a corner with his eye ·
I will be there, tho' it were but to die !

We wrangle not for Mammon's dignity,
 Nor windy honors that in titles lie ;
The soil shall be our bullion, boys, and we
 Will coin us comforts from it that shall buy
 Heart's ease, and that bright varnish for the eye

They cannot sell us here.   Fie on the art
    That mounts a mocking smile upon a sigh !
Give me that commerce where the mind's a mart,
Where the glad eye hath dealings with the heart.

O ! for a cot whose threshold takes the sun,
    When day is deepening into the decline ;
Back'd by a wooded mountain, towering dun,
    And fronted by a meadow that is mine,
    Crown'd with the oak and whisker'd with the vine.
Then, where an infant river sings, and plays
    Its sweetest to the twilight, I'd recline,
And on my native melody I'd raise
A song to Heaven of gratitude and praise !

And is this all I wish or hope to find ?
    No, to the sunrise often would I look ;
Longing to welcome those I left behind ;
    In sooth, I cannot, like the selfish rook,
    Mutter and munch my morsel in a nook ;
But could I raise a gathering song, would bring
    All the fond hearts are written in the book
Of my affections.—Heavens, how I'd sing
Till Susquehanna's echoes all should ring !

And I have many a vow, and many a band,
    The knot of friendship, love's devoted pledge,
That there shall come the essence of this land,
    All that I love it for.   Then let the rage
    Of party madden, or let it assuage,
It boots not, my heart's cargo is ashore ;
    And thou, companion of our pilgrimage,
Come, tho' the breast may heave, the eye run o'er,
We must not part as those who meet no more.

THE LINKER'S ADIEU TO HIS BROTHER, JINGLING JOCK.

The judgment's best decree, Jock,
　Aft banishes the heart ;
Sae it hath far'd wi' me, Jock,
　For thou and I maun part.

O, ye are ane o' twa, Jock,
　That I can weel ca' brither :
Whaur the saul's strong outs an' ins, Jock,
　Clink fine wi' ane anither.

I've ha'en mony canty days, Jock,
　An' merry nichts wi' thee,
Wi' storms o' witty fun, Jock,
　An' spates o' barley bree !

Tho' noo in parting grief, Jock,
　I wring thee by the hand,
I hope we yet shall meet, Jock,
　Within a better land.

Then I'll brew a browst for thee, Jock,
　Will kill thy cankers a',
An' I'll redd room for thee, Jock,
　Or else my mailin's sma'.

An' the billy o' our heart, Jock,
　(That saul o' the right breed),
Shall match wi' me, an' we shall be
　Three canty carles indeed.

Syne we will twine a bower, Jock,
　O' the forest's living boughs,
An' baptiz't in our joy, Jock,
　The Pilgrims' Repose.

POEMS

Additional to those included in the foregoing
" Pilgrimage."

*Reproduced from the portrait of Hew Ainslie
in the New York Volume 1855.*

POEMS.

THE TWA MAIDENS AND THEIR MEN.

FIRST MAIDEN.

" If Heaven a draught of heavenly pleasure spare,
   One cordial in this melancholy vale,
'Tis when a youthful, loving, modest pair,
   In other's arms, breathe out the tender tale,
   Beneath the milk-white thorn that scents the evening gale."

SLOW o'er a sky young May had drest,
The glow o' day was gathering west,
Where darkly 'gainst the deepening glare
Rose the rough ruins o' St. Clair.

It was an eve that grief had chose,
When time had master'd half her woes,
To give to sorrow's mellowing dye
A scanter tear, a softer sigh.
Nor was it fitted less
For love's delicious tenderness ;—
The very whisperings o' the gale
Seem'd soften'd for a lover's tale.

When down the lane young Maggie's gane
  Wi' step as she were dancing,
Her rosy cheek, like e'ening's streak,
  Like stars her e'en are glancing.
She's in her shoon, her task is dune,
  The foddering an' the milking,
A ribbon rare is in her hair,
  An' canty lays she's lilting.

MAGGIE'S SANG.

THE laverock awakens the welkin,
  Our mavis he sings down the sun,
An' he's the braw bird o' my likin',
  That tells us the day work is done.

    Then hey for the sang o' the gloamin,'
      The laverock awakes us to work ;
    While the mavis sings, "Johnny's a comin',"
      To meet wi' his Meg when it's dark.

There's bonnier blooms in the simmer,
  Than craw flowers an' gowans, we ken,
An' statelier trees amang timmer,
  Than bushes are busking our glen.

    But hey for the birk hings sae featly,
      The primrose an' genty hare-bells !
    That scent our wee bourock sae sweetly,
      When cracking at e'en by oursel's.

Near whaur the burnie takes a crook,
Ye'd found their cosey canny nook ;
The row'ntree nodding owre the brae,
Right gallantly to thorn an' slae ;

While a' around, sae fresh an' fair,
Told Spring had been right busy there.
True to his tryst, wi' loup an sten,
Young Jock came whistling up the glen ;
Light to the trysting-tree he sprang,
Venting his spirit in a sang.

JOHNNY'S SANG.

THE wind it cam' saft frae the southart,
   Awakening the bird an' the bee ;
Cleeding bourocks were sair winter wither'd,
   An' busking our bonny hawtree.
An' fee-day will soon follow on it,
   When down come the pennies an' poun's,
Our lads then will don a new bonnet,
   Our lassies new ribbons an' gowns.
     Then hey for the time cowes the claver,
      The tedding an' bigging o' ricks !
     When auld bodies take to their havers,
      An' youngsters to tousling an' tricks.

Brown hairst, when the weather is lythsome,
   An' out come the bansters and baŭns,
Our lassies they kythe then sae blythesome,
   It's hard, man, to haud aff your han's !
An' syne when we're dune wi' the leading,
   An' a' things comes bien to the birn,
Our laird he sits king o' the feeding,
   But Maggie's the queen o' the kirn !
     Then hey for a bab at the babby,
      The tousling, the boosing, an' a',

An' hey for my bonnie wee Maggie,
    The pride o' the rig an' the ha'!

But hark, ye! on the nether bank,
Whaur supple saughs are waving rank,   .
There's rustling o' a petticoat—-
Weel Johnny kens the owner o't—
A laugh—a loup—a shout o' glee—
An' Meg the dawty 's on his knee.

Then came the squeezing an' the smack,
Nae sic as cauldrife wooers tak';
But that lang kiss, an' hearty grip,
Tells how the bosom works the lip—
Till Maggie, gasping out o' breath,
Declares he'd worry her to death.

Belyve, he's calm an' doucer grown,
An' then, wi' earnest words, an' lowne,
He's tald her hoo the clachan wright
Was bandit in a paction tight,
To hae a' ready, reel an' rock—
The aumry an' the aucht day clock—
Wi' ilka loom auld kimmers ken
Is mensefu' in a butt-an'-ben.

Forby, frae Rab o' Whinnyhause
He'd rentit 'gainst next Martinmas
A cot-house an' a hawkie's grass.

But safe us! when the lad was led in
To mint at bridal day an' beddin'
When Maggie would be a' his ain,
He tint his tether stick again,

An' took to ranting an' to singing,
Till Roslin's echoes a' are ringing !

The sma' kittie wran has quattit her nest,
A wondering what din's been breaking her rest,
An' flitter'd about on her windlestrae legs
In mortal dread for her wee pea eggs.

Ye needna be frightit, my bonny bit hen,
But haud awa hame to your saft foggy den,
For weel it's been kent, this warl out thro',
In days lang syne as in days e'enoo,
When maidens are leaning on lovers' breasts,
It's little they think o' herrying nests.

SECOND MAIDEN.

" O had I wist, afore I kist,
    That love had been sae ill to win,
    I'd lock'd my heart in a case o' goud,
    An' pinn'd it wi' a siller pin."—*Old Song.*

But another sight was seen that night,
    Where the grim auld castle stood,
An' the restless linn sent an eerie din
    Thro' the howlet-haunted wood.

For there 'midst the wrack o' auld ruins black,
    A lonesome maiden sat ;
On her heaving breast her hands are press'd,
    An' her wan young cheek is wat.

An' aft her sad eye takes a range o' the sky,
   Or sweeps by the Harper's ha',
But it hurries aye back, to rest on the wrack
   O' the grim auld castle wa'.

Then closing her eye, wi' a moan an' a sigh,
   Her head on her bosom she hung;
Like the wailing dove, o'er her long lost love,
   This dowie sang she sung.

HELEN'S SANG.

SWEET May, fair nursling o' the Spring,
   In bonny bygane years,
What merry hours ye wont to bring,
   But now, alas! it's tears.

When ha's are bright, an' spirits light
   Are glancing butt an' ben,
It's then I haste, like conjur'd ghaist,
   To seek this gloomy glen.

For lonesome bowers, an' ruined towers,
   Are fittest mates for me;
The roaring flood, the soughing wood,
   The broken, blasted tree.

Ah, Walter Weir! fause Walter Weir,
   Could ye but see me now!
The spirit dead, the roses fled,
   The wither'd lip and brow!

Yes, rough and reckless as thou art,
   Mate o' the wild corsair—
This faded form would chill thy blood,
   If human blood ran there.

Hadst thou been slain on battle plain,
   Or slept beneath thè sea,
A thought that you in death were true,
   Had laid me soon wi' thee.

But ah, a fond forsaken thing,
   O' lightlied love the wreck—
It's bred that wither o' the heart
   That winna let it break.

Alang life's lonely road I look,
   It's fenc'd wi' grief an' care ;
My rest lies in yon cauld kirkyard—
   O God, that I were there !

Now leave we this maiden, her woe and her wail,
And away wi' the wind o' the night let us sail,
Nor stop, nor stay, till we list the tide,
That mutters and moans around Galloway's side ;
There mark we an old baronial keep,
The storms are crumbling it into the deep ;
But there's sturdy vaults in the rock below,
That few have seen, and that fewer know ;
Fashioned and framed in days long gone,
By willing hands from the stubborn stone—
Sanctuary meet for a chosen band,
When red persecution flooded the land.
   Ah, little reck'd they, those holy men,
They were wairing their work on a smugglers' den ;

For hark ye! it is no holy hymn
That echoes along these vaults so dim,
But the ribald song and the loud hurrah,
'Tis carousing night o' the wild outlaw.
    The torch and lamp send a dark red glare
Thro' the thick and long imprisoned air ;
By fitter light who'd seek to view
A smugglers' den and a rovers' crew ?
And there, 'midst spar, an' oar, an' sail,
Run'let an' cag, an' box an' bale,
Spoils of many a distant land,
Sits Walter Weir and his ruffian band.
    But where's the winning, the wiling look,
Fair Helen's heart and her honour took ?
'T is hidden beneath that dark moustache,
And buried in scars of many a gash ;
So chang'd, estrang'd, in eye and brow,
Could maiden, or mother, have known thee now ?
As wild in word, and loud in cheer,
He urges his mates in their mad career,
While rocky roof and cavern rang
To the roving chief's carousing sang.

THE ROVER'S SANG.

Come launch the big brimmer, my boys,
    Wi' the brandy and wine we will spice it,
And if night is too short for our joys,
    Wi' the best o' to-morrow we'll splice it.
When broad moons are sailing on high,
    Your Rover he's swinging at anchor ;
When black winds are sweeping the sky,
    Then hurrah for the boom and the spanker !

Who'd live a dull landlubber's life,
   When there's money and mirth o'er the waters?
Who'd hitch to one wearisome wife,
   When France hath such frolicsome daughters ?
Ay, gi'e me the beauties o' Brest—
   They're the darlings for fun and for freedom.
What's sweeter, when lovingly prest,
   Than the frauleins that waltz it in Schiedam ?

Bale, bale then the brimmer to-night,
   While we tell o' our cruising an' kissing ;
How press-gangs were shov'd out o' sight,
   And gaugers were found 'mong the missing ;
Ay, roar up some jolly old runs,
   When the sea was a-scouring our scuppers,
How we dodged the old Commodore's guns,
   And bedevil'd His Majesty's cutters.

Then here's to our roving marine,
   He's the jolliest mate that's a-going ;
Right end up, wherever he's seen,
   Be't the wave or the wine cup that's flowing.
All flags but his lost country's own,
   With a rousing hurrah he can hail her ;
And his motto, wherever he's known,
   Is, Free trade and the rights o' the sailor !

THE TROKER.

A WEE the harvest side o' Yule,
As frost was flooring burn an' pool,
An' king's hie way an' cottar's lane
Were stiffened like the quarry stane—
The day was dour, an' as the light
Was hurrying hillward out o' sight,
As gif it seem'd it were nae thrift
To shine on sic a dirty lift—
A carle came tramping up the way
That hauds awa' to Ballantrae.

A man he was o' stalwart mak,
If ane might gauge him by the pack
That hint his buirdly shouthers hung,
As weel as by his muckle rung.
His step was steeve, his leg was trim,
But what aneath his bonnet rim,
Should been a Christian face, I vow,
It kyth'd the grunzie o' a Jew !
A beard, would make a pony's tether,
An' then, twa wally cowes o' heather
Had effigied his whiskers.—Truly,
He'd made a brainger in a brulzie.

Right on he strade, till he cam' tae,
The wastling shouther o' the brae ;

Then like a man o' stane he stood,
Glowering outowre the corbie's wood,
To where, a wee ayont the howe,
A sma' farm house stood on a knowe.
It seem'd a lane but cosey biggin',
Wi' wa's o' stane an' theekit riggin'.

Our Laird's herd, Jock, cam' whistling by,
As he drave hame the nowt an' kye ;
On him our Troker coost a look—
Jock's mou' that moment tint the crook,
An' stoitering, stammer'd out "Gude e'en,"
Thinkin' his life no worth a preen.
The carle leuch, to see the chiel
Boggle as he'd run owre a de'il ;
An' syne, in words o' lawland sough,
Speer'd wha might win in yonder cleugh ?

The lad took heart, as soon's he faun'
The carle spak like Christian man.
" It's auld Rab Glen, wha 's no been fier
Since tawtie lifting was a year ;
An' mair an' waur, his gude auld kimmer
Has no been just hersel' sin' simmer,
While Jean—their bonny daughter Jean—
Keeps spinning there frae morn tlll e'en,
Striving, as a' around can tell,
To fend twa sick folk an' hersel'.

The warst is owre tho', for we hear
Our Laird, wha's fleech'd for three lang year,
Has gat her trysted, an' next owk
She'll be the Lady o' Carnook."

"When I said this," quo' Johnny Tamson,
"He look't as he'd hae thrash't a Samson ;
An' utter'd words I'se no be naming,
Seem'd unco like downright blaspheming."

But soon our anger't carle grew douce,
An' airting towards Robin's house,
Took sic lang strides, an' strade sae fast,
A lang Scots mile was shortlin's past.

He 's tirl'd gently at the pin,
An' Jeanie saftly said, "Come in ; "
An' in he gaed a' gruff an' grim—
Jean laid her han' on the wheel rim,
An' star'd as he his "Gude e'en " shor'd
In words as calm 's he could afford.

"The weather's coorse, an' lang's the way,
That I hae trampit out the day ;
Sae wi' your will, as gane's the light,
I'd like to shelter here the night."

"Gudeman," said Jeanie, an' her e'e
Grew watery, as the carle could see,
"I'm laith to bid ye streek your gait
On sic a night, sae cauld an' late ;
But waes me, sir, lang months o' ailing
Hae scrimpit sae our ance gude mailing,
That little's left, as ye may see,
To entertain the stranger wi'."

The carle look'd sad an' sair at Jean.—
"I'm seeking nought, my comely quean,
But just aside your ingle nook,
Till daylight, frae the blast to jouk ;

An' gif it be, as ye would mint,
This house has lang had trouble in't,
I'm blyth to say that I hae airts,
Whilk I owretook in foreign pairts,
That mak' me maister o' a' sickness,
Like racking pains an' inward weakness ;
Sae wi' your will, I'se do my best
To gi'e them ease, if sae distress'd."

Our auld wife, wha sat in the dais,
Gat up an' show'd her runkl'd face ;
Poortith had eaten deep, and grief
Had bleach'd it like a frostit leaf.
Her words came howe, as she'd been boss,
She tald hoo mickle scaith an' loss
Had follow'd her gudeman's mishap,
As loss o' nowt an' waste o' crap.
She spak too o' the waesome brash
Had left her feckless as a rash.
"Their gear was poindit ; but Carnook,
The Laird from wham the lan' was took,
Was boun', when Jeanie was his bride,
To lay the poinding plea aside ;
An' Jeanie, tho' he was a coof,
Had plighted him her word an' loof ;
As her braw sweetheart, Willy Grame,
Had perished far awa' frae hame."

Poor Jeanie moan'd a sad " Alas ! "
An' threw the apron owre her face.
The Troker stampit wi' his fit,
An' gi'e his teeth a grewsome grit,
As our auld wifie gather'd breath
To sum the upshot o' their scaith.

12

"Sair hae we suffer't, tho' we've tried
The skill o' a' the country side,
An' wair'd on doctors far an' near
The feck o' our hard-gotten gear.
Sae, whatsome'er your airts may be,
As we hae nought to mense ye wi',
An' tint a' faith in drug or pill,
It's needless here to waste your skill."
"Sit down," quo' he, "an' haud your tongue,"
As aff he laid his pack an' rung—
"They're sair to blame, and gi'e offence
To ane owre-watching Providence,
Wha fleer at ony mean that's offer'd,
Whan, wi' gude will, it's freely proffer'd."

Our wifie calm'd, an' Jeanie sigh'd,
As wakenin' up the winkin' light,
While frae his pack our Troker brought
A gardevine, right-queer owrewrought
Wi' images o' awsome brutes
As e'er were seen in horns or clutes ;
Bang'd out a bottle, syne a caup,
An' stroan'd it reaming to the tap—
"Hae, haud that, kimmer, to your lips,
An' tak' it doon wi' canny sips!"

The ingle noo bleezed bright, an' Jean
Had made the hearthstane snod an' clean ;
Whereon she stood, as in a swither,
'Tween hope an' fear, she e'ed her mither.

On her our Troker stell'd his e'e.
And comely was that maid to see—
Tall, straught as ony willow wan',
An' gracefu' as the sooming swan.

Aneath her locks o' raven hue,
Like lily blossom kyth'd her brow,
A cheek, smooth as the polish'd stane—
But, *och-an-ee !* the rose was gane.

Our wifie gied a wee bit hoast,
Like ane wha's drink the gaet has lost ;
Gat up, an' straught began to hirple
Across the floor, to hand a sirple
O' the gude gear to her gudeman.
Our Troker couthly took her han',
An' led her where, upon his back,
Auld Robin lay, the waesome wrack
O' pains an' poortith—grewsome pair,
Hounds mony a stout heart to despair !

Wi' tenty han' they set him up
An' steadied to his mou' the cup.
He preed an' pech'd, an preed again,—
Said he could haud the cup his lane—
Declar'd baith taste an' smell were gude—
He faund it working thro' his blood.

Our Caird was growing fast a pet—
When clank ! a rap comes to the yett.
" Up, Jeanie lassie ! draw the pin,
An' let the Laird o' Carnook in."

A fearsome glowre our doctoring Caird
Let out, as she brought ben the Laird,
Wha fidg'd about, an' sought a seat,
Vow'd he was vext to be sae late,
But he'd been to the Borristoun,
An' coft for her the bridal gown,
Sae could na rest, nor think o' meat,
Till he cam' wast to let her see't.

Syne clapt his loofs, an' winkt, an' cackl'd,
While Jeanie stood like ane hapshackl'd,
Gi'eing her answers wi' a stare,
Like ane wha's mind's some itherwhere.
His e'e at last fell on the Caird—
" An' wha may ye be ? " quo' the Laird.

" I'm Frank the Troker, Frank MacFee,
A chiel wha'll neither cheat nor lee."

Our Lairdie gied his mouth a thraw,
An' open'd wi' a loud guffaw.—
" This warld maun sure be near an' en'
When Trokers turn up honest men.
But come, as words are win', let's see
How ye'll pit this in prief to me."

Kytching his pack, our Troker said,
Gif he'd be wairing on that maid
The price o' bracelet, brooch or pin,
An' were a judge o' gauds, he'd fin'
He was to Johnny Cheats nae kin ;
Nor mell'd wi' sic as lee'd an' blether'd,
But kept a conscience tightly tether'd.

" Aweel, aweel—to stap your snash,
Let's look at this same wally trash."

A box, a' laid wi' goud an' green,
Was set afore his Lairdship's e'en,
Pang'd fu' o' jewels rich an' rare,
As ever glanc'd on lady fair—
Bobs for the lugs, an' finger rings,
Wi' leeming pearlings, strings on strings.

The Lairdie gied a start an' stammer,
Like ane whas e'en are fasht wi' glamour,
But soon as he cam' to his breath,
He boutit up an' swore an aith
He was nae Caird, but some deceiver,
A cheat-the-woody, hie-sea riever ;
" An' ere the morn is on the lift,
I'se hae ye by the huggars tight,
'Less ye can mak' it plain to me
Hoo ye cam' by this gauderie."

The Troker heard the body's yaup,
As gorhawks listen to a whaup.—

" Hout, Laird, ye're like a tap o' tow,
An' unco easy set alowe ;
But no to hunt about the buss,
An' straughten crooks wi' sma'est fuss—
The comely lass sits by your side,
Her that ye ca' your trystit bride,
Can tell ye, as ye'll shortlin's hear,
Hoo I cam' by my gauds an' gear."

Jean rais'd her hands, like ane wad pray—
" Ah ! wicked man, mind what ye say ;
For here, as God's aboon us a',
His face afore I never saw ! "

" Enough, enough, it's easy seen,
What this same honest Troker's been—
A midnight merchant.   Ay, an' further,
I sudna swear he's clean o' murder.
I'm aff this minute for the Shirra'—
He'll board ye whaur ye should be, Sirrah ! "

"Anither moment," cried the Carle,
"This is a wae an' weary warl'!
Hoo bairnly friendships are forgot,
An' bands o' love grow frush an' rot—
But, laying wrangs an' waes aside,
Hae, hand that to your bonny bride."

A box was raxt as he was bid,
Jean tremblin' lifted aff the lid—
A saxpence, an' a lock o' hair,
Were a' that ane might reckon there.
It was enough ; she raised her e'e,
An' sank doon by her mither's knee.

"O, God aboon ! O, well-a-day,
He's slain my bairn, our stoop an' stay !"

Up lap the Laird, an' made a glaum
At Troker's head, an' aff there cam'
A bannet, wig, an' slough o' hair,
Like peltry o' a norlan' bear.

"Is that your gaet, ye greedy grew ?
Then tak' my gaberlunzie too."
He lows'd a buckle, drew a brace,
An' flang the rauchan in his face—
Strade owre the hearthstane at ae stap,
An' lifted Jeanie in his lap ;
Waffing her wan face wi' a claith,
As she began to get her breath,
And as he watch'd her reddening cheek,
A braver lad ye mightna seek.

Our wifie glower'd, an' glower'd again,
Dightit her e'en an' quat her maen,

Syne brak' into ae great exclaim :
" As God's my judge, it's Willy Grame ! "

The screech brought Jeanie frae her dwam,—
She boutit up, an' tried to stan'—
Will twin'd his arms about her waist,
An' drew her saftly to his breast,
Muttering between ilk lengthy kiss—
" O Jeanie, what an hour is this ! "

The draps now ga'e her heart relief
Had na their fountain-head in grief,
But sprang frae that sweet well o' tears
Had been seal'd up for five lang years.

Like some great gumphy o' a fule
Wha sticks his carritches at schule,
Or her wha for a woman's faut
Was bang'd into a lump o' saut,
Our Lairdie stood in dreeping dread,
His whilk e'en sticking out o's head,
Like mousie thrappl't in a fa',
Or looñ that's loopit by the law ;
Glowering across the kitchen floor—
Gauging the shortest to the door—
At last he makes a brainge an' break—
But Willy's han' is in his neck.

" Ah, Satan's tacksman ! Rogue accurst !
I've gat ye, ere ye've dune your warst.
Heaven that's outowre us! what should hinner
This rung frae ending ye, ye sinner ?
Doon to the yird, ye ravening shark,
An' tak' the wages o' your wark ! "

As Willy's words grew hie an' hi'er,
The body he grew wee and wee'er.
Till hunkert doon, aside the dais,
He seem'd a bunch o' dirty claes.

Will's rung was liftit to the riggin'—
The Lairdie for his life was priggin'—
When Jeanie, dinless as a ghaist,
Slipt up an' wrathsome Willy fac'd ;
She raised her hand an' said a word—
" O, Willy, leave him wi' the Lord ! "

Like frostit claith afore the fire,
Out fell the lurks o' Willy's ire ;
The cudgel drapt aside his leg,
His hand slipt frae the body's craig—
A smile cam' owre his comely lip,
An' Jean's again within his grip.

Our Lairdie, as ye may expect,
Soon had his fingers on the sneck ;
Lap thro' the door, as baudron's loups
Whan boustit frae the pats an' stoups ;
But ere that he the door could bang,
Sharp at his heels auld Bawty sprang.
Will hirr'd him on, an' when the light
Show'd hoo the body clear'd the height,
They faund ae gay weel stampit spot,
Wi' blauds o' breeks an' wyliecoat.

HARVEST HOME IN AMERICA.

THE barley's in the mow, boys,
　　The hay is in the stack,
An' grain o' a' kinds now, boys,
　　Snug under rape an' thack.

Then streek the harden'd hand o' toil,
　　An' broach the treasur'd hoard ;
We bent us bravely to the soil,
　　Let's bend noo owre the board.

Owre aft hath Labor sown, boys,
　　The crap that ithers reap ;
Seen grain that he hath grown, boys,
　　But fill a landlord's heap.

But stent or tax or tythe, boys,
　　Our girnals daurna spill ;
These burdens were bought aff, boys,
　　Langsyne at Bunker's Hill.

Then upward let the spirit leap,
　　An' spread the waukit han',
Gi'e thanks to heaven we sow an' reap
　　Within this blessed lan'.

What tho' the han' be like a hoof,
   The cheek be like the grun',
The weary'd shank be kicking proof
   An' rather stiff for fun.

Ne'er fear we'll get the slight o't—
   An' tongues shall wag like flails,
An' faith we'll hae a night o't,
   Or punch an' pantry fails !

When hearty health is given, boys,
   To season life's dull lease,
An' plenty comes frae heaven, boys,
   To mate wi' gentle peace,

The soul that winna glow then
   Is chill'd wi' gripping greed,
An' the heart that winna flow then
   Is a stony heart indeed.

A RETROSPECT.

WHEN up fifty years I look,
As ye'd trace a restless brook,
Up glen and cataract,
Thro' some wild and desert track,
With here and there between,
Some spot of pleasant green,
Till in mead or flowery dell
Lay its native crystal well ;

Thus my wand'ring ways I trace
To my spirit's starting place,
When burn an' grassy lea
Were world enough for me ;
Each blossom on the wold
Was my silver and my gold,
The birch and mossy stone
My canopy, my throne !

But the spirit who can still ?
The spring will be a rill,
Let us dam it as we will,
And the din of busy men
Will reach the deepest glen ;
A strange exciting noise,
Rousing boyhood from his toys—
Painting, glorious to behold !
Scenes of pleasure, heaps of gold.

Yes, I own it with a sigh,
The glitter took mine eye,
And with HOPE—a wily guide—
Strange lands and plans I've tried,
Till I've found each sunny height
Take the color of the night.
But the " rolling land " is past !
I have reach'd the shore at last ;
Merging calmly to thy sea,
Dark, dumb, ETERNITY !

A KIFT OWRE A CHAPPIN.*

ADDRESSED TO JOHN PRENTICE.

LET's tell auld tales o' far awa',
　　While streeking our auld legs ;
An' tho' our drink's no usquebaugh,
　　'T will ser' to weet our craïgs.

Wake up ! ye spirits o' the past
　　That hauntit life's braw morn,
An' gif a girning ghaist looks in
　　We'll lay him wi' a horn.

Ay, let our youngsters kick the mools,
　　They're gear'd for life's braw race ;—
The goud and siller's at the dools—
　　Hie honors, post, an' place.

But stoutest tree e'er stood on lan',
　　At last comes to the grun' ;
An' biggest blether e'er was blawn,
　　What ends it, but in win' ?　　　　·

We ken hoo things are handl'd here,
　　Howe'er we puff or pech ;
Sae, " saving win' to cool our kail,"
　　Let's toom anither quaich.

* A talk over a tankard.

It's right, bee-like, to fill the byke,
    An' keep things het at hame ;
But weary on your niggard drone
    That never prees the kame.

Glauming at a' thing in his grip,
    Blin' onward bores Sir Greed,
Nor recks the coof some sliddery loof
    Will soon skail a' abreed.

It's lang been said, what's cross'd the craig
    Can ne'er be testamented,
An' sages hint that what is tint
    Is twice tint when lamented.

But saws o' age, an' counsels sage,
    Are no aye owre weel ta'en ;
Sae here we'll quat—haud in your caup—
    Here's to ye, Jock, again !

AULD HAME YEARNINGS.

ADDRESSED TO JOHN GIBSON.

I'VE green'd to see ance mair, John,
   Our brave auld countrie ;
The stately towers, the bin'wood bowers,
   I haunt in memorie ;
I haunt in memorie, John,
   As ghaists, auld minstrels say,
Will wander round the hallow'd ground
   That kent their earthly day.

Lang thirty years are gane, John,
   Since in your wastlin sea,
Auld Scotia's hills sank down, John,
   Nae mair to rise on me ;
Nae mair to rise on me, John,
   Tho' sadder sets I've seen,
The set o' beaming eyes, John,
   That gilt this earthly scene.

But blessed be that Power, John,
   That gied us power to raise
The dear departed dead, John,
   The joys o' ither days.
Ay, thoughts o' sunny hours, John,
   In days o' darkest hue,
Can make a rift in dimmest lift,
   An' let a star look thro'.

Thus in my midnight ponderings,
  In sleep or waking dream,
I range the glen by Hawthornden,
  Or sport by Girvan's stream ;
Dear " Girvan's fairy-haunted stream,"
  Bargeny's banks sae braw ;
The auld ash tree that cosilie
  Leant owre my daddy's ha' ;

The bleaching haugh, wi' fencing saugh,
  The garden tosh an' trig,
Wi' divot edge, an' clippit hedge,
  Where linties loved to bigg ;
Where linties loved to bigg, John,
  An' merry sangsters meet,
Syne yoking tilt, wi' mony a lilt
  Made April mornings sweet.

Sic scenes are hoarded up, John,
  In memory's sacred ben ;
This thriftless heart wi' a' may part,
  But them I manna spen' ;
O, them I daurna spen', John,
  Or what were left to me
But frostit crops o' early hopes
  That sicken ane to see.

Dear sainted Eleanora !
  Sweet sister o' my heart,
It was thy gentle whisperings
  First made this spirit start ;
First made me wondering see, John,
  The lovely things that lie
Around us, on the earth, John,
  Above us, in the sky.

Ay, bravely broke my dawing,
   A mild an' pleasant glow ;
Now wintry winds are blawing,
   My day is wearing low.
But hush ! I've said an' sung, John,
   An' sing it yet again :
Howe'er the heart is wrung, John,
   The word is—Ne'er complain.

COME AWA TO THE WEST.

Come awa to the bonny green West !
  Where the bauld an' the brave hae thriven ;
Come, see our braid valleys still drest
  In the crap that was planted by heaven.

Come, leave the dull gear-getting crew,
  Come away frae the lordling an' slave—
It is not a right land for you,
  Wha canna bow down wi' the lave.

Tho' wealth hath delayed yet to deck
  Our valleys wi' taste and wi' art,
Yet the head o' ilk freeman's erect,
  And his language still empties his heart !

Come, come to our bonny green West,
  Whaur liberty soughs in the breeze !
O, the flesh, Jamie, never can rest,
  Till the heart an' the spirit's at ease !

A FOREIGNER'S FEELINGS IN THE GREAT WEST.

YE vales of this wide western land
　May be richer than those gave us birth ;
Your rivers, majestic and grand,
　The bravest that water the earth.

And the blossoms your May can awake,
　May outrival old Albion's rose ;
Your mornings more lovely may break,
　And softer your twilights may close.

But the heart hath a time when it fills,
　And the spots where our infancy pass'd,
In the glen, or the wild heathy hills,
　The memory will part with them last.

Thus we miss, when Spring tenderly throws,
　On the brown earth her first cheering look,
The brown furze and white-coated sloes,
　Unpacking their buds by the brook.

While the daisy comes forth like a bride,
　As the woodbine is thatching the bower,
And the meek primrose shoulders aside
　Withered leaflets, to hang out her flower.

And when day breaks away from the night,
  Where's the birds used to pipe it aloud ?
Where's the lark, that blythe herald of light,
  Pouring melody down from his cloud ?

It is vain.—But the heart still will roam
  To the sweets of its own native plain,
Tho' reason hath found it a home
  Where RIGHT and EQUALITY reign.

A DECEMBER DITTY.*

THE merry bird o' Simmer's flown
　　Wi' his brave companions a' ;
Gruff Winter has the green leaf stown,
　　An' gifted us the snaw.

The pine tree sings a sober sang,
　　As it swings in the deepening drift ;
An' the glint o' day it creeps alang
　　The ledge o' the leaden lift.

But swith wi' words in wint'ry weed !
　　An' thoughts that bode o' ill.
What ! are we o' the forest breed
　　To dow wi' the daffodil ?

Let's raise up merry days we've seen,
　　When carping Care was dumb ;
Let's talk o' flowers an' Simmer's green,
　　There's Julys yet to come.

Tho' my lair is in a foreign land,
　　My friends ayont the sea,
There's fusion in affection's band
　　To draw them yet to me.

---

* This and the seven following pieces were written by the
author while wandering in the New World in search of a home for
those " he'd left behind him."

THE LADS FAR AWA.

WHEN I think on the lads an' the land I hae left,
An' how love has been lifted, an' friendship been reft,
How the hinny o' hope has been jummelt wi' ga',
Then I lang for the lan' an' the lads far awa.

When I think o' the days o' delight I hae seen,
When the sparks o' the spirit would flash frae the e'en,
Then I say wi' a sigh, as I think on them a',
Where shall I find hearts like the hearts far awa?

When I think on the nights that we spent hand in hand,
When love as our solder, an' friendship our band,
This warld gets dark—but ilk night has a daw',
An' I yet may rejoice wi' the lads far awa.

I'M LIVING YET.

THIS flesh has been wearied, this spirit been vext,
Till I've wisht my deeing day were the next ;
But sorrow will flee, an' trouble will flit—
Sae tent me, lads, but I'm living yet.

When days they were dark, an' the nights were grim,
When the heart was dowff, an' the e'e was dim,
At the tail o' my purse, the end o' my wit,
It was time to quat—but I'm living yet.

Ay, pleasures are weakly, an' gi'en to disease,
E'en Hope, poor thing, gets dowie an' dees ;
While dyester Care wi' his darkest litt
Keeps dipping awa—but I'm living yet.

A wee drap drink, wi' a canty chiel,
Gars us laugh at the warl', an' snock at the Deil,
Wi' a blink o' sense, an' a flaught o' wit—
Ay, that's the gear keeps me living yet !

THE ABSENT FATHER.

THE friendly greeting of our kind,
  Or gentler woman's smiling,
May soothe the weary wanderer's mind,
  His lonely hours beguiling;

May charm the restless spirit still,
  The pang of grief allaying;
But ah! the soul it cannot fill,
  Or keep the heart from straying.

O, how the fancy, when unbound,
  On wings of rapture swelling,
Will hurry to the holy ground
  Where loves and friends are dwelling!

My lonely and my widow'd wife,
  How oft to thee I wander!
Re-living those sweet hours o' life,
  When mutual love was tender.

And here with sickness lowly laid,
  All scenes to sadness turning,
Where will I find a breast like thine
  To lay this brow that's burning?

And how are all my pretty ones?
  How have the cherubs thriven,
Who cheer'd my leisure with their love
  And made my home a heaven?

Does yet the rose array your cheek,
  As when in grief I bless'd you?
O, are your cherry lips as sweet
  As when in tears I kiss'd you?

Can your young broken prattle tell—
  Can your young memories gather
A thought of him who loves you well—
  Your weary wandering father?

O, I've had wants and wishes too,
  This world has check'd and chill'd;
Yet bless me but again with you,
  And half my prayer's fulfill'd.

LIFE'S SUMMER TIDE IS GOING.

LIFE's Summer tide is going,
　And those fancies droop and die,
Kept my spirit's springs a-flowing
　Like the streams that never dry.

Yes, the bosom's glow is cooling—
　Affection runs to wreck—
And disappointment's schooling
　Kills where it should correct.

The cup hath lost its flavour ;
　Even mirth forgets to move ;
And my creed begins to waver,
　Upon friendship, upon love.

Can it be that years have done it ?
　My locks have still their jet ;
And tho' roughly I have run it,
　My limbs are limber yet.

Can it be that change and distance
　This spirit hath unmann'd ?
Yes, the stays o' my existence
　Are in another land.

Thus the chill of early Winter
　Hath settl'd in my breast—
I've fallen like those that venture
　Too far beyond the rest !

TO AN OLD FRIEND.—1825.

HERE's to thee, Jemmy lad,
  Here's a health to thee an' thine ;
An' when I drink to *thy* friends,
  It's then I drink to *mine.*

Here's to them from whom we parted
  As our twain had been the grave ;
Here's the leal, the honest hearted,
  Wha will seek us 'yont the wave.

Here's the gowans, lad, that studded
  The braes where youth was spent ;
Here's the blossoms, yet unbudded,
  That *our* wilderness shall scent.

Ay, dear the heathy lan' is,
  Where our fathers had their home !
Yet here's to the savannahs
  Where our children yet shall roam !

Here's the gallant bark that brings ye ;
  May its speed be like my prayer !
And every wind that wings ye,
  Be like thy Annie—fair !

TO JAMES WELLSTOOD,

HECH ! but it's heartsome to look owre
  The days sae firmly fixt
In memory's map, when thou an' I
  Our mirth an' madness mixt.

Taking the braidside o' the lan',
  Nae bank at braes an' birns—
At bridals branging for the broose,
  Wild ranting it at kirns.

'Twas then our spirits took the twist
  That they maun aye retain ;
An' there we felt, when first we kisst,
  As we'll ne'er feel again.

An' hae na we seen fairer sights,
  Where the June rose scents the vale,
An' the watches o' the Simmer night
  Are cheer'd wi' the nightingale ?

'Twas there we felt those friendly dews
  Gar the affections start ;
An' muckle gear we gather'd there,
  For the girnal o' the heart.

An' Jamie, up thy bonnet, man !
   Hae we nae twasome stood
Upon that holy hallow'd lan'
   Was coft wi' freemen's blood?

That land where honour's mair than name,
   Where honesty's renown ;
Where the EAGLE made the LION tame,
   An' the CAP has cow'd the CROWN !

O Jamie, hie thee to this lan',
   An' gar my heart rejoice !
For there's a virtue in thy han',
   A cordial in thy voice.

TO A FRIEND.

Last time thy honest face I saw,
Auld Caledonia's usquebaugh
Gart thy brave spirit toom its ga'
   On priests an' kings,
While wally words thy heart let fa'
   On better things.

Far distant frae us baith are now,
The broom buss an' the heather cowe,
The gowan'd greens, the streams that row
   Sae clear an' saft ;
An' queans hae set this heart alowe,
   Gude kens hoo aft.

There's brawer countries on the map,
An' richer too in kine an' crap ;
But while this heart contains the sap
   O' life, by Jing !
Auld Scotland still maun stand the tap
   O' a' the bing.

Some gowk has said, for gowks will bode,
That 'twas the reckless inward goad
O' norries sent my banes abroad,
   Some waff desire,
Wi' nought o' reason in't.—'Fore God,
   That gowk 's a liar.

No, John, my saul was sick to see
The dowie look o' Liberty,
While curs'd Corruption's badger e'e
  Glowr'd hale and healthy,
An' lick-lip loons, wi' supple knee,
  Grew bein an' wealthy.

But swith, wi' words that grip the gizzard—
Venom's a sleeking, slimy lizard,
That wi' the cantrips o' a wizard,
  Would soak an' sour us ;
Crumple us up like ony izzard,
  An' then devour us.

Altho' Gude kens, I hae been needy,
I ne'er was in my greening greedy ;
Ne'er glunsht whan chiels, mair douce an' steady,
  Shot up the brae ;
But wi' a hearty hale " God speed ye,"
  E'en let them gae.

This gaet my prayer has ever run
" O, for a cot, a wee bit grun',
" An' twa three lads, that trade in fun,
  " To be my marrows.
Then let the warld lose or win—
  I've clear'd the harrows.

Part o' my prayer has noo been grantit,
But still the better part is wantit—
O for the day that I shall rant it,
  An' roar to see
The kindred o' my spirit plantit
  Aneath my e'e.

TO MY FAVORITE NOOK.

SWEET sober solitary nook,
  Where oft at eve I've stole,
To read, as in a written book,
  The records o' my soul.

Ay, oft when morn came down yon cleugh
  To gild those waters clear,
An' birds sent up their merry sough,
  Thou'st found me pondering here ;

Pushing my restless spirit forth,
  Thro' paths that lay before,
And praying they might be more smooth
  Than those I've wandered o'er.

Those days are done, and I draw near,
  My last fond look to take ;
Yet I can think of one who here
  Will wander for my sake.

And when gruff Winter, sad an' sour,
  Bids birds an' blooms depart,
She'll find, within this wither'd bower,
  An emblem of my heart.

TAKING THE WARLD.

SMA' praise has he can only strut
　　Whan birn an' barnyard's bulky ;
Wha gecks, when Fortune smiles, the slut,
　　But cowers when she gets sulky.

But here's to him—the heart o' proof—
　　When Fortune sulks the sourest,
Can cock his bonnet, spread his loof,
　　An' daur her do her dourest.

There's some, when ill fa's in their gaet,
　　As rocks in roads will tumble,
Will worry at it aire an' late,
　　An' grunt, an' grane, an' grumble.

But here's to him, when trysted sae,
　　Ne'er tries to sap or sound it—
Just gies his naigs a hap or gee,
　　An' canny drives around it.

Some gowks will wrangle out their tack,
　　In din would deave a miller ;
While ithers will their conscience rack
　　To catch that dirt ca't siller.

Wae worth sic loons will haul an' harl
　　At dirty dubs to net it ;
But here's to him wha taks the warl'—
　　Faith, just as he can get it.

TO THE NIGHT WIND.

WHEN the Winter's at his strength,
And the night's a weary length ;
When outlyers on the brae,
Lea' their tates o' tedded strae,
And scour across the field
To the planting's lownest bield,
Then look, ere midnight's past,
For a stour frae the nor-wast.

Aft wi' thuds, hae gart me growse,
Thou hast shook me frae a drowse,
An' wi' eerie rair an' rowt
Cried the wakrife spirit out,
To mark the mighty aik
Whaur he lords it owre the brake.
How he shoggles in the grun',
As his monarchy were done,
An' bends his giant might
To the black wind o' the night.
But heavier is the thud
That shakes the ancient wud,
An' howls 'mang ruined wa's,
Through lang deserted ha's,
While the brown stream, dashing on,
Gi'es a thickening to thy moan.

And hark ! a wailing note
Has borne me to the spot
Where the dead an' buried rot,
Where the auld ghaist-haunted isle
Stands a black an' grewsome pile,
Where the yew tree branches wide
O'er the vaults of rotting pride,
Where broken mossy stanes
Lean o'er lang-forgotten banes,
An' the deadly hemlock rears
His stem 'mang tangled briars.

Hush ! o'er the dead man's lea
Sweeps a mournful melodie,
As the voices o' the slain
Were mingled in the strain !—

A flutter o' the heart—
A shudder and a start—
The wild unearthly din
Scares the wandering spirit in.

MAY WASHING.

About the time the mavis sings
　　His sweetest frae the brake,
And primroses around the springs
　　Their scented blooms awake ;

When craiks are heard among the braird,
　　And bats get rife at e'en—
Ay, that's the time, by burn and swaird,
　　To make the linen clean.

The light had jimply broke aboon,
　　The east begun to clear,
When our gudewife was in her shoon,
　　An' a' her maids asteer.

They've ta'en the naip'ry braid an' wide,
　　The sarks, the sheets, an' a',
An' they're awa to yon burnside
　　To make them like the snaw.

And brightly did that burnie play,
　　And heartsome was its croon,
For saft the pleasant month o' May
　　Was slipping into June.

The gauzy mist began to streek
  Owre haugh an' howe sae fair,
And mixing wi' the big pat reek,
  Soom'd up the caller air.

Our lassies then for boyne an' tub
  Their coats began to breek,
Lads, haud aback ! for sic a sight
  Has spoilt my rest a week.

Now jibe an' joke an' canty laugh
  Rang loud owre banks an' braes,
As ankles like the barkit saugh
  Gaed splashing 'mang the claes.

Ay glib the wark gaes frae the han'
  Whan some delight's in view,
An' weel the lassies kent that e'en
  Would send them joes anew.

O ! for the jolly days o' youth,
  Whan love swalls frae the bud !
Life's lythe win' settled in the south,
  The lift without a clud !

Wisdom that lies 'neath lyart locks
  Anither saw might say,
But wha wi' cauld December blasts
  Wad scathe the flowers o' May ?

TO MY FIRST AND LAST TRUE LOVE.

I HAE wish'd thee a lang fareweel,
    We hae parted to meet nae mair,—
The wounds that we canna heal,
    We maun season the spirit to bear.

We were bairns, Jean, o' ae burnside,
    An' grew up like sister an' brither,
Or like twa Spring buds wha's pride
    Is to flourish an' fade thegither.

But the warld came atween us, Jean,
    An' it twain'd what it couldna shift—
For I lov'd thee, my bonny quean,
    Wi' that love that we canna lift.

Noo, I'll wear on awa to the grave,
    Like the tree has been wrack't in the win';
It may hing out a leaf wi' the lave,
    Tho' it's dosen'd an' dead within.

Ay, the spirit may swell an' set,
    Gi'e an outward to joy or pain,
But the heart that is filled an' shut
    Maun burst ere it open again.

Fare-ye-weel, Jean, a long fareweel,
    We have parted for evermair,
The wounds that we canna heal
    We maun season the spirit to bear.

A PARTING SONG.

To part wi' those our years hae blest,
An' those in rapture's hours we've kisst,
O, sair's the rive that breaks the twist
  Which binds our hearts in ane, O.

    Yet sing wi' me this ae night,
    This ae, ae, ae night,
    O, rant an' sing this ae night,
      We yet may meet again, O.

Our bosom friends, our native shore—
There's few, there's nane hae lov'd them more,
Yet tho' it wring me to the core,
  We maun be owre the main, O.
                Then sing, &c.

For when our fortunes tak' a fit,
An' sense an' freedom bid us flit,
Shall we on sic' a warning sit,
  Whate'er be parting's pain, O?
                Then sing, &c.

Tho' farewell grief may make us lower,
Yet hope can paint a meeting hour,
When grinding despots lose their power,
  An' tyrants' threats are vain, O.
                Then sing, &c.

Tho' stormy seas between us boil—
Tho' this may be our parting bowl,
We'll yet hold fellowship in soul
  When we're ayont the main, O.
                              Then sing, &c.

MY BONNY WEE BELL.

My bonny wee Bell was a mitherless bairn,
Her aunty was sour, an' her uncle was stern,
While her cousin was aft in a cankersome mood,
But that hindered na Bell growing bonny an' gude.

When we ran to the schule, I was aye by her han',
To wyse off the busses, or help owre a stran',
An' as aulder we grew, a' the neighbours could tell
Hoo my liking grew wi' thee, my bonny wee Bell.

Thy cousin gangs dinkit, thy cousin gangs drest,
In her silks an' her satins, the brawest an' best,
But the gloss o' a cheek, the glint o' an e'e,
Are jewels frae heaven nae tocher can gi'e.

Some goud, an' some siller, my auld gutcher left,
An' in houses an' mailins I'll soon be infeft—
I've a vow in the heaven, I've an aith wi' thysel',—
I'll mak' room in this world for thee, bonny Bell.

MY LAST SANG TO KATE READ.

I'll sing a sang to thee, Kate Read ;
  It may touch a lonesome string ;—
I maun sing a sang to thee, fair Kate,
  Be't the last that e'er I sing,
                  Kate Read,
    Be't the last that e'er I sing.

For I hae sung to thee, sweet Kate,
  When the young Spring, like thysel',
Kyth'd bonnily by Roslin lea,
  By Gourton's flowery dell,
                  Kate Read,
    By Gourton's flowery dell.

An' Simmer e'ens have seen us, Kate,
  Thy genty hand in mine,
As by our water's pleasant side,
  I mixt my heart wi' thine,
                  Kate Read,
    I mixt my heart wi' thine.

When day was doun, the braw hairst moon
  Has seen thee in yon glen,
Sitting, my sainted idol Kate—
  Did I not worship then,
                  Kate Read,
    Did I not worship then?

Thrice seven lang years hae o'er us past
  Since thae braw days gaed bye ;
Another land's around me, Kate—
  I see another sky,
                Kate Read,
    I see another sky.

Yet fresh as when I kiss'd thee last,
  Still unto me ye seem—
Bright'ner o' mony a weary day—
  Sweet'ner o' mony a dream,
                Kate Read,
    Sweet'ner o' mony a dream.

THE LAST LOOK O' HAME.

Bare was the burn brae,
　　December's blast had blawn,
The last flower was dead,
　　The brown leaf had fa'n ;
Twas dark in the deep wood,
　　Hoary was the hill,
An' the wind frae the cauld north
　　Cam' heavy and chill.

I had said fare-ye-weel
　　To my kith an' my kin',
My bark it lay ahead,
　　My cot-house behin' ;
I had naught left to tine,
　　I'd a wide warld to try,
But my heart it wou'dna lift,
　　An' my e'e wou'dna dry.

I look'd lang at the ha'
　　Thro' the mist o' my tears,
Where the kind lassie liv'd
　　I had ran wi' for years,
An' the braes where we sat,
　　An' the broom-covered knowes,
Took a hank on this heart
　　I ne'er can unlowse.

I hae wander'd sinsyne
  By gay temples and towers,
When the ungather'd spice
  Scents the breeze in their bowers.—
Sic scenes I can leave
  Without pain or regret,
But that last look o' hame
  I ne'er can forget.

TAKE ME HAME TO GLENLUGAR AGAIN.

Your big town is braw,
Ye're kind to me an' a',
An' try aye to make me feel fain ;
    But my heart it winna flit
    Frae our auld water fit—
Tak' me hame to Glenlugar again.

I hae been to your shore,
Where the big billows roar,
An' ships' haud awa to the main ;
    But gi'e me the shady pool
    Was on Simmer e'en sae cool—
Tak' me hame to Glenlugar again.

I've been within your ha's
Where music swells an' fa's,
Thro' many a sweet new strain ;
    But gi'e me the hamely things
    My kindly mither sings—
Tak' me hame to Glenlugar again.

Your winning words an' arts,
May be sproutings o' your hearts,
But to me they seem hollow an' vain ;
    Ay, sadly I can see,
    There's naething here for me—
Tak' me hame to Glenlugar again.

TO S——N——

WHEN first we met, and that dark eye
Disturbed me, yet I know not why,
I said, 'fore heaven, "There is a snare
That thoughtless boyhood should beware";
Nor did my thinkings wander then
To harder hearts or older men.

But when that lovely eye of jet
In swimming tenderness was set,
When thy lip quiver'd in the breath
That heav'd those heav'nly hills beneath,
Then rush'd those feelings on the heart
To which we cannot say, Depart:
Yes, Nature unto some hath given
Gems from her jewelry of heaven,
And he can calmly look on such
Hath felt too little,—or too much.

Farewell, I would not have thee feel
Those pangs I may not bid thee heal,
Nor offer thee, fair as thou art,
Love's lees—the embers of a heart.

A MIDNIGHT MEETING.

LAST night as my dreaming soul
  In the wildness of fancy roamed,
Commingling the present and past,
  The living and long entomb'd,

I came on a beautiful dell,
  The green beech at midsummer cools,
And the brook leaves the flower-border'd well
  To dimple the valley with pools.

In the west lay a dark purple glow—
  The last bird of eve was awake,
And I gazed as the night settled slow,
  In the heart of a neighbouring brake ;

When, as angels are said to have come
  On the night path of wandering seer,
A form seem'd to grow from the gloom,
  And I shook as the vision drew near ;

For in form, and in face, it was you—
  It was you—O, and lovely as when
You wept with me a sad adieu,
  And we vow'd ne'er to weep it again.

But a smile banished all but my love—
   All barriers that war with the will—
Strong bonds that we may not remove,
   Have sever'd—must sever us still.

Then raptures mere flesh cannot give,
   Were mingled with bursts of delight—
'Tis an angel's life that we live,
   When we live in the spirit at night.

MARY.

THE TIME FOR LOVE TO SIGH.

Is it a time for love to sigh
When the sun is blazing high ?
No ; but when ev'ning cools the sky,
  And day hath lost its dazzle,
Meet me where the willow droops,
Where the bird o' gloaming whoops,
Meet me where the tendril loops
  The branches o' the hazel.

Then will I tell of love as deep
As ever broke a wooer's sleep,—
I've given thee, love, a heart to keep,
  The fondest e'er was given.
My love ! It's like thy loveliness,
The very utmost of excess !—
O, Mary, how can it be less,
  Thou fairest out o' Heaven.

JEAN THAT'S AWA.

AIR, *Robin Adair.*

BLYTHE were the days I've seen
    Wi' her that 's awa ;
Fair mony a Simmer e'en
    Set on us twa.

    Sad noo by yonder burn,
    Lanely I stray and mourn
    Days that will ne'er return,—
        Her that 's awa.

Jeanie, thou aye wert dear,
    Dear still to me ;
Ne'er did this bosom fear
    Falsehood from thee.

    False now I find thou art,
    Sair has it griev'd my heart.
    Who thought that aught could part
        Jeanie an' me ?

ANDRO KEIR.

WHEN corbies lea' their clecking cleughs,
　An' falcons flap the wing,
It is nae for the feckless bird
　To cock his head and sing.

Brown Winter spates may flood our gaets,
　An' smoor the meadows wide ;
But bide aback frae ford or track,
　They'll 'swage ere Beltane-tide.

The Lord o' Wharrie's ta'en his steed,
　Wi' five gude men o' wier ;
An' angry man he's ridden forth,
　In search o' Andro Keir.

Noo Keir was wight, an', tho' nae knight,
　Could handle targe an' glaive,
An' our Lord's daughter he has ta'en,
　Nor speer'd her father's leave.

Our Lord he's ridden braid an' wide,
　Owre frien' an' fremmit grund,
But less might sairt, for Andro Keir
　Is nae where to be fund.

He's boun' his men to Wharrie's ha',
   An' hied him to Kilquhae,
To fee the Warlock o' the glen
   To tell where Andro lay.

" Noo tell to me thou Warlock wight,
   An' say thy guerdon then :—
Whaur will I find this Andro Keir,
   The orts o' lawless men ? "

" It's wherefore seek ye blood, Sir Knight ?
   It's wherefore would ye kill ?
It's wherefore seek the blood o' ane
   That never did ye ill ? "

" Nae words to me but what I want,"
   Replied our Knight sae bauld,
" Or else by a' that bides aboon,
   I'll lay thy body cauld."

" Then work your worst," the Warlock said,
   An' off his rachan fell ;—
Stout Wharrie ga'e a start an' stride,
   'Twas Andro Keir himsel' !

" Riever an' rogue ! "—'twas a' the win'
   Our wrathsome Knight could spare,
Till swords were gleaming in the sun,
   An' blows fell fast an' sair.

Wi' thrust an' hack, stout Wharrie strack,
   He strack wi' might and main ;
At guard an' wier lay Andro Keir—
   He faught to haud his ain.

Slee canny airt will tak' our part,
  It's no aye wrath that wins ;
Stout Wharrie's brand has left his hand,
  An' flown out owre the whins.

"Strike now, thou Riever ! "—Wharrie cried,
  " I'll neither flinch nor flee."
" 'Twill ne'er be said, that my gude blade
  Was stain'd wi' blood o' thee."

Bauld Andro's dightit his red brow,
  An' then his trusty sword ;
He's turned him lightly on his heel,
  Withouten sign or word.

He's raised his bugle frae his belt,
  An' blawn baith loud an' shrill ;—
Our Lord's brave daughter an' her maids
  Came tripping down the hill.

" Twa choices ye hae, Lady love,
  Twa choices, Marion dear ;
Whether wi' your brave father gae,
  Or bide wi' Andro Keir."

She's lookit in her father's face ;
  The tears are streaming fast ;
She's turned her e'e on Andro Keir,
  An' drappit on his breast.

Stout Wharrie spak'—" I dool'd the wrack
  O' a my heart hings on ;
Noo find I here, a daughter dear,
  But an' a gallant son."

Twa weeks owre this a noble feast
    Was held in Wharrie's ha',
Fair Marion an' bold Andro Keir
    Stood bravest 'mang them a'.

LADY ELLEN'S LAST NIGHT.

THERE leem'd a light frae yon high tower,
    When the sun had sought the sea ;
There came a sang frae Ellen's bower,
    When the bird had clos'd his e'e.

An' first it sweet and blithely rang,
    Like the chirm to the early light ;
But ah ! it grew a dowie sang,
    Like the bird that sings o' night.

" Gae busk my bower wi' roses white,
    Pu' lilies frae the rill ;
Sir Richard he'll be here this night,
    Ere the moon has left the hill.

" My father's gone for stern Lord John,
    An' says I'll be his bride,
But Richard he has Ellen's vow—
    Her vow, and heart beside."

The moon swam up the cludless lift ;
    Night's lonesome hour has rung ;
While sad, and sadder grew the sang
    Fair Lady Ellen sung.

"O, what can stay my wandering Knight?
  Can love so soon grow cold?—
Or thinks he Ellen's heart is light
  Without her father's gold?"

It's lang she sobb'd an' sorrow'd there;
  The moon in clouds has set;
The 'kerchief o' her bridal robe
  Wi' many a tear is wet.

When hark! there comes a heavy step,
  Fair Ellen rais'd her head,—
Sir Richard stands in her bower door,
  His cheek like the sheeted dead.

"O Richard, ye hae tarried lang,
  See yonder breaks the day;
My father's gone for stern Lord John—
  Away my love! away!"

"I've met thy father and Lord John,
  We met in yonder howe;
And I hae come my bride to claim,
  They cannot follow now."

"Here, Lady, we hae often met,
  An' here we twa maun part;
O, there's a wound in this left breast
  That dries up Richard's heart!

"O, bed me in thy bower, Ellen,
  An' make thy maidens speed,
An' hap me wi' thy hand, Ellen,
  The last that e'er I'll need."

They've made a bed, he's laid him down,
   Nor word again he spak' ;
An' she has sat an' sobbit there
   Until her young heart brak'.

An' there they lay, in others' arms—
   O, 'twas a waesome sight !—
A pair o' Simmer's blighted blooms,
   The red rose and the white.

THE CADGER O'KERRY.

The Cadger O'Kerry cam' hame yestreen,
   His cuddy, his creels, an' a' ;
Sair toutit an' tasht, the body came wast,
   For the gaet it lay deep in the snaw.

Noo the Cadger's wife an' her kimmers war met,
   They'd a browst in the big berry pan,
An' seated sae snug by the het ingle lug,
   She's lightlied her drookit guidman.

Our Cadger he sat, he was cauld, he was wat,
   But asteep he is laying his brain,
Till he's cleckit a plan to break up the clan
   An' make the braw panfu' his ain.

Sae out he's gane to fodder his brute,
   An' whan he came back to the door,
He raised a big rowt, crying, " Kimmers, come out,
   An' look at this awful uproar."

The carlins strade out wi' a wonnerfu' speed,
   Our Cadger sae sly slippit in,
Syne cannilie shot, the muckle door slot,
   Made a ranse o' a big racking pin.

The Cadger he leuch as he rypit the ribs,
  Set the winking ingle ableeze ;
An' then he began on the rare berry pan,
  An' mixt it wi' bread an' wi' cheese.

But losh ! whan the luckies they faund out the trick,
  They were neither to haud nor to bin',
An they stampit an' flet, at a' tear-in-twa rate,
  An' bann'd whan they couldna win in.

" Let's in," quo' they, " ye auld Cadger loon,
  Or we'll rive your auld cantle bare."
" E'en do sae," quo' he, " an' he leuch merrilie,
  "Whan your han's they can win àt my hair."

" Let's in," quo' they in a cannier sough,
  An' we'll a' be gude companie."
"I'm right fond o' your crack, there ahint the door back,
  As we aiblins might no here agree."

" But here's to ye, kimmers," quo' he wi' a rift,
  As a tilt gat the twa luggit cap ;
It's weel wal'd gear, an' right heartsome cheer,
  For a carl that's baith drouthy an' wat.

The night it was dour, the drift flew like stour,
  An' whan they saw a' thing was gane—
The howdy strade hame, wi' the ither dry dame,
  Left the Cadger's wife freezing her lane.

" O' maun I dee here at my ain door cheek ?
  O, Willie, hae mercy on me ! "
" Aye, the win's in an' airt that will saften your heart,
  Ye'll fin noo what poor Cadgers dree."

Sae he never let on till her win' it grew weak,
    Then stauchering he airtit her in.
Her nose it was blae as a big partan tae,
    An' an icicle hung frae her chin.

" Ye'll ken noo," quo' he, an' he winkit his e'e,
    " What frost-bitten gangerels crave."
She dightit her snout, said she had just found it out,
    An' she'd mind it as lang as she'd leeve.

Our leal Cadger syne grew baith couthy and kin',
    When he found her sae cow'd and sae tame,
An' in trouth our gudewife put a loop in her life,
    An' turn'd out a right decent dame.

THE DAFT DAYS.

THE midnight hour is clinking, lads,
An' the douce an' the decent are winking, lads ;
   Sae I tell ye again,
   Be't weel or ill ta'en,
It's time ye were quatting your drinking, lads.

Gae ben, an' mind your gauntry, Kate,
Gi'es mair o' your beer, an' less bantry, Kate,
   For we vow, whaur we sit,
   That afore we shall flit,
We'se be better acquaint wi' your pantry, Kate.

The "daft days" are but beginning, Kate,
An' we're sworn.   Would you hae us a sinning, Kate ?
   By our faith an' our houp,
   We will stick by the stoup
As lang as the barrel keeps rinning, Kate.

Thro' hay, an' thro' hairst, sair we toil it, Kate,
Thro' Simmer, an' Winter, we moil it, Kate ;
   Sae ye ken, whan the wheel
   Is beginning to squeal,
It's time for to grease an' to oil it, Kate.

Sae draw us anither drappy, Kate,
An' gie us a cake to our cappy, Kate ;
   For, by spiggot an' pin !
   It's waur than a sin
To flit when we're sitting sae happy, Kate.

LET'S DRINK TO OUR NEXT MEETING.

Let's drink to our next meeting, lads,
   Nor think on what's atwixt;
They're fools wha spoil the present hour
   By thinking on the next.

     Then here's to Meg o' Morningside,
       An' Kate o' Kittlemark;
     The taen she drank her hose and shoon,
       The tither pawned her sark.

A load o' wealth, an' warldly pelf,
   They say is sair to bear;
Sae he's a gowk would scrape an' howk
   To make his burden mair.
                  Then here's, &c.

Gif Care looks black the morn, lads,
   As he'd come doon the lum,
Let's ease our hearts by swearing, lads,
   We never bade him come.
                  Then here's, &c.

Then here's to our next meeting, lads,
   Ne'er think on what's atwixt;
They're fools who spoil the present hour
   By thinking on the next.
                  Then here's, &c.

MAGGIE M'GEE.

Aye gi'e me auld Maggie McGee, man,
Wi' her cozy auld howff at Knockree, man ;
   For gin ye want a drap,
   Be't frae stoup or frae caup,
Seek the gauntry o' Maggie McGee, man.

Should your head be as dowff as the daigh, man,
An' your heart in your fecket lie laigh, man :
   Gae down to Knockree,
   Speer for Maggie McGee,
An' lay your lugs deep in a quaich, man.

Ay weels on ye, Maggie McGee, lass,
Tho' ye're runkl'd, an' short o' an e'e, lass ;
   I mind the day, Meg,
   When the birkies would beg
Your braw sappy lips for to pree, lass.

It's kent ye had proffers enew, lass,
An' our Laird, baith whan sober an' fu', lass,
   Aft vow'd wi' an aith,
   Shou'd his Kate slip her breath,
Ye should lady it doon at Cardoo, lass.

Tam Dudgeon wha dealt wi' the Manks, lass,
Him ye led like a shelty in branks, lass ;
   Was right tight in your loop,
   But a Revenue Sloop
Settled that an' the rest o' his pranks, lass.

Rab the drover, wha cam' frae Carstair, lass,
Kept cramming your lug late an' aire, lass ;
   Rab's han' wou'd na keep,
   Was owre fond o' the sheep,
An' gat hangit, ye'll mind, down at Ayr, lass.

But gi'e me auld Maggie McGee, man,
Wi' her cozy auld howff at Knockree, man ;
   For gin ye want a drap,
   Be't frae stoup or frae caup,
Seek the gauntry o' Maggie McGee, man.

THE TINKLER'S SANG.

WHEN birds in bands, frae foreign lands,
   To hill an' howe are hieing ;
When goudspinks neat, and linties sweet,
   Their bravest sangs are trying.

It's then I see our greenwood tree,
   Where wives an' weans are howdering ;
A-scraping spoons, an' crooning tunes,
   While pats an' pans we're sowdering.

Owre brae an' bank, our youngsters spank,
   To hunt the brass an' pewter ;
For faith, the mill may weel stan' still
   Has neither grist nor muter.

Syne hares frae glens, an' fat muirhens,
   Are in the caldron boiling ;
While braxy hams, an' Hieland drams,
   Weel pay us for our toiling.

When gloaming still, creeps up the hill,
   The birns were set a-glowing ;
Screw up the pegs, an' shake our legs,
   'Till a' our hearts are glowing.

Ilk girn an' line's inspeckit syne,
 An' gif we've no been lucky ;
The farmer's barn, afore the morn,
 May aiblins lack a chucky.

But spoons a' made, an' fortunes spaed,
 Wi' little left to fen' us ;
We hoist our creels, tak' to our heels,
 An' howff where less they ken us.

Nor stent nor cess our minds distress,
 We're clear o' lords or gentry ;
In cove or glen, we make our den,
 An' a' the warld's our pantry.

THE BACHELOR'S ADVICE TO THE BOYS.

Air, " I HAD A HORSE."

IT's sad to see the bauld an' slee,
  The lads ance bravely mettl'd,
Gang douf an' douce about the house,
  By wedlock's cantrips settl'd.

  But the free, the free, the cowt that's free,
    Nae tow, nae tether ga's him ;
  While the halter'd brute maun gee his clute,
    Just as his driver ca's him.

Lord, see him there, wi' sich an' prayer,
  A fleeching some dresst draigle
To come an' keep his aumry bare,
  Or daud him wi' the ladle.
                    But the free, &c.

Syne see him weary out his life
  On weans, to keep an' clout them ;
Or fechting for a fractious wife,
  When ane can do without them.
                    But the free, &c.

Horn daft is he wha greens to gie
  A liferent to some gipsy,
To clash wi' cronies owre her tea
  An' scauld ye whan ye're tipsy.
                    But the free, &c.

Gae hame an' tend the mill an' mow,
  Nor mair o' love be talking,
We've fools an' beggars' brats enew ;
  Sae, youngsters, quit your jauking.
                    For the free, &c.

TO AN OLD PACK OF CARDS,

THAT AMUSED US IN CROSSING THE ATLANTIC.

PEACE to his spirit did devise
    These most amusing things ;
And taught us, democratic wise,
    To play with queens and kings.

When winds were loud as woman's grief,
    When the dark wave was rude,
And our good bark, like drifting leaf,
    Drave o'er an angry flood ;

Or when the elemental fray
    Was o'er, and winds asleep,
And like a little isle we lay,
    Still, rooted in the deep ;

'Twas then ye *cut* old crusty Care
    Of half his killing power,
And *tricked* and *shuffl'd* daddy Time
    Out many a weary hour.

But cards, like creatures, will grow old,
    Yea all things must decay ;
And carnal kings, like kings o' cards,
    Last not, thank God ! for aye.

Ye're merry toys, in sooth, yet still
  Ye've bred no little grief;
Strange this ! that kings occasion ill
  In boards as well as beef !

But then this solace to the mind
  Our best attention craves ;
For mark, their mischief is confined
  To those who are their slaves.

THE MERRY MAIDS O' SCOTLAND.

Ye merry maids o' Scotland,
    Dear lasses o' langsyne,
How turns o' some auld melodie
    Will bring you to my min'!
Wi' your daffin' an' your laughin',
    Frae glint o' day to gloam,
Whan corn was whitenin' on the lea,
    An' hay was on the holm.

At Martinmas and Whitsunday,
    At bridal or at fair,
Wi' Sunday braws like drifted snaws,
    Ye wore a doucer air;
But smirks aroun' your rosy lips,
    Wi' glintin's o' the e'e,
Tauld ay how soon a canty tune
    Could wake ye into glee.

Whan dreary days o' Winter
    Were scailin' sleet an' snaw,
Your fresh unfrosted merriment
    Sent Simmer thro' the ha';
Your kind "Gude e'en" an' winsome mien,
    Would thow the plowman chiel,
While merry sang, the lee night lang,
    Was chorused wi' your wheel.

I'm far awa', I'm lang awa',
    An' muckle's cam' atween
The nights we reel'd it in the ha'
    Or link'd it on the green ;
But sowth we get a canty lilt,
    Ye're a' afore my min'—
Dear merry maids o' Scotland,
    Sweet lasses o' langsyne.

LINES,

WRITTEN ON THE ANNIVERSARY OF BURNS'S BIRTH-DAY,
WHEN WANDERING BELATED IN THE MOUNTAIN GORGES
OF VERMONT.

LAST time my feeble voice I raised
    To thy immortal dwelling,
The flame of friendship round me blaz'd,
    On breath of rapture swelling.

Now far into a foreign land,
    The heavens above me scowling,
The big bough waving like the wand,
    The forest caverns howling.

No kindred voice is in mine ear,
    No heart with mine is beating ;
No tender eye of blue is near,
    My glance of kindness meeting.

But rocky mountains, towering rude,
    Dim heaven with their statures ;
Grim Winter in his wildest mood,
    'Midst Nature's roughest features.

Yet thou who sang of Nature's charms,
    In barrenness and blossom,
Thy strain of love and freedom warms
    The chill that's in my bosom.

And here, where Despotism's mute,
　　And Right hath the ascendance—
O where's the land could better suit
　　The hymn to independence?

Thou giant 'mongst the mighty dead,
　　What bowls to thee are flowing!
What souls of Scotia's *noble* breed
　　With pride this night are glowing!

THE PIONEER.

Spring awakens the wilds of the West,
  Gruff Winter has ceased his roar,
For the green leaf hath burst the bud
  Of our white-limb'd sycamore.

And fairest of wood flowers blow,
  Where prowls the sly racoon,
And the sumac hath trimm'd its bough
  In the glass of the clear lagoon.

There's a sound in the upper air,
  The rush of a thousand wings,
'Tis our brave Summer bird, he's away
  With his songs to the northland springs.

And hark ! 'tis the cheer of our bold pioneer,
  He's away in our venturesome van ;
He is bluff, he is rough, but he's made of the stuff
  That's widening the world for man.

Free and fearless he treads, thro' prairies and glades,
  His face to the set of the sun,
The red man and brute may his passage dispute,
  But his charter's his axe and his gun.

Far, far from his home, where wild buffaloes roam,
  See his crackling camp-fire shine,
While he halloos aloud to the forest and flood,
  " This slice of the world it is mine !"

Let thirty long years, with their comforts and cares,
  Pass, as thousands have passed before,
Then as evening sets in, let us eye him again
  As he sits by his cottage door.

There are deep furrows now in that cheek and that
    brow,
  Still he's stalwart, stout, and hale ;
By his side take a rest—he is proud of a guest,
  And list to a squatter's tale.

" The first time I plodded this plain,
  I was six feet and rising of twenty,
Being raised on the mountains of Maine
  Ye may guess that the boy wasn't dainty.

" My neighbours—then wild cat and bear—
  Were brutish and sometimes uncivil,
But my sleeping companion, old Tear,
  He fear'd neither bull, bear, nor devil.

" On the ground floor old Tear and I fix'd,
  We'd the ' might is right ' title to take it,
The squirrels and coons had the next,
  The turkeys they rented the attic.

" We had room in our lodge, ye'll suppose,
  It was airy tho' none of the cleanest ;
The rafters were sturdy old boughs,
  Well shingl'd with leaves of the greenest.

" Our Summer arrangements got thro',
    I began for to think of December's ;
So some jolly old settlers I slew,
    And penn'd in a patch with their members.

" We'd corn soon, and deer came in flocks,
    I was carpenter, farmer, and hunter ;
So when old Johnny Frost shook his locks,
    We'd a cabin to keep out the Winter.

" Soon movers came tumbling in,
    And squatted without e'er a ' thank ye ; '
Well, Tear and I thought it no sin
    To be swapping a bear for a Yankee.

" Ye'll guess then the trunk and the limb
    Of our forest Goliahs got shattered ;
And daylight look'd bloody and grim
    As they blaz'd and their ashes we scatter'd.

" While cabin and corn crib arose,
    Like tents of the mighty invader ;
And craftsmen came following close,
    With preacher, and doctor, and trader.

" Then clubbing the means and the mind,
    Together all pulling and drawing,
A lively young creek we confin'd
    And set it to grinding and sawing.

" Frame fabrics then rose in a twink,
    For stores and for matters domestic ;
We'd one temple for talk and for drink,
    Another for things 'clesiastic.

"Thus chopping and cropping ahead,
  Continually scratching and scheming,
What a gash in the forest we've made !
  While drones are a drowsing and dreaming.

" Our youngsters, too, rise in the ranks,
  Ourselves we grow greater and greater ;
I've got shares in your railroads and banks,
  And a seat in the State Legislature."

THE KEBBOCK, THE CAKE, AN' THE COG.

THERE's fun in your frolics, an' Thanksgiving Day
Is famous for feeding an' great in its way;
But gie me the lan' whaur auld plays are in vogue,
An' the cake an' the kebbock gae down wi' a cog.

Your Frenchman can kick ye a neat pas de deux,
Your Dutchman can waltz it an' booze himself fu';
But gie me a fling in the kilt an' the brogue
While the cake an' the kebbock gae down wi' a cog.

Your bridals by bishops look stately and fine,
But they're mocks to our weddings o' canty langsyne,
Whan the bride's brimming bowl set the birkies agog.
An' the cake an' the kebbock gaed down wi' a cog.

Then here's to the lan' o' the butter an' brose,
An' here's to the lan' o' the kilt an' the hose,
Whaur the reel an' strathspey gie the spirit a jog,
An' here's to the KEBBOCK, the CAKE, an' the COG.

A MORNING WAKE UP.

THE morning star is hidden
  In the dawing's ruddy flake,
An' the laverock has bidden
  His merry mates awake.

Then up, the lamb has shaken
  His fleece an' ta'en the knowes ;
An' sounds o' gladness waken
  Frae heights an' hazel howes.

Come, see the burnie keeking
  Thro' boughs o' blooming thorn,
See merry May unsteeking
  Her beauties to the morn.

Come, while the leaf is laden
  Wi' gems that brightly glow,
For ah ! they're quickly fadin',
  Like a' that's fair below.

ROSABELL.

[*Pure* in *spirit*, but *cut* to the *heart* by the *pure* in *blood*, she died of the wound.]

IT was not well, sweet Rosabell,
  It was not well for thee,
When the English rose for a heart-mate chose
  A flower of the forest free.

The golden tinge, thy eyelids fringe,
  Tell of thy mother's race;
The crimson glow, the noble brow,
  The father's in thy face.

Fresh in all woman's loveliness,
  A ban is on thy birth,
Thy dawn's o'ercast, alas thou hast
  No kindred upon earth !

I see it in thy shudderings,
  The flush, the blush, the start ;
The death-worm's on thee, Rosabell,
  The canker's at thy heart.

Sweet Rosabell, it was not well,
  It was not well for thee,
When the English rose for a heart-mate chose
  A flower of the forest free.

TO A FAIR FOREST BUD ON HER WISHING
TO FLOURISH IN TOWN.

THE garden hath its blossoms rare,
  With many a cultur'd gem ;
But forests have their flowers as fair,
  And thou art one of them.

Here buds receive the dews of eve,
  Thro' purer, sweeter air,
Than when the breeze thro' tainted trees
  Plays round the gay parterre.

Then keep the shade, my pretty maid,
  Nor tempt the unclouded rays,
For wither'd bowers, and wilted flowers,
  Are found in July's blaze.

BUCKWHEAT PANCAKES.

WHOE'ER he was had wit, or luck,
To take this victual of the buck,
And put it to the use of man,
O ! noblest product of the pan !
Deserves to have his lucky name
Stuck in the premises of Fame ;
There let it blaze, with buck to bound it,
And flourishes of cake around it.

I'd question him who's had a stuff
Of cakes till he's cried " Hold, enough,"
Where is the truck, whate'er ye call it,
That slips so sweetly o'er the palate ?
Or where's the broil, the boil, the sop,
That sits so lightly on the crop ?
Ye gourmand gods ! whoe'er ye are,
Oh, listen to your votary's prayer ;
Give me, when from her eastern gate
The Morning issues pale and late—
I mean when days are sour and short,
And feeding fun is fittest sport—
Oh, give me then, when I awake,
To snuff the savor of the cake ;
To spy ye thro' the greasy fog,
Like pretty toadstools on a log ;

Hissing and singing out by fits,
And dimpling into little pits ;
Until, oh, rare ! ye take at last
A chestnut-pale mulatto cast.
Then, then behold ye on the plate,
Piled up in savory smoking state !
Alternating with layers of butter,
Drench'd in molasses, till a gutter
Of sauce surrounds ye !—O ye gods,
Or godlings, in your bright abodes,
Or Paynims in your bower of bliss,
Say—
Is aught in Paradise like this ?

MAY COLZEAN.

The fause Sir John a wooing came,
  To a maid of beauty rare ;
Fair May Colzean was the maiden's name,
  Lord Cassills' only heir.

He's woo'd her butt, he's woo'd her ben,
  He woo'd her in the ha',
Till our bonny fair maid at last has said
  She'd mount an' ride awa.

She's mounted on a milk-white steed,
  Sir John on a dapple grey ;
An' wi' wylie word he cheer'd the road,
  Till they came to the raging sea.

Till they came to a girt an' gruesome rock,
  'Twas frightsome for to see ;
" Light down, light down, fair May Colzean,
  Your bridal bed to see.

" Cast off, cast off, now May Colzean,
  Your hood an' silken gown,
For they're owre rare and costly gear
  To rot in the salt sea foam.

"Cast off, cast off, my May Colzean,
    Thy pearls an' jewelrie,
For they're owre rare an' costly ware
    To be rusting aneath the sea."

"O, turn about, thou fause Sir John,
    Gae turn your back on me,
For a belted knight it is not right
    A naked maid to see."

He's turned him right an' round about,
    Nae dread nor fear had he;
Sae swift as the win' fair May Colzean
    Has plunged him in the sea.
"Now, lie ye there, thou fause Sir John,
    Whaur ye thought to hae laid me."

"O help, O help, my May Colzean,
    Take pity upon me;
I'll take you home to your father's ha',
    Wi' your weight in jewelrie."

"Nae help, nae help, thou fause Sir John,
    Nae help expect frae me,
For seven braw brides thou'st drownéd here,
    But the eighth I shall not be."

She's mounted on her milk-white steed,
    Sae lightsome an sae gay;
And she's come hame to her father's tower,
    Lang ere the break o' day.

Up then spak' her pretty parrot
"Where has May Colzean been?
An' what's become of the bold Sir John,
   That woo'd ye sae late yestreen?"

" O, hold thy tongue, my pretty parrot,
   An' dinna talk sae loud ;
Your cup shall be o' the sandal tree,
   Your cage o' the beaten goud."

Up then there spak' the Earl himsel',
   In the chamber where he lay ;
" What ails May Colzean's bonny bird,
   To talk sae lang ere day?"

" There came a cat to my cage door,
   A' for to worry me ;
An' I cried on my May Colzean
   To kill the cat for me!"

THERE'S WAR IN THE WORLD.

1822.

THERE'S war in the world—What, still?
  Why, the despots of Europe have said
Their motto's no longer "Let's kill,"
  And rapine they've quit as a trade.
Aye, aye, they may scabbard the blade,
  But tyrants for ever must fight
Till the last freeborn spirit is laid
  To slumber with reason and right.

There's war in the world, and will be,
  While despot and potentate reigns;
Till men learn to value and see
  Wherein lie true glory and gains;
Till burst are the bonds and the chains
  Keep brother and brother apart;
Till we *be* what hypocrisy *feigns*,
  And words are the fruit of the heart.

ON THE FLY-LEAF OF THE POET'S EXPENDITURE-BOOK.

THE BLACK BOOK FOR 1819,

Containing an account of provisions, liquors, clothing, etc., destroyed by Hew Ainslie, his wife, children, servant, and the stranger that cometh within his gate.

O THAT a man could live without
  Shoes, clothing, or a hat ;
That breezes might his belly fill
  And water make him fat.
Were this invented, where would be
  The use of a black book like thee ?

LOVE AND FRIENDSHIP.

YOUNG Love is like the tender vine
  That springeth sweet in May,
But Friendship like the stable pine
  That keepeth green for aye.

Then train and twine the pretty vine
  When Summer suns are warm ;
But ne'er neglect the noble pine,
  'Twill shield ye from the storm.

SECRET LOVE.

A SECRET love, a hidden love,
  A love maun shun the light,
Like miser's gold is often told
  In the watches o' the night—

Recounting o'er the precious store :
  The grasp, the clasp, the kiss,
That marked the mingling o' the minds,
  The oneness o' the wish.

Built from this secret treasury,
  The heart enshrines a saint,
Garnished wi' a' the loveliness
  Love's partial eye can paint.

Life's wants and wishes, hopes and fears,
  May crowd and cloud the brain ;
But evermore, in thy heart's core,
  That image must remain.

FAREWELL TO SCOTLAND.

Our sail hath ta'en the blast,
　Our pennant's to the sea,
And the waters widen fast
　'Twixt the fatherland and me.

Then, Scotland, Fare thee well !
　There's a sorrow in that word
This aching heart could tell,
　But words shall ne'er record.

Our love should make us veil,
　From the heart's elected few,
Our sorrows : when we ail,
　Would we have them suffer too ?

No ! The parting hour is past—
　Let its memory be brief ;
If we monument our joys
　We should sepulchre our grief.

Now your misty mountains fail,
　As the breezes give us speed—
Up, my spirit, with our sail,
　There's a better land ahead !

LINES FROM THE LINKER, ON EDIE'S LANDING IN NEW YORK CITY.

WELCOME, Edie, owre the sea,
Welcome to this lan' an' me,
Welcome from the warl' whaur we
    Hae whistled owre the lave o't.

Auld Scotland has some cosy biels,
An' owns a fowth o' canty chiels,
But blast her birn! She's whalpit deils
    Can cheat an' " do " the lave o't.

Come, gie your banes anither hitch,
Up Hudson's stream, thro' Clinton's ditch,
An' see our watlin meadows rich
    Wi' corn an' a' the lave o't.

We've hizzies here baith swank and sweet
An' birkies that can stan' a heat
O' barley bree, or *aqua vit*,
    Syne whistle owre the lave o't.

Gude kens, I want nae better luck
Than just to see ye, like a buck,
Spanking the haughs o' auld Kentuck,
    An' whistling owre the lave o't.

THE BLACKBERRIES O' BETHEL.

ADDRESSED TO MISS KATIE H. CRIST, MONTGOMERY, N.Y.

O THE berries o' Bethel, they're sappy an' sweet,
Be they fresh, be they dry, they are ever a treat ;
They're rich from the bush, but superb on a plate
When sugar'd and cream'd by the hands of dear Kate;
They're fine in a pie, in a pudding they're fine—
Ah ! what can compare with the blackberry wine ?
But 'twas not the berries, tho' ardently prized
Like nectarines nearly, with grapes fairly sized—
Delight must have ever an adequate cause.
'Twas the " picker " in garment of billowy gauze,
Yet better arrayed in a sheen that would wear—
Her own native innocence, modest and fair ;
Her round arm uplifting, with triumph aglow,
To show you the bank where the dear berries grow ;
Aye ! that was the secret, aye ! that was the spell
Made the berries o' Bethel all berries excel.

TO SAM^L^ B. CRIST.

DEAR SAM,
 WHEN Winter winds are rude and rough,
 A city stove does well enough,
 An' paper'd halls and painted flowers
 May serve for Simmer's leafy bowers.
 But when, from Southern solitudes,
 The breeze brings beauty to the woods,
 It's then I long to hear the din
 O' lammies " loupin' o'er a linn,"
 An' list an opera in a glen,
 Instead o' squallin' foreign men,
 Or hearken to the bleatin' lamb
 An' hae a crack wi' Uncle Sam.
       Quoth Hew Ainslie.

Jersey City, March 27, 1855.

GLENLIVET REVISITED.

CHRISTMAS DAY, 1853.

WHEN last I saw this cosy bield,
   'Twas Simmer-tide wi' me,
The corn was waving in the field,
   The leaf was on the tree.

An' kind an' canty faces then
   Gaed glancing thro' the ha';
But like the forest's Simmer flowers,
   They're a' noo wede awa.

The saughs that beautified the burn,
   Tho' noo a' dow'd an' dead,
Hae frae their roots sent sturdy shoots
   To flourish in their stead ;

Even as the dear departed dead
   Hae left memorials here,
Wherein I see, wi' sadden'd e'e,
   " The lost but ever dear."

The noble sire in the sons
   With anxious eye I trace,
And in each maiden's lineaments
   I see a mother's face.

And pleasant 'tis in thought to turn
Frae what ye are e'en noo,
To when your sweet wee cherry lips
First mutter'd " Uncle Hew."

TO STEPHEN WELLSTOOD ON HIS FORTY-THIRD BIRTHDAY.

DRUNK WITH ALL THE HONOURS, NOVEMBER 1, 1854.

Upon this night, when fairies bright
    Dance over banks an' braes,
Our Steenie chiel began to squeal
    An' spartle 'mang the claes.

" I'm three-an-forty noo," he'll state,
    " An' neither lame nor lazy,"
An' yet the laddie lacks a mate !—
    Folk wonner gif he's crazy.

It's true auld sparrows ken the cauff
    Fu' brawly frae the grain,
An' trouts that hae been hookit ance
    Are hard to hook again.

He's maybe chosen the better " part,"
    For dinsome weans an' wife
Are nae great comfort to a chiel
    Wha lo'es a canny life.

Then here's to Stephen, honest man,
    An' whether pair'd or single,
Lang may he craw, in his ain ha',
    Aroun' his canty ingle !

SONG OF ST. STEPHEN,

OR THE PILGRIM'S RETURN FROM THE FATHERLAND.

THE Exile will be wearying—
  His spirit aften greens
To see the brave auld fatherland,
  Some dear remembered frien's ;
But wander east, or wander west,
  He'll wander far an' wide,
Ere he forget his happy home
  An' canty ingle side.

We've pu'd the heather on the hill,
  The gowan in the dale ;
We've seen the rose o' England blow,
  We've heard her nightingale ;
We've wandered east, we've wandered west,
  We've wandered far an' wide, -
But ne'er forgot our happy hame
  An' canty ingle side.

We've fed on Scotia's wale o' food,
  Her crowdy an' her kale ;
We've dined on Johnny's boasted beef
  An' swigged his nappy ale ;
But wine an' wassail, meat an' maut,
  In raxin' routh beside,
We ne'er forgot our happy hame
  An' canty ingle side.

We've gazed on mighty monuments,
    The pride o' priestly days ;
We've marked the splendour o' the prince,
    Seen crowns an' coronets blaze ;
In holy wa's an' lordly ha's
    Been stunned wi' pomp an' pride,
But ne'er forgot our happy hame
    An' canty ingle side.

The welcome warm o' former frien's,
    The kindness o' the new,
May freshen up the dowie heart
    Like herbs wi' e'ening dew.
Yes ! frien'ly grips an' beauty's lips
    Our hearts did charm and cheer,
But ne'er forgot this happy hame
    An' frien's that we hae here.

TO THE LITTLE LADY ALICE, BORN FEB. 16, 1855.

"IN THE INCIPIENT STAGE OF HER EXISTENCE."

My pretty pet ! I vow ye get
　Aye dear an' dearer still—
Come make your nest upon this breast,
　And kick an' crow your fill.

Now gie's a sip o' that sweet lip—
　But, Alice, what is this?
Ho, mother, bring some wiping thing,
　And then we'll have a kiss.

Now heave and set, my pretty pet,
　And show your bends and becks,
But, look ye there ! she's in my hair—
　And dash, there go my spec's !

Well, never fret, my pretty pet,
　Just work your ain wee will,
And run an' tug, an' scout my lug,
　And crow an' kick your fill.

TO MASTER ANDREW SPENCE

ON POKING HIMSELF UPON US ON MARCH 21, 1856.

WELL, Master Andrew Spence, so you're there !
Wi' your little poke-up nose and your little lock o' hair !
    I daresay,
    Master A.,
  You think yourself right smart,
     Tho' ye might hae gi'en
     My little queen
 A little better start.
    But I'm dumb,
    And succumb.

    We remark,
    My little lark,
There's a something all about ye
    Looks so cunning
    And so winning,
We could never do without ye.
    And so trim
    In each limb,
It marks ye o' the breed
    That wi' daring,
    And wi' tearing,
Are sure to go ahead.

For we know,
'Tis the " go "
Now-a-days to foot it fast,
To be rushing
And pushing
And laughing at the past.

So dash along
And head the throng,
And let your motto be :
The Rights o' Man,
The Social Plan,
With the Largest Liberty !

TO OUR LITTLE LADY ANN

ON HER INTRODUCTION TO DORKING VILLA, AUGUST 1, 1857.

THE ancient Greeks and Romans,
 We learn from historie,
Had faith in signs and omens
 And held the number three
  A myth and mysterie.
 And well may we
  Respect the " three "
And count the number cannie, O,
 For aint the third,
 Our pretty bird,
The smiling dimpled Annie, O ?

  And tho' that ye
   Stand Number Three,
'Tis plain to wife or man,
  That ye should be,
   Not Number Three,
  But big A. No. one.

Then cock your noddle, Annie,
 An' gie's a canty craw ;
For Uncle Stephen says that ye're
 The sweetest o' them a'.

TO THE LATE MISS ALICE SPENCE.

Now Mrs. William Wellstood.

When girls are tender, young and green,
'Twixt sunny twelve and sweet sixteen,
  We treat them to such stuff, then,
As tells of pretty doves, and darts,
Sly Cupid's bow, and bleeding hearts,
  And count it good enough, then.

But when the maid becomes a dame,
Her spirit changes with her name,
  And " Jim," instead of Cupid,
Is then the pretty word ; and so,
To palter about Cupid's bow
  Would sound extremely stupid.

So, being now a wedded wife,
I pray the balance of your life
  May be as free from sorrow
As when, beneath the moon of May,
Ye kiss'd the " spoony " hours away,
  Wi' Will, your winsome marrow.

BLOOMINGDALE.

WE may live in marble halls
  In homes of stately stone,
But Bloomingdale's dear walls
  I must ever think upon.

Rich Summer blooms were rife,
  When first ye met my view,
And I, a new-made wife,
  Had Summer in me too.

It may be the *inner* eye
  Makes the *outer* often see—-
But Bloomingdale and beauty
  Are synonyms with me.

Maggie, per H. A.

TO STEPHEN WELLSTOOD.

GLENLIVET, JANUARY 2, 1862.

IF my lungs had been strong enough,
Or your lugs had been long enough,
   Yesterday,
Ye'd heard me sing or say :
" A gude New Year I wiss ye, Steenie,
  An' ditto to your marrow ;
An' may there never come atween ye
  Aught sour to breed ye sorrow—
Wi' routh o' meal and rout o' maut,
Haddocks fresh and herrings saut,
Carvie cakes an' curran' bun,
Lots o' kissing—lots o' fun.
  An' may the Deil
  Rock him in creel
That doesna wiss ye weel ! "

THREE LIVES, THREE WIVES.

A DROLL old Pagan sage,
I don't recollect the age
Or reign in which he flourished,
Some right funny notions nourish'd
Touching *homo* as a whole,
Touching body, heart, and soul.
     As this brave old sage, or hero,
Lived before the Christian era,
He'd neither doubt nor dread
Of dogma, bull or creed,
But fearlessly, untrammel'd,
Thro' all sorts of subjects scrambled ;
Proving, to *his* satisfaction,
By putting it in action,
That all right-minded men,
Who lived threescore years and ten,
Lived three distinctive lives,
And, of course, should have three wives !
'Twas a pretty stout assertion,
As you'll gather from this version :
     When the boy becomes a man—
We'll say he's twenty-one—
The Academic grove
He quits for courts of love ;
When he singles from the ring

Some pretty, giddy thing
That can chatter, dance, and sing;
Wooes, weds, and blesses fate
For such a matchless mate!

    But the boy becomes a father,
And clouds begin to gather ;
Sweet fairy idealities
Grow rough and tough realities :
A squalling litle baby
A nervous little lady—
Ah ! the fairyland is gone !
The dreamer finds he's on
A world of earth and stone.

    Then give the man a wife
To aid him in the strife
Thro' the battle day o' life—
A woman that can brighten,
A woman that can lighten
His spirit and his load
As he foot's life's rugged road ;
A woman that can reason,
A woman that can season
The often mawkish cup
Your married man must sup.

    Now say the man has thriven
And some fifty-five or seven,
Soul sicken'd with the bustle,
The wrangling, the tussle,
With men of major keenness,
With men of minor meanness,
His spirit—as the grub,
Tho' its motherland's the dub,
When wing'd, despises mud—

Soars, seeks beyond the mire
Something finer, fairer, higher.
 Then match him with a mind,
Enlightened and refined ;
Let her have a little store
Of ancient song and lore,
To while his mind away
From the rude and rough to-day ;
Then gently let her raise
And train his eye to gaze
On truths that Nature preaches,
On truths that Science teaches,
Till his world-wearied eye
Sees another earth and sky.
 Aye, happy man is he
Who findeth such a *three !*
But happier still the man
Who finds the *three in one !*

THE LEDDY MACMEEKEN.

THE Leddy Macmeeken
　　Was touching twa score,
Her neibour Miss Witherspoon
　　Said she was more ;
But it's needless to spier,
　　If ye're seekin' the truth,
An auld maiden's age
　　Frae an auld maiden's mouth.

But forty or fifty,
　　Her leddyship fan',
Tho' walthy and furthy,
　　She wanted a man ;
So the bauld Laird o' Chang,
　　Tho' sair sottert in sin,
And rough as March weather,
　　She set on to win.

She met him at preachin's,
　　She plied him at fairs,
Wi' meek pious looks
　　And wi' maidenly airs ;
She trockt wi' his man,
　　But Jock privily swore,
Nae leddy nor limmer
　　Should darken his door.

At last she bethought her
O' Lucky Macteer,
Whaur the laird spent the feck
O' his time and his gear :
And wi' presents sae timely,
And fleechin's sae fine,
She seasoned and sautit
The wife to her min'.

The laird quaffed his brandy
And tootit his yill,
As he'd aye dune before ;
But ae night he fell ill,
Wi' a head on the rive
And a coal in his craw—
The laird, sair forfoughen,
Maist slithert awa'.

Wae saeks for his lairdship,
The business was bad—
Nae doctor nor druggist
Was near to be had ;
But our brewster wife mindit,
While basting his brow,
Our Leddy Macmeeken
Was skeely, I trow.

The leddy was sent for,
The laird soon gat ease ;
Sae weel kent the leddy
Whaur lay the disease.
Wi' kind, gentle treatment,
And womanly airt,
His hoastin' she lowsed
While she tethered his heart.

19

The laird saw his errors,
　　And started anew ;
Nae mair is the croak
　　In his craw or his brow.
Ae bright Simmer morning
　　The bridal bells rang—
The Leddy Macmeeken
　　Is Leddy o' Chang.

SIR RINGAN.

Sir Ringan came o' gentle blood,
    But wild as the Winter wind,
Nor honours gay, nor lover's pledge
    Would young Sir Ringan bind.

His father gae him sword an' steed,
    For a valiant Knight was he;
His mother gae him book an' bead,
    For a leal Lady was she.

But seek nae him at wapinschaw,
    Where gallants run their steeds;
Nor look for him in holy ha',
    Where gownsmen tell their beads.

But where the wassail bowl is bright,
    And harpers twang the string,
Where lossels swagger out the night,
    And wantons fill the ring—

There, wi' the wine cup in his hand,
    His leman on his knee,
Up rolls Sir Ringan's ribbald song,
    Loud o'er their revelrie.

Aye loudly sing, Sir Ringan, sing,
  And drown the memory
Of perjured vows to Lady Jane,
  And wrangs to mony mae.

This night, Sir Ringan, is your ain,
  Let hall and bower resound ;
Drink deep, drink deep, no pause for sleep,
  To-morrow you'll sleep sound.

The tether ye hae taen, Sir Knight,
  Has baith been lang an' wide ;
An' dark an' deep the waters be,
  Sir Ringan, that ye ride.

A wizard frae the misty land,
  Hath cast and read thy weird ;
That eye so bold is closed and cold,
  Thy coronach's been heard.

At dead of night, an armed Knight
  Strides up the banquet floor :
A shout, a scream—a purple stream—
  Sir Ringan's in his gore !

And well Sir Ringan knows that Knight,
  His lineage and name—
A brother's hand was on the brand
  That 'veng'd a sister's shame !

Thy tether, Ringan, has been wide,
  Thy tether has been long ;
Stern Justice watches step an' stride,
  Her red right arm is strong.

THE SWEETEST O' THEM A'.

When Springtime gi'es the heart a lift,
Outowre cauld Winter's snaw an' drift,
An' April's showers begin to sift,
   Fair flowers on field an' shaw ;
Then Katie, when the dawing's clear,
Fresh as the firstlings o' the year,
Come forth my joy, my dearest dear,
   O sweetest o' them a' !

When pleasant primrose days are dune,
When linties sing their saftest tune,
An' Simmer, nearing to his noon,
   Gars rarest roses blaw ;
Then, sheltered frae the sun an' win',
Beneath the buss, below the linn,
I'll tell ye hoo this heart ye won,
   Thou sweetest o' them a'.

When flowers hae ripened into fruit,
When plantins wear their Sabbath suit,
When win's grow loud an' birdies mute,
   An' swallows flit awa'—
Then, on the lea side o' a stook,
Or in some calm an' cozy nook,
I'll swear I'm thine, upon the *Book*—
   Thou sweetest o' them a'.

Tho' black December binds the pool
Wi' blasts might e'en a wooer cool,
It's them that bring us canty Yule
   As weel's the frost an' snaw !
Then, when auld Winter's ragin' wide,
An' cronies crowd the ingle-side,
I'll bring them ben a bloomin' bride—
   O, sweetest o' them a' !

SOBER SAWS.

"Hae a warl' o' your ain."

Wi' beauty an' wi' barrenness
  This wondrous warl' is rife,
As wi' sadness an' wi' gladness
  Is striped our web o' life :
E'en dourest days will hae a glimmer,
An' sourest years hae aye a Simmer.

Rare plants that beautify the Spring
  Aft sprint frae roughest spot ;
Sae, dainty blooms keep gathering,
  Let briers an' dockens rot,
An' ne'er in July's crystal pool
Be spying icicles o' Yule.

Doomed for to battle wi' the warl',
  Brace ye to bear the brunt,
An' e'en, tho' worsted in the quarrel,
  Keep an unconquer'd front,
An' ne'er let man or woman know
How deep hath gone their stab or blow.

Nor like the hunter-smitten bird,
  Flee frae the flock apart,
Letting a green untended wound
  Eat festering to the heart ;
No, promptly ply the leech's skill—
'Tis *inward wounds* that surest kill.

Dreary o'er barren moor an' dale
   Life's highway often lies,
Unshelter'd frae the scorching sun,
   Or Winter's blustering skies ;
But still your weary, way-worn wight
Has aye his resting hour at night.

Then start the soul a travelling,
   While lith an' limbs repose,
No tangled paths unravelling,
   No forging future woes ;
But, letting Hope an' Fancy lead,
Build ye a braw wee warl' ahead.

Wants, wishes, aspirations, all—
   Give thy full spirit vent ;
Up wi' the castellated hall
   Or cottage o' content ;
For certes, while the dream endures,
The castle or the cot *is yours.*

What tho' they perish wi' the light—
   Does Summer last for aye ?
Your granite walls and marble halls
   Have but a longer day ;
And ask them who their temples boast,
What was the trouble, toil and cost ?

Yes, keep a wee warl' o' your ain,
   The big warl' ne'er maun see ;
There congregate an' entertain
   Your heart's dear companie ;
Then, blow an' bluster as it will,
Your heart's wee warl' is sunny still !

"IT SEEMS NAE SAE TO ME."

THE sun may shine as brightly, May,
  As when here it shone on thee,
An' a' things look as sightly, May—
  It seems nae sae to me.

An' the grassy seat, my winsome mate,
  We raised beneath the tree,
May look mair fresh in its April dress—
  It seems nae sae to me.

Does the lintie's throat have the selfsame note
  As when wi' his melodie
Ye mixt your sang, till the wildwood rang?
  It seems nae sae to me.

Yes, birds may sing, an' glens may ring,
  Wi' a' their wonted glee,
An' fields may wear their gayest gear—
  It seems nae sae to me.

THE CURLERS O' CURRY.

Stout sons o' the stane an' the besom,
   Wi' bruks fu' o' brave Scottish blude,
The win o' the North's to ye loesome,
   It's breath floors the face o' the flood.
It's heartsome to see the burns purling,
   In Summer when woodlan's look weel,
But carles wha delight in the curling
   Rejoice when they're stiffen'd like steel.
     Then up wi' the Curlers o' Curry !
       An' Duky the King o' the core,
      Auld Roslin, tho' ne'er in a hurry,
       Is famous at wicking a bore.

Weel bouden in bonnet and rachan,
   Our caigie auld curler sets out ;
A cog o' fat brose in his pechan,
   A dribble o' drink in his snout.
His kimmer may kick up a cungle,
   The outlyers for fodder may rowte,
But soon at his stanes on the channel
   He thinks nae o' women or nowt.
     Then up wi' the stane an' the besom,
       An here's to the frost an' the snaw,
      An' hey ! for a brange at the lousing,
       The saut beef, the lang kail, an' a'.

They're gleg han's, they say, at Lochsterrick,
   An' Duddistan bodies will blaw,
But gie me the pick o' North Berwick,
   And hey ! for a rink at the Law !
Bowd Benjie's the first I sou'd ca' on,
   An' siccar is Wat o' Langwhangs,
While Bauldy the King o' Tantallon
    Is H—— on a hammer an' tangs !
     Then hey ! for the dregs o' December,
      It brings out the stanes an' the broom ;
     An' wha is't that fails to remember
      Our boosing in Mungo's ben room ?

THE FISHWIFE'S ADVICE TO HER BAIRN.

Ken the kintra, Kirsty
    Ken it wide an' weel,
Ere ye cry a codling,
    Ere ye back a creel.

Lithe be wi' the leddies,
    Win' is easy war'd ;
But for flukes or haddies,
    Bargain wi' the laird.

Cosh be wi' your kimmers,
    Whether auld or young,
But wi' flyting limmers,
    Min' your mither's tongue !

Let the poor and needy
    Ken ye hae a creel,
But the grippin' greedy,
    Pit it to them weel.

To swankies free an' funny,
    Dit nae up your lug ;
Gif lavish o' their cunzie,
    Let them hae a rug.

Freely birle your boddle,
   When the wark gaes weel,
But ne'er lade your noddle
   Till ye've toom'd your creel.

Learn to blaw an' blether,
   Baith wi' lad an' lass ;
Gie your tongue nae tether,
   Lang's it brings the brass.

Ken the kintra, Kirsty,
   Ken it wide an' weel,
Ere ye cry a codling,
   Ere ye back a creel.

GENTLE VERSUS SEMPLE.

GENTLE.

Ho! ye delvers and dibblers—
  Grim warrers wi' the weeds,
Can any thing of wit or worth
  Spring frae your dirty heads?

Wi' clutes a' clottert wi' the clods,
  Your rumples to the sun,
Your digits diggin' in the dirt,
  Your grunzies like the grun.

Say, dirty, delving dibblers,
  Grim sextons to the weeds,
Can cleanly things, or seemly things,
  Sprout frae your dirty heads?

SEMPLE.

My valiant catechiser,
  Ye break right bauldly oot,
Tho' what is fair, and what is foul,
  Has aften stood dispute.

The tiger and the spotted pard
   May boast a comely skin,
An' sae may painted Jezebels,
   But what are they within?

Our dirt an' muck that mak's ye bock,
   An' filth that gars ye grue,
Will nourish roots an' juicy fruits
   To gust your dainty mou'.

The singing bird maun eat his grub
   Before he sings his tune,
And seeds hae dealings wi' the dirt
   Before they burst aboon.

'Neath roughest rhind we aften find
   The soundest, sweetest nit ;
An' heat and light, yea, diamonds bright,
   Are found in darkest pit.

Your dainty sense may tak' offence
   At wights that war wi' weeds,
While we that toil see nought sae vile
   As filthy words and deeds.

WRONG AND RIGHT WEDLOCK.

O, WEDLOCK's oft a dreary drag ;
   He wales a luckless lot
When gentle blude, or tocher gude,
   Has handlin' o' the knot.

And hot calf-loves o' tender doves
   Are unca apt to cool ;
The tane may grow a puttin' coo,
   The tither turn a mule.

But mark the marrying o' minds !
   Youth's foolish fondness past,
When heart and brain hae forged the chain—
   Aye, thae's the links that last.

A HAIL FRAE THE LAND O' CAKES TO OUR FRIEN'S IN THE LAND O' CORN.

HEALTH and Wealth to ye a'
   On your side o' the sea !
Is our cry on this birthday
   O' young Sixty-three.

An' we wish and we pray
   That ye soon may get thro'
The black job ye began
   In the year Sixty-two.

The fierce fire-eaters—
   Vile dealers in men—
Your boys o' the North
   Hae got snug in a pen.

And before they walk over
   That strong living wall
The King and the Kingdom
   Of Cotton must fall !

Then back not, and slack not
   Till slavery's o'erthrown,
'Tis the holiest of wars
   That this world yet has known.

20

SIGHINGS FOR THE SEA.

At the stent o' my string,
 When a fourth o' the earth.
Lay 'tween me and Scotland,
 Dear lan' o' my birth—

Wi' the richest o' valleys,
 And waters as bright
As the sun in midsummer
 Illumes wi' his light ;

And surrounded wi' a'
 That the heart or the head,
The mou' or the body
 O' mortal could need—

I hae pined in this plenty
 And paus'd in my track,
As a tug frae my tether
 Would make me look back—

Look back to auld hills
 In their red heather bloom,
To glens wi' their burnies
 And hillocks o' broom,

To some loop in the loch
  Where the wave gaes to sleep,
Or the black craggy headlands
  That bulwark the deep ;

Wi' the sea lashing in
  Wi' the wind and the tide—
Aye, 'twas then that I sicken'd,
  'Twas then that I cried :

O, gie me a sough o' the auld saut sea,
  A scent o' his brine again,
To stiffen the wilt that this wilderness
  Has brought on this bosom and brain.

Let me hear his roar on the rocky shore,
  His thud on the shelly sand,
For my spirit's bow'd and my heart is dow'd
  Wi' the gloom o' this forest land.

Your waving woods and your sweeping floods
  Look brave in the suns o' June,
But the breath o' the swamp brews a sickly damp
  And there's death in the dark lagoon.

Aye, gie me the jaup o' the dear auld saut,
  A scent o' his brine again,
To stiffen the wilt that this wilderness
  Has brought on this bosom and brain.

REFLECTIONS FOR THE AFFLICTED.

SINCE this world's an estate,
  And Fortune and Fate
Are the ladies that slice it and share it,
  It is bairnly to fret
  Against fortune and fate,
But manly to grin and to bear it.

  And philosophers say,
  If in frolic and play
We mortgage the mirth o' to-morrow :
  Don't be making a noise—
  Wait for future supplies,—
Justice says we must pay if we borrow.

    Good and true,
    Says Uncle Hew ;
    Ne'er-the-less,
    Some stress
    Should be laid
    On what's afterwards said.

  If our nose gets a bash,
  Or our thumb gets a gash,
We ken how to plaister or patch it ;
  But invisible pain,
  Tearing body and brain,
What plaister or poultice can catch it ?

Some reckon a roar
Is right sanative, for
See a wifie gae gyte,
L—d hear hoo she'll flyte
An' tear like a brute in a brulzie !
Gie her tether an' vent,
The storm is soon spent,
An' she's calm as an e'ening in July.

Sae when they've a tout
O' rheumatics or gout,
An' neither can stand, lie, nor go it,
They'll roar and profane,
An' it slackens the pain—
At least it mak's ither folk know it.

And whether it's best,
When pain'd or distressed,
To thole or to kick up a clatter,
Is a question that still
Maun depend on the will—
For me, I make rhymes and drink water.

ALTERATION SUGGESTED BY " MINE ENEMY."

Now whether it's best,
When pain'd and distress'd,
To thole or to rant like a randy,
Is the question that will
Aye depend on the chiel—
For me, I sing sangs and drink brandy.

NUT

FOR THE AUTHOR O' " THE KISS AHINT THE DOOR."

I HAE nae wuss, 'hint steekit door,
   Or door that's haflin's open,
When tulyin' wi' a bonny lass,
   For kisses to be gropin'.
It isna there that sud come aff,
   Sound than sweet music deeper,
Wi' ten horse power an' hearty baff,—
   A smourock or a cheeper.

Na ! na ! while there are gowden whins
   Breathin' their fragrance balmy,
'Tis there that I wad draw my dear,
   My artless-heartit lammie.
There sou'd she stan', her only words
   Shot thro' the blue e'e's glintie,
Nif-niflin' at her apron-strings
   An' watchfu' as a lintie.

If some wee burnie rippelt on,
   Or birk it's croon were bendin',
It wadna interrupt the job
   My boldness was intendin' :
To tak' her as her fingers fine
   In apron-strings were lockit,
An' print on her warm lips the sign
   Our hearts an' han's were yokit.

"O AS HE KITTLED ME."

WHASAE may threep an' loud insist
On Robbie's faut, I shanna list ;
Wha couthier ere a lassie kiss'd ?
 No you, lad, staun'in' by.

Chorus :—
 For O as he kittled me,*
  He kittled me, he kittled me ;
 O hoo he kittled me,
  But I forgot to cry.

Sae weel he kens the way to woo ;
Nae blackfit comes tweesh him an' you ;
He settles on a gilpie's mou'
 Ere she can say " O fie."
 Chorus :—
 For O as he kittled me, &c.

He kittles but he disna skaith ;
The touzle is a treat to baith ;
On that I'll tak' my bible aith ;
 Judge for yoursel's an' try.
 Chorus :—
 For O as he kittled me, &c.

* This chorus is very old, but is none the less lively for that.—Ed.

Na ! no ae hint o' Robin's faut,
The wee drap or the peck o' maut,
Frae lass in his strang airms he caught
   When " Comin' thro' the rye."

Chorus :—

For O as he kittled me, &c.

A MAN BEFORE THE MAST.

FAREWELL.

I DAURNA say my fare-thee-weel
    Afore your kith an' kin',
The word would choke me in the throat
    An' tears would mak' me blin'.

They maunna see my watery e'e,
    My tender term is past ;
Noo I maun be a man, Minnie,—
    A man before the mast.

But when the sun's aneath the sea,
    The moon aboon the hill,
Ye'll find me i' the holme, Minnie,
    The holme below the mill.

There in that saft an' silv'ry licht
    Nae earthly list'ner near,
I'll lay my last kiss on thy lip
    An' drap my hindmost tear.

Then steel'd an' strengthen'd to my trade,
    I'll brave it to the last,
My heart wi' you an' country, too,—
    A man before the mast.

THE RETURN.

WAKED by the sang o' Simmer birds,
 I raise wi' heartsome glee,
Right glad to fin' some ither din
 Than soughin's o' the sea.

A plower o' the watery waste
 Three lang years I had been,
Sae grassy howes an' whinny knowes
 Were dainties to my e'en.

Tho' decks an' wales an' spars an' sails
 My darg had daily been,
My dreamin' hours were aye 'mang flowers
 An' holmes o' glossy green,

Watchin' the birdies by the burn,
 The wanton lammies play,
Or pu'in' nits or haws an' hips
 For sweet wee Minnie Gray.

In leavin' hame for gear or gain,
 We haud a headlang track,
But wi' a hank about the heart
 We'll aye be keekin' back.

An' wha'd hae thocht a lad had wrocht
 On nocht but stane an' lan',
Would, on a rovin' privateer,
 Turn out a hearty han'?

But the bold Captain o' our crew
   Wha's word was life an' law,
Soon put a spirit in my pith
   An' ripen'd what was raw.

Sae, fechtin' wi' the Spanish don,
   Or slavers, doomed to die,
There were but few amang our crew
   More ready, stieve than I.

But death, or peace gars warfare cease ;
   Sae, on the Spanish main,
In boardin' o' a Buccaneer,
   Our gallant chief was slain.

Then hameward, hameward was the cry
   Frae stem to stern it flew,
For swords an' guns an' birslin' suns
   Had thinn'd an' cowed our crew.

Like caller trout I'd gane thereout
   Wi' fresh an' ruddy cheek,
Noo brunt an' tash'd afore the mast
   Like speldrin' in the reek.

An' hoo will bonny Minnie stand,
   Her gentle bosom bide
A wight brown-beardit like a bear
   An' tann'd like barkit hide ?

Sae, worn an' weary, dowf an' daz'd,
   I wander'd 'mang the braes,
An' pond'rin' 'bout my alter'd look
   I met wi' ane amaze !

A lady like a buskit bride
  Lap lichtly frae her steed—
O blessin's on that head an' heart,
  She scatter'd doubt an' dreid.

For ere that I could trust mine eye,
  Or gather breath to speak,
Her lily arms were roun' my neck,
  Here lips were on my cheek.

Some said it was a sight to see,
  Some said it was a sin
To see that lovely lady fine
  Cling to my cheek an' chin.

But Minnie Gray soon chang'd me sae
  That neibors wink'd an' ask'd:
Can that be him, sae tosh an' trim,
  Wha focht afore the mast?

BABBY O' BARLEE.

Lang hae I wantit,
Days graned an' gauntit,
Nights lain dementit,
  Heart sair for thee.
        O, gin I had her,
        Eh, gin I had her,
        O, gin I had her,
            Babby o' Barlee.

Aft to my sighing,
I've thought her complying—
Whan, huff! aff she's flying,
  Flaff, like a flee.
        O, gin, etc.

Rab Muir the miller,
Says it's the siller
Tethers me till her ;
  Rab Muir, ye lee.
        O, gin, etc.

Hear to me, Rabby,
Gie me bonny Babby,
Then tak' a' her daddy
  O' money has to gie.
        For O, gin I had her,
        Eh, gin I had her,
        O, gin I had her,
            Happy wou'd I be.

MEG O' MINNYBOLE.

TRIPPING to the well,
  Stepping up the causey,
I've maunder'd to mysel',
  "Meg's a bonny lassie."
    But tho' she took my e'e,
      Tho' I praised her carriage—
    Sound, heart-hale, an' free—
      Never thought o' marriage.

Riding to the fair,
  Flourishing a feather,
Gallant, ripe an' rare,
  Sweet as Summer weather.
    Then she took my e'e,
      Then I prais'd her carriage,
    But bent on being free,
      Never thought o' marriage.

Scraping a strathspey,
  Wha sou'd be my dancer?
Meg, our flower o' May !
  Wasna she a prancer?
    The pride o' Minnybole
      Gae my heart a wringing,
    Sapped my very soul—
      Floor'd me wi' her flinging !

KATIE KINNAIRD.

HERE'S a health to thee, Katie,
　　Sweet Katie Kinnaird ;
Thou wert born for a Lady,
　　Thou'st married our Laird.
Tho' my blanket wi' thee
　　I ance thought to hae shar'd—
Here's a lang lightsome life
　　To thee, Katie Kinnaird.

Some gouks wou'd gane gyte,
　　Were they trystit like me ;
They would talked o' a rape,
　　Or wou'd ta'en to the sea ;
While I to the alehouse
　　Right doucely repaired,
An' drank to thee, Kate,
　　An' thy wee junkit Laird.

The Laird keeps thee dinkit
　　As Lady need be,
But whyles at the kirk
　　When I meet wi' your e'e,
It kythes nae sae blythe
　　As when on the green swaird
Ye reel'd wi' Pate Lowrie,
　　Sweet Katie Kinnaird.

It's true that my liking
   Lay long to thee, Kate ;
But liking, like living,
   Ye ken has a date.
Tho' the Laird's got the crap,
   I'd a pree o' the braird ;
So, here's to thee, Katie,
   Sweet Katie Kinnaird !

YOUNG AND OLD LOVE.

Young love it may be hot,
　Young love it may be strong,
But the love of riper years
　Is the love that lasteth long.

Young love it lives on lips,
　Or comely cheek an' chin,
But unco soon it flits
　When nae deeper than the skin.

Youth catcheth at the flower
　That shows a pleasant shoot ;
His elder maketh sure
　There's no poison in the fruit.

Still doubt the wily word,
　Distrust the fervid vow ;
Our gaudiest of flowers
　Are flowers that soonest dow.

Stan' steeve afore ye start—
　Haste seldom maketh speed—
And ever keep the heart
　In a halter o' the head.

TO THE GHOST O' AULD JEANIE, MY SPIRIT'S NURSE.

THE last o' a line,
  A break in a breed,
A stalk that hath flourished
  But shedded nae seed.

'Twas thy doom an' thy dool,
  A lone wearysome path,
Frae the gasp o' thy birth
  To the groan o' thy death !

Earth's mighty magnifics
  May ask wi' a sneer—
Their names made for monuments—
  Why *thou* wert here.

Ask the waves o' the deep,
  " Why incessantly toil ? "
Their Tasker's the Lord,
  They are building an isle.

Man measures a moiety,
  Heaven surveys the whole ;
Flesh genders with flesh,
  Soul generates soul.

And the soul seeds ye sowed,
  Thro' some hamely auld rhyme,
May yet crop out in thinkings,
  High, noble, sublime.

Tribes, nations, are gulph'd
  In the world's turmoil,
But the fruit of the spirit's
  Eternity's spoil.

Thou hast passed from thy place
  Like a leaf from the bough,
But thy spirit still lives—
  Hark ! *It speaks to thee now !*

WHA WILL BE THE WISER?

GENTLE Jeany Glen,
    Talks o' ceremonie,
Fears that folk sou'd ken
    Hoo weel she lo'es her Johnny.
Sae, noth the plantin' park—
    Naething could be nicer—
Meet me when it's dark—
    Wha will be the wiser?

Market day's the morn—
    Feign ye're sick or ailing ;
Soon's they've cleared the corn,
    Meet me noth the pailing.
Don your auntie's cap—
    Naething cou'd be nicer—
Tho' they see your step—
    Wha will be the wiser?

Clean across the muir—
    Sure that nane has seen ye—
We'll beveridge the bower
    I've buskit for my Jeany.
Kissing 'neath the tree—
    Dear, what cou'd be nicer?
Nane but heaven to see—
    Wha will be the wiser?

STANDS SCOTLAND WHERE IT DID?

Hoo's dear auld mither Scotland, lads?
   Hoo's kindly Scotland noo?
Are a' her glen's as green's of yore,
   Her hare-bells still as blue?

I muckle dread the iron steed,
   That tears up heugh an' fell,
Has gien oor canny auld folk
   A sorry tale to tell.

Hae touns ta'en a' your bonnie burns
   To cool their lowin' craigs?
Or damm'd them up in timmer troughs
   To slock their yettlin naigs?

Do Southern loons infest your touns
   Wi' mincin' cockney gab?
Hae "John and Robert" ta'en the place
   O' plain auld "Jock and Rab?"

In sooth, I dread a foreign breed
   Noo rules o'er "corn an' horn,"
An' kith an' kin I'd hardly fin',
   Or place whaur I was born.

They're howkin' sae in bank an' brae,
    An' sheughin' hill an' howe,
I tremble for the bonnie broom,
    The whin an' heather cowe.

I fear the dear auld " Diligence"
    An' " Flies" hae flown the track,
An' cadgers braw—pocks, creels, an' a'—
    Gane i' the ruthless wrack.

Are souple kimmers, kirkward boun',
    On Sabbath to be seen,
Wi' sturdy carles that talk o' texts,
    Roups, craps, an' days hae been ?

Gang lasses yet wi' wares to sell,
    Barefittit to the toun ?
Is wincie still the wyliecoat
    An' dimity the goun ?

Do wanters try the yellow leaf
    Upon the first o' May ?
Are there touslins on the hairst rig
    An' houtherins 'mang the hay?

Are sheepshead dinners on the board
    Wi' gusty haggis seen ?
Come scones an' farls at four-hours?
    Are sowens ser'd at e'en ?

Are winkin's 'tween the preachin's rife,
    Out-owre the baps an' yill ?
Are there cleekin's i' the kirk gates
    An' loans for lovers still ?

Gang lovin' souls in plaids or shawls
   A-courtin' to the bent?
Has gude braid lawlan's left the land?
   Are kail an' crowdy kent?

Ah! weel I min', in dear langsyne,
   Our rantin's roun' the green,
The meetin's at the trystin' tree,
   The " chappin's oot " at e'en.

O bootless queries, vanish'd scenes!
   O wan an' wintry time!
Why lay alike on heart an' dyke
   Thy numbing frost an' rime?

E'en noo my day gangs doun the brae,
   An' tear-draps fa' like rain,
To think the fouth o' gladsome youth
   Can ne'er return again.

NEW LEAVES, NEW LIVES.

THE robin's left the ha' door,
  The meycock he's come back ;
While sparrows, chirping cheerily,
  Sit pyking at the thack.

Then doff your duffles, deary,
  An' kist the Winter claes,
For laverocks are in the lift,
  An' gowans on the braes.

Up, leave the reekit rafters,
  The din o' warldly men,
Let's see what April's canny han'
  Is doing in our glen.

Where snaw lay deep in Winter,
  In the howe below the linn,
Sweet primroses are coming, love,
  Wi' a' their comely kin.

There's music in the loan, love,
  There's dancings o'er the dubs,
There's wooings in the sunny nooks,
  There's weddings in the woods.

A' living things sae gay, love,
  A' growing things sae green,
Ye'd hardly trew, to see them noo,
  That snaws had ever been.

Our surly win's o' Winter
  Scoup windlestraes awa,
That ither sprouts may spring, love,
  That ither buds may blaw.

Sae let us blaw the griefs awa',
  That sorrow bred, or sin,
And wi' this New Year o' the Lord
  A braw new life begin.

COURTING IN THE CAULD.

THE neibors kent, the parish kent,
  An' weel I kent mysel',
Hoo deep in love, hoo steept in love,
  I was wi' Annie Bell.

An' weel she kent what nichts I'd spent
  In traikin' up her tracks
To feasts an' foys, to plays an' ploys,
  Or boglie roun' the stacks.

Oh ! licht o' heart an' licht o' limb,
  Sae winsome, fresh, an' fair—
Could ye hae seen that fairy queen
  She'd gart ye stan' an' stare !

The robin haps into our ha',
  An' whistles in the hedge,
A dainty bird, a genty bird,
  But winna brook a cage.

Sae, tho' the pride o' our burnside
  Wi' me was frank and free,
Whene'er I'd mint my love to hint,
  She'd cock her head an' flee.

Yet smirks and smiles at antrin whiles
   Would gie my heart a heeze ;
Then jokes an' jeers would start my fears,
   An' gie my hopes a freeze.

At last ae nicht, a wintry nicht,
   It fell my place and pride
To see the dawty ower the dale,
   An' up our waterside.

My gude grey plaid, baith syde an' wide,
   I airtit to the wun' ;
She took my lee richt cheerilie,
   An' leuch as it were fun.

In stoppin' at the steppin'-stanes,
   I bode to back her o'er ;
But no, she'd tak' the steps her lane—
   She'd ta'en them aft afore.

Wi' skip an' spring, like thing on wing,
   She made the middle stane ;
But there she met a sliddery step,
   An' in the burn she's gane !

Ye needna dou't I had her out
   As fast as bird cou'd flee ;
But such ado !—she'd lost a shoe,
   An's droukit to the knee.

Richt gentilie an' tentilie
   I bore her to a biel',
An' wrappit her and happit her
   Wi' carefu' swath an' sweel.

I took my cosey frae my craig,
  My bonnet frae my pow,
An' buskit up her sweet wee fit—-
  The deftest that I dow ;

Syne, eased her up an' heezed her up
  To haud her feet frae harms,
Till, by lifting an' by shifting,
  I gat her in my arms.

She raised her head, an' saftly said—
  " Oh ! Will, ye're wondrous kin' "—
I fan' her dear wee bosey then
  Was melting into mine.

It warmed me, it charmed me,
  To fin' her grow sae fain,
An' just afore we made the door
  I kent she'd be my ain.

She's spinning there fornent me noo,
  Ayont the ingle lowe,
The neatest thing, the sweetest thing,
  That ever tuggit tow !

RALPH PETERS' FAREWELL TO THE REGIONS
OF RASCALITY.

CONGREGATE, congregate,
　Saint with the sinner.
Jar it and war it,
　The strongest's the winner.

Wrangle it, jangle it,
　Elbow and squeeze,
Fight till ye swelter
　Like maggots in cheese.

Yes, prison the earth
　And distemper the air—
I'm clear of your shoutings
　Of joy or despair.

Winds from the timberlands
　Breath o' the plain,
Ventilate, renovate
　Bosom and brain.

Ambitious frail fabrics,
　Away with the winds ;
Fond loves and friendships false,
　Down to the fiends.

Off, off, old habits vile,
　　Off with a sweep ;
Plague-stained habiliments,
　　Bury them deep !

Sons o' the wildwood,
　　Tho' rough is your cheer,
If there's room in your lodges
　　A brother is here.

THE HOOSIER.

WE lads that live up in the nobs,
　　Tho' our manners might yet bear a rubbing,
We're handy at neat little jobs
　　Such as chopping and hewing and grubbing.

Tho' we roost in a cabin of logs,
　　And clapboards lie 'twixt us and heaven,
Our mast makes us fine oily hogs,
　　And from hoop-poles we pick a good living.

Right quiet—to a decent degree—
　　It's seldom we guzzle it deep, Sir,
Tho' we don't mind a bit of a spree,
　　Provided the liquor is cheap, Sir.

Our neighbours, that live 'cross the drink,
　　May laugh at our fondness for cider,
But so long as we pocket their clink
　　They may laugh till their mouths they grow wider.

Our gals make our trousers, you see,
　　From that beautiful stuff called tow linen,
And in coats of the linsey—dang me,
　　If we don't look both handsome and winning.

Our wives are our weavers, to boot ;
  Ourselves are first rate on a shoe, Sir ;
We can doctor a tub with a hoop—
  And hark ! we're our own niggers too, Sir,

So here's to our Hoosier land,
  The sons of its soil and its waters !
May the " nullies " ne'er get it in hand,
  Nor demagogues tear it in tatters.

But still may it flourish and push,
  Thro' vetos and all such tough cases,
Till railroads are common as brush,
  And the nobs are as sleek as your faces.

SPRING THOUGHTS.

'Tis now the full fresh Spring,
And earth, from all her pores, is pouring forth,
A flood of living beauty.   Tender buds,
Doffing their Winter gauntlets, spread abroad
Their leafy fingers to the mellow air,
Wafting the pretty minstrels to their boughs,
While songs and sounds of merriment awake
Earth's subterranean sleepers.   Then man,
Heaven's latest miracle below, comes forth,
Touched with the living sap that seems to fill
The very firmament.   Laying aside
His musty leaves of macerated rags,
Darken'd with stuff from theologic brains,
He takes a lesson from the living leaves—
God's fresh edition of His wondrous work.
Joining the joyous throng " How fair, how grand,
How glorious!" he cries.   When lo! behold!
The grub hath smote the germinating herb,
The bird hath quit his morning song and pounced
On the devouring worm, while from his poise,
The falcon stoops and makes the bird his prey!
So swiftly death and desecration pounce
And prey upon the living!   What then?
Death gives no jar to the almighty plan.
Death's only change or absence—
For in the bulk of the Eternal whole

22

There cannot be a leak.   All that's past
Or present stands recorded, the *to come*
Sleeps in the unsprouted seed ;
While from the crop this globe hath garner'd,
Hopefully we see a braver future still.
And thus our loved and lost we hoard away
Like precious seeds, waiting our will
To moisten them into life.

SUMMER SAYINGS.

THE birds have sung our Queen o' the Spring,
The gentle Lily, and her lady train,
To sleep in their leafy beds ; while Gillyflowers,
And gallant Marigolds are heralding the Rose ;
For merry May, sweet teen time o' the year,
Hath pass'd her ripening beauties all to June.
Come then, my spirit's mate, let's sit us down
And feast on the young Summer.
    Yes, 'tis a joyous sight to see the sun
Swim from his morning cloud and burnish all
His wondrous wealth of leaf, and flower, and fruit,
With living gold.   It is a sight
That touches every sense ; the very soul
Seizes and soaks it in, till it becomes
Part of our living selves.
    Gazing on such fair scenes we oftimes sigh
To think our earth-life is so limited, so pent,
Wishing for wings to give us all the globe.
For even now, some pretty warbler's song
Will sweep us up and bear us far away
To some old mead, or glen, or grassy rill,
Where first we play'd "and pu'd the gowans fine."
    Aye, Memory, and her co-mates, Hope and Fear,
Tho' spurs and curbs to rein or urge us on,
Oft mar and spoil our present, shutting and sealing up
The immediate eye with picturings of the past

Or shadowings of the future.   Dear childhood,
And those pretty birds that fill
Yon thicket with their songs,
Record no Winters and forestall no Springs.
They'll droop in fogs and shiver in the storm ;
But then a sunny hour can make all well
And wake at once their merriment and song.
   Sing then, my pretty mate, a Summer song.
Let's live with the birds and gather flowers again.

AUTUMNAL MUSINGS.

Now, like some noble lady of the land,
Robed for a festival, comes Autumn on ;
Spring's pleasant gleams and Summer's fervid glow,
Temper'd and soften'd to an amber hue,
Tell us it is the evetide of the year.
The work and warfare of the year is o'er,
And peace and plenty tell of harvest's home.
. Then let us leave the jolly husbandman
Counting the stock and store his brawny arm
Hath garner'd up against the siege of Winter,
And hie us to the woods—the grand old woods—
Dame Nature's clerks, that tally on their trunks
The rounded plunges that our bowling globe
    Takes in the eternal void.
They've doff'd the modest vesture that they wore
When flowers brought out the bee ; and now,
Gorgeous with robes of purple, gold and green,
They mock the marble temples and the fanes
That priests and potentates, with gauds and gilt,
Dress up for rites and revelrie.
'Tis Nature's holiday and farewell feast
To her fair commoners.   And hark !
Soft western winds, balm'd with the breath
Of fragrant fruitage, sweep along the land
And pipe them to the banquet.   But see,
They shun our sight.   We drove them to the wilds

And stained their bowers with blood.   Alas the day !
   We're not invited guests.*
Now fully fledged our Summer visitants
Collect their scatter'd families and sit
Trimming their feathery oars to stem the surge
Of the etherial sea and silent watch
The signal to depart.   Sudden a blast,
Sharpen'd on face of some high icy peak,
Comes crashing thro' the valleys and the glades,
Tossing the grand old foresters like reeds
And giving all their glories to the ground.
   Up thro' the painted cloud the feather'd fleet
Shoot for a calmer sky, chirp their adieus,
And give our land to Winter.

---

   * " I'm unco sorry man's dominion
   Has broken Nature's social union."
                Burns.

WINTER.

Were't not for Winter's curb, and man and beast,
With all the unnumbered hosts that Summer sends
To feed and breed, to raven and destroy,
Our teeming earth would grow itself to death,
As, at the first, Nature in her hot youth
Piled ponderous burdens on the infant isles
And steaming continents, till the unwieldly bulks
Toppled and plunged into the gulphing depths.
Now, tamed and temperate grown, one crop complete,
And all her numerous families supplied,
Silent but sharp upon the twilight air
Steals on her crispy rime, shutting life's gates ;
And with a hand, practised in rarest tracery,
Dresses with glittering jewels all the land.
But see, my musing mate, they're not the gems
That virgin May hangs on the blushing buds,
But gauds to deck the dead.
A few pale moons gleam o'er the silent scene
Like funeral lamps on beauty balmed in state.
Then came her mighty harvesters abroad,
Whirlwinds like giant scythmen, raking storms,
With gouts of thrashing hail, till breathless, spent,
The exhausted hosts dissolve in curdling sleet,
As if they wept the ruin they had wrought.
Nor aught that breathes might brave such sweeping wreck,
But that the eternal mother, ever awake,

Laps up her houseless flocks in suits of proof,
Or chambers them beneath the threshing floor
Till her rough harvest's home.
While we, her joint co-labourers i' the earth,
Secure within our castle or our cot,
Hear unconcerned the mighty Reaper's rage,
Knowing the awful arm that racks our roofs
And bares our sheltering oak, is sowing seeds
To grace another Spring.

A WINTER DOGGEREL.

(Written in a letter to Samuel B. Crist, on hearing that he had traded, or " swapped," his farm in Bethel, Sull. Co., N.Y., for a house in New York City, Feb. 24, 1862, and just as the author was about to start on a visit to his native land.)

WHEN Winter, the ice makker,
Wi' auld Boreas for a backer,
Comes raging frae the north,
Shooin' a' our birdies forth,
Drivin' brutes to holes and kennels,
An' auld bodies to their flannels ;
Then dinna spare the fuel,
Pit a poker in your gruel,
And gin ye've laid away
Aught again' a rainy day
Mak' it usefu' noo I say.
Now our lads o' Yankeeland,
When swapping's at a stand,
An' rain an' slush an' snow
Make peddling craft " no go,"
Set their busy brains a-thinking—
They're not sleeping when they're winking—
Hatching out some new design
In the "ham" or "nutmeg" line ;

While our pioneers and hunters
Tak' "rint" out of their Winters
An' wi' many a grunt and growl
In the tempest's angry howl,
Don their buckskins, boots and mits
An' gie "the varmin" fits ;
We, the planters and the sowers,
The weeders and the hoers,
Groan to see the Wintery wun'
Dash our beauties to the grun',
But grin to see the grubs,
An' fell enemies, the bugs,
Erst laid our borders waste,
Slain in the selfsame blast—
Making steive the proverb still,
That gude grows out o' ill.

MARIGOLD.

Why did he love that yellow flower,
  Whose fringes, bright, unfold,
Reminding all of glittering ore,
  And hence call'd—Marigold?
In fragrance lacking, as he knew,
  No buds it might disclose,
While vernal zephyrs gently blew,
  Could match a wither'd rose.

Perhaps a subtle meaning, quaint,
  Might from his whim be wrung,
Unmarked by hint, however faint,
  From "canny" Scottish tongue.
That maid, who in the garden bends,
  An inkling could unfold;
Mary, she's hailed by all her friends,
  And she is good as gold.

THE PLEASANT PAST.

OH for the sunny afternoons,
  When the roses were in blow,
When the birds began their e'ening sang
  And the win' was saft and low;

When my heart's delight, in the mellowing light,
  Would trip it wi' me to the green,
Rehearsing o'er some bliss in store
  Or the joyous days we'd seen.

E'en our Winter nights had their warm delights
  Tho' the snows were a' drifting deep;
For the din an' the shout o' the storm without
  But made us the closer creep.

Hold fast, hold fast to the pleasant past,
  Its sweet and unfading flowers;
The seeds that we sow may never never grow,
  But the crop o' the past is ours.

TO JAMIE TAMSON.

*(Some attempt at commemoration of the notorious and glorious occasion when Messrs. M*Ritch, James John Ritch, James Macdonall, James Wellstood, Thomas Dick, and Hew Ainslie had the pleasure of feasting at his board.)*

A TOWMOND nearabout has run
    Sin' last we saw thy face, man,
An' mony an up an' down has been
    Amang the human race, man.

It's laid some white hairs on thy pow
    An' brocht some sorrows hame, man,
But, faith ! thy e'e has yet its lowe
    The head is aye the same, man.

The blackbird has gi'en up his bower
    To the robin for to sing in,
An' hawthorns, lately in the flower,
    Wi' yellow leaves are hingin'.

We're like the buss, an' Care, like cauld,
    Can bore us like the timmer,
But Friendship's blink or Beauty's wink
    Can bring again our Simmer.

This nicht thy south shall be our sap,
Thy face shall be our sun, man ;
Pride, mirth an' glee our leaves shall be,
Our blossoms shall be fun, man.

O bliss to them that, stowlins, meet
When day to gloamin' slips, man,
Whaur hearts are pair'd, e'en thochts are shar'd
An' lips are laid to lips, man.

An' joy be wi' ilk merry core
That spend a social hour, man,
But here's to them this nicht shall roar
Within thy hallowed bower, man.

A RHYME TO OUR KINAWA.

WE'VE birds that come frae 'yont the sea
　An' raise a bonny brood,
Syne feather'd fu' an' fit to flee,
　They're aff an' owre the flood.

Like them ye've rais'd some dainty doos,
　Tho' they were nae your ain ;
Noo, cuckoo-like, ye tak' a fyke
　An', flaff ! ye're owre the main.

Weel, gang your wa's, we ken the cause
　That gars ye flee an' flit,
But word o' blame around thy name
　Nae man shall ever pit.

To the Almighty dollar, lad,
　Had ye bent down the knee,
A wally crust o' gowden dust
　Had sure surrounded thee.

Wae worth the dirt ! ye reckon'd right
　A spotless heart an' han'
Are richer treasures, day or night
　Than lots o' gowd an' lan'.

Noo when ye beek in Embro reek,
  Or soak in Glory's dew,
Think o' the kin ye've left behin',
  An' whiles o' Uncle Hew,
  For they'll remember you.

HEW GREY.

YE'RE no for this warl', Hew Grey, Hew Grey,
Ye're no for this warl', I say;
    Wi' your crazy auld brain,
    Biggin' castles in Spain,
Instead o' the biggin's that pay, Hew Grey,
Instead o' the biggin's that pay.

Ye're no for this warl' or day, I say,
Ye're no for this warl' or day;
    Wi' pouches an' wallets
    Fu' o' rhymes an' auld ballats,
Instead o' "I promise to pay," Hew Grey,
Instead o' the papers that pay.

Ye're a waif in this warl', this day, Hew Grey,
Ye're a waif in the warl', I say,
    An' your auld-warl' rhymes
    Are no for thae times,
They are na the blethers that pay, Hew Grey,
Sae lay your auld whistle away.

AN ANSWER TO "HEW GREY."

(Lines on Hew Ainslie which appeared in the "Scotsman" some years before his death.)

BY ANNIE WELLSTOOD JOHNS.

LAY not your "auld whistle" aside Uncle Grey,
 Hush not its soft melodie ;
 Tune it again in sweetness to glide
Away o'er the ocean to me, Uncle Grey,
 Away o'er the ocean to me.

Your name awakes my bairn-dream, Uncle Grey,
 Sets my heart astir in its place ;
 Sends the ripples in memory's stream
To flow in waves o'er my face, Uncle Grey,
 To flow in waves o'er my face.

A "waif" in the world you're not, Uncle Grey,
 Glad actor in joyous scenes ;
 Hair may be white, heart partially shut,
Still soul is yet in its teens, Uncle Grey,
 Still soul is yet in its teens.

Lengthen your *pilgrimage* here, Uncle Grey,
    Add to its pages a few ;
  For fain would I grasp the hand so dear,
That wrote the old verses and new, Uncle Grey,
    That wrote the old verses and new.

You were one of the first who gave, Uncle Hew,
    A welcome to life and to light,
  To the child of friends long in the grave,
And she has not bid you good-night, Uncle Grey,
    And she has not bid you good-night.

So keep your "auld whistle " in tune, Uncle Grey ;
    Let the *Scotsman* tell from afar,
  Fixed in the *West*, near the setting sun,
There burn the rays of a *star*, Uncle Grey,
    There burn the rays of a *star*.

HEW AINSLIE.

DEAR, cherished friend of thirty years and more !
   Sad sinkings of my heart thy loss bewail :
   Alas ! we "swap" no longer song or tale,
As in the merry days and nights of yore.
Yet, though the parting I must aye deplore,
   To thy immortal carols, hail, all hail !
   Thy canvas swell'd by Fame's propitious gale,
Thou'rt safely landed on the restful shore.
Now does a grateful people understand
   The Muse's heritage *not* scoff and scorn :
The hills and dales that gem our native land
   Boast added grace that thou 'midst them wert born,
And Patriotism feels a soul revived
A thousand fold that brave HEW AINSLIE lived.

THOMAS C. LATTO.

NEW YORK, FEB., 1892.

HEW AINSLIE.

(BORN 5TH APRIL, 1792.)

SWEET singer at " the hint o' hairst,"
　　And rover of the sea,
What name soever else thou bear'st,
　　These be thy names to me.
What though the wide engulfing West
　　Endowed thee with a grave,
Thine elegy is chanted best
　　By Ayrshire wind and wave.

An hundred years have swept the scene,
　　With April floods of flowers,
Since by Bargeny's bourocks green
　　Awoke thine infant powers.
And to thy birthday festival
　　Spring comes again to-day
To twine with tender blossoms small
　　Thy slender wreath of bay.

An hundred years ! but fresh and strong
　　Thy notes above their din :
Immortal as the soul is song,
　　And singers all of kin.

And Girvan water e'en as Ayr
  Reflects a poet's smile,
And Dailly's purpling woods are fair
  As those of Ballochmyle.

O Scotland, on thy sacred breast
  There's not a stream that flows,
There's not a hill whose haughty crest
  Salutes the Winter snows,
There's not a margin of the sea
  That wraps thee with its tide
As with a plaid—but there for thee
  Thy sons have sung or died.

                    JANET LOGIE ROBERTSON.

Scotsman, APRIL 5, 1892.

MARY WELLSTOOD.

BY A FRIEND.

MOTHER, sweet sister, daughter, darling dear!
   Whose quiet dignity and loving heart
   So often cause the tear unbidden start,
Encourage hope, dispelling doubt and fear.
I marked the promise of thine opening year;
   Its petals saw the rosebud gently part,
   The splendours of rich womanhood to dart,
Unconscious that she stood without a peer.
Where art thou, Mary? Where those varied graces
   By the bright eyes of genius once so prized?
A vestal veiled from wistful human faces,
   By "shining ones" alone seen, recognized;
No violet, half-hid by mossy stone,
Has left a fragrance sweeter than thine own.

www.ingramcontent.com/pod-product-compliance
Lightning Source LLC
Chambersburg PA
CBHW021341110726
47900CB00005B/1562